THE THEORY AND INTERPRETATION OF NARRATIVE
SERIES

MATTERS OF FACT

Reading Nonfiction over the Edge

Daniel W. Lehman

OHIO STATE UNIVERSITY PRESS
Columbus

Library of Congress Cataloging-in-Publication Data
Lehman, Daniel W. (Daniel Wayne), 1950–
    Matters of fact : reading nonfiction over the edge / Daniel W.
Lehman.
        p.   cm.—(The theory and interpretation of narrative series)
    Includes bibliographical references and index.
    ISBN 0-8142-0760-X (cloth : alk. paper).—ISBN 0-8142-0761-8
(pbk. : alk. paper)
        1. Journalism—United States.   2. Reportage literature, American—
History and criticism.   3. Feature writing.   4. Nonfiction novel—
History and criticism.   5. Books and reading.   6. Literature and
history.   I. Title.   II. Series.
PN4867.L43   1998
071'.3—dc21   97-26663
                                                        CIP

Text and jacket design by Donna Hartwick.
Type set in New Caledonia by Graphic Composition, Inc.
Printed by Cushing-Malloy, Inc.

The paper used in this publication meets the minimum requirements of
the American National Standard for Information Sciences—Permanence
of Paper for Printed Library Materials. ANSI Z39.48-1992.

9 8 7 6 5 4 3 2 1

YOU CAN TELL A TRUE WAR STORY BY THE QUESTIONS YOU ASK. SOMEBODY TELLS A STORY, LET'S SAY, AND AFTERWARD YOU ASK, "IS IT TRUE?" AND IF THE ANSWER MATTERS, YOU'VE GOT YOUR ANSWER.

—TIM O'BRIEN, *THE THINGS THEY CARRIED*

Contents

ACKNOWLEDGMENTS

MY FATHER AND MOTHER TAUGHT ME first that truth matters and that, despite the "sticks and stones" cliché, words have the power to hurt or to heal other people. And so my first thanks go to them for the ethical grounding of this study.

My years as a reporter offered a rich foundation of practical experience in life writing and fact checking. Of the many reporters and editors who taught me, I would particularly like to acknowledge Jack Newfield, Wayne Barrett, and Beverly Cheuvront in New York City, as well as Bob Gibson and the late Elizabeth Wilson in Charlottesville, VA. Robert McGovern at Ashland University took a chance on a veteran reporter and encouraged my scholarship at every turn. The Ashland University Deans Council provided a Summer Study Grant that enabled me to finish this study; particular thanks go to former Arts and Humanities dean John Stratton. Valuable responses to many of the ideas of this book were offered by Ashland University journalism and English students in a seminar on nonfiction narrative, especially Traci Blanchard and T. J. Moraco. At Ohio State University, I learned from John Hellmann, whose *Fables of Fact* was the starting point for this study; from Walter A. "Mac" Davis, who encouraged an active mind and a restless heart; from Debra Moddelmog, the best reader I've met in journalism or academia; and from James Phelan, who offered patient encouragement at every turn.

Portions of this book concerning Freud's Dora and the nonfiction of Tom Wolfe appeared in *Style* 29:1 and in *Prospects: An Annual of American Cultural Studies* 21, respectively. I thank those editors for their permission to reprint and would particularly like to acknowledge Claire Kahane, Audrey Jaffe, and Steven Joyce for their assistance with the Freud project. Peter J. Rabinowitz, James Phelan, and an anonymous reviewer produced particularly helpful readings of the text at several stages of this project. That this book reached publication is due to them and all remaining missteps and flaws are mine. At Ohio State Press, I would like to thank Charlotte Dihoff, Ruth Melville, and especially Barbara Hanrahan, who encouraged this project when things seemed dark. Tonia Payne found my mistakes, and Beth Ina devoted extraordinary personal care to the project and provided first-rate insights into its ideas.

As always, Hadley Lehman shares her wisdom and keeps me honest, while Barbara Lehman provides my scholarly example and is my best friend. This book is dedicated to them.

1.

Nonfictional Narrative and the Problem of Truth

THE CALL CAME LATE AT NIGHT, as I remember it, long after my wife and daughter had gone to bed, and I was alone with the crickets and mosquitoes in the humid Virginia night. On the other end of the line was a distraught woman, a woman whose father had committed suicide the night before. He had scrambled out the window of a center for the treatment of chronic alcohol abuse, walked slowly and deliberately onto a nearby inter-state highway, and died—head up and arms outstretched—on the grill of a twenty-ton semi truck. I had written the story of his death for the afternoon newspaper, and the daughter was calling to dress me down.

Her father had been a bank president and church deacon in life. His alcohol problems, she said, had been kept quite private, and his admission to the sanatorium had been a secret to all but his closest family members. My story that day, sketchy though it was, had aired some of these secrets, even to his own grandchildren, and the daughter could not understand why. Was the idea, she asked, to destroy her family? To parade her father's pain for profit? What gave me the right, she demanded to know, to have the final say on her father's life? I tried to explain that I had stuck to official sources, to easily verifiable facts. I told her that the fatality had snarled highway traffic for an hour, that people had the right to know why they were inconve-nienced, that the police had the obligation to state publicly that the truck driver was not at fault, that we had to try to explain to our readers why a man might scramble over a fence and walk onto the highway to die.

But her voice became louder as the conversation grew longer, and I began to wish that I had taken my editor's advice and ordered an unlisted home telephone number. How much safer it would be, I reflected, to write fiction, to hide characters (or myself for that matter) behind assumed names or narrative postures. If I could only guard my privacy, my vulnerability.

What I yearned for, in short, was the very same protection—the veil of persona, the cloak of anonymity—that I had denied the caller's father in death.

It was in that recognition—reached in the early hours sometime past the midpoint of a professional reporting career—that I first really understood the stakes of writing nonfiction. I as a writer, the woman as a reader, her father as the subject of the narrative—each one of us was implicated materially and historically by the words on the page. Whether the narrative I had written of the father's life could be defined as true was not the only point. Certainly it had many elements of fact; in no way had it been exposed as lies. It was marketed as truth by the author and by the newspaper that profited from its publication. And yet it had the indeterminacy of text as well, a text produced from other texts like police reports, medical records, morgue files, memories, observation, eyewitness accounts, telling details, quotes. I could no more guarantee it was the true account of her father's death than say it was false.

The Implicating Power of Truth

But these conventional generic markers—of truth and falsity, of fact and text—were, finally, almost beside the point that night. They had triggered the discussion, but what counted was how this story had implicated its writer and its reader. That anguished call in the night was proof that what I had written that day, while its facts may have been presented in textual form, had a social and material effect different from fiction. On the one hand the circumstances of its research, writing, publication, and consumption were, and are, deeply intertwined with what literary critics traditionally have called the "text." But its full power and problems cannot be understood until the discursive relationships among author, subject, and reader that undergird nonfiction are read as closely as the words and images that make up the narrative itself.

This book therefore grows from my interest and training as both a professor of literature and as a journalist, in which latter occupation I worked for fifteen years as a reporter and editor for daily and weekly newspapers. Because I was engaged for so long in the research and writing of narratives that claim to be "history," I have some working understanding of the way that writing and reading nonfiction differs from writing and reading fiction.

The writer of nonfiction produces a document for an audience that reads history as both text and experience, an audience that is engaged over the edge, by which I mean both inside and outside the story. This audience will be drawn by the lure of the narrative and by the direct or indirect knowledge of the events and people on which the narrative is based. Certainly such considerations are never foreign from many forms of realistic fiction, which depend on mimetic communication to create possible worlds that interplay with actual worlds. And that outside engagement in fictional texts will become more "thick" or complicated by outside experience if the events are widely known or if the reader has a direct, material interest in those events. But nonfiction depends on a materiality of its characters' bodies and on a reference to outside events that is more powerful than most forms of fiction. Even the reader who had never heard of the bank president before his suicide would have some understanding, no doubt, that an actual person had died and not merely a character of the writer's imagination. And the fact of the resulting traffic jam had affected actual readers in ways that helped to determine the way the scene could be reported.

No journalist or historian can work for long without discovering, as I did during that late-night telephone call, the deep stakes that her readers have in the history she attempts to capture in text. The production and consumption of such nonfictional narratives, therefore, is a site of both artistic and social engagement, an engagement that contests the manner by which we apprehend and communicate experiences. Reading history over the edge of text and experience blends the forms of close reading and analysis that allow us to get "inside" the narrative, while at the same time we understand that the narrators and subjects of nonfiction—in a way less true for fiction— live "outside" the narrative as well. Reading over the edge is alive to the complications inherent in the matrix of inside and outside forces at work and at play in the text.

Given contemporary critical theory's obsession with discourse, popular culture, social history and practice, and the extension of semiological readings to "noncanonical" texts, reading over the edge is a long-overdue project. As a decade closes during which nearly everyone seemed to complain about the nightly news and in which media coverage of events like the Gulf War or the O. J. Simpson trial verged on self-parody, the dearth of recent critical writing on the theory of nonfiction reportage has been almost astonishing. Within traditional English disciplines, scholars who specialize in nonfiction seem to have turned their attention to such worthy areas as journal or travel writing—perhaps because those subgenres raise timely issues of gender self-construction or postcolonial discourse relations. Meanwhile, the theoretical criticism of narratives that emphasize close reporting of public events seems to have been tossed in the closet along with the well-thumbed copies of *The Electric Kool-Aid Acid Test* or *Armies of the Night*— relics to be considered in bursts of 1960s-era New Journalism nostalgia, if at all.

The recent publication of Phyllis Frus's *The Politics and Poetics of Journalistic Narrative* provides a welcome exception to that fitful record. In her study, Frus prowls through reportage by Stephen Crane, Ernest Hemingway, Tom Wolfe, Truman Capote, Norman Mailer, Joan Didion, and Janet Malcolm in an effort to obliterate what she considers artificial boundaries between literature and journalism, between fiction and nonfiction, and between canonical and noncanonical narratives. Rather than perpetuate what she argues are these false critical dualities, Frus urges critics of nonfiction to read reflexively, to "expose the construction of the objective or factual, so that the tension between referential and reflexive levels becomes palpable" (121). Her argument echoes and extends earlier ideas discussed most fruitfully by John Hellmann in his *Fables of Fact: The New Journalism as New Fiction* (1981), wherein the wall between fiction and nonfiction is breached to analyze both forms as exercises in mythmaking—the telling of stories to account for events that surround us.

This project, *Matters of Fact: Reading Nonfiction over the Edge*, enters into a sustained conversation with these theories, providing what I think is a bit more bite to Frus's valuable notion of reflexive reading but specifically countering her assertion that, in all important respects, "the experience of reading an invented tale is identical to that of reading a historical one" (160). While I don't argue that fiction should be read outside history or that it never makes use of "actual" names and events, my contention is that the experience of reading the invented and the historical tale normally is anything but identical. Nonfiction is a form of communication that purports to reenact for the reader the play of actual characters and events across time. What counts is not so much whether these phenomena can be empirically known but that they are also available to and experienced by the reader outside the written artifact. The resulting transaction among writer, reader, and subject forces the nonfictional narrative onto a multireferential plane that I would call "implicated": a term I use for the sense that it has of one being "deeply involved, even incriminated" in both history and text and for the way it complicates more traditional or tidy literary notions of "ideal" or "implied" authors and readers.

By denying any distinction between reportage and fiction, Frus would refuse the most powerful tools that her reflexive approach offers. Her analyses, with their wonderful potential for reading the referential (outside) against the reflexive (inside), stop too often at the level of textual formalism because she won't allow herself to wander outside the written text into the domain where the accuracy or adequacy of representation is always at issue. For example, in her discussion of *Fatal Vision,* the writer Joe McGinniss's account of convicted murderer Jeffrey MacDonald, Frus criticizes MacDonald's legal case against McGinniss for its "common displaced emphasis on the error and falsity of a narrative account" and finds "more desirable" the writer Janet Malcolm's "simple acknowledgment of 'the difficulty of knowing the truth about anything,' the fact that there are very few incidents about which we can know what 'really' happened" (193). To Frus, "arguing over which parts a writer 'got right' in terms of accuracy is a hopeless exercise because we have no primary or original text to compare later versions to, and these narratives are paramount in determining the history we have of events in the past; in fact, they are all we have, for we cannot retrieve the past except from texts, including our memory as a text" (229). I will certainly grant Frus's desire not to return to some sort of safe empirical realm wherein the genre police—upon finding error or an imaginative author—would consign a narrative to "fiction" and declare it irrelevant to history. But I will not grant her accompanying conclusion that arguing about accuracy is a hopeless exercise. Indeed, elsewhere in *The Journalist and the Murderer* Malcolm makes clear that she respects some essential differences between fiction and nonfiction—no matter the difficulty of constructing a true account. "The writer of fiction is entitled to more privilege," Malcolm says. "He is the master of his own house and may do what he likes with it; he may even tear it down if he is so inclined. But the writer of nonfiction is only the renter, who must abide by the conditions of his lease" (153).

The confession that, finally, it is impossible to delineate an exact boundary between fiction and nonfiction does not mean that the boundary does not matter. For example, if it matters that at least 343 Vietnamese women, infants, teenagers, and old men were killed by Americans at My Lai—as Tim O'Brien reports in "The Vietnam in Me," his recently published narrative of his return to Vietnam's "Pinkville" district—in contrast to their being eliminated from the imaginative plot of O'Brien's written text, then it follows that nonfiction, its writers, and its readers are implicated by experiences off the page. To write or read nonfiction for its implication in history opens up Frus's valuable notion of reflexivity to an even more troubling level.

For not only will readers read to "discover how a text, through its style, 'makes' reality" (Frus 5), but also how the play of history, or "reality," if you will, makes or adjusts a text. In this sense "text" is never held hostage to literary form but is a fluid interchange of events and their telling: history over the edge.[1] In such a project matters of accuracy, though slippery and seldom proven, are anything but irrelevant. For example, when Jane Tompkins struggles to engage competing nonfiction accounts of Native American captivity in her essay "'Indians': Textualism, Morality, and the Problem of History," she finds herself implicated by the narrative of an enslaved girl whose nose was burned repeatedly by a firebrand. Does it matter if that smell of singed flesh was invented or took place in history, Tompkins asks herself, then concludes that "arguments about 'what happened' have to proceed much as they did before post-structuralism broke in with all its talk about language-based reality and culturally produced knowledge. Reasons must be given, evidence adduced, authorities cited, analogies drawn. . . . If the accounts don't fit together neatly, that is not a reason for rejecting them all in favor of a metadiscourse about epistemology" (76).

Matters of Fact: Reading Nonfiction over the Edge explores the theory of nonfictional narrative as implicated text: my argument is that an implicated reading becomes all the more valuable and troubling if we explore some distinctions between nonfiction and fiction at the level on which the narrative interacts with historical experience and if we examine that interaction for its practices and ideology. I don't wish to reconstruct an absolute division in my bookshelf between fiction and nonfiction, but I do want to look at the range of narratives along the shelf and describe how my very desire and difficulty in building such a division affects me as a reader.

To that end, in addition to joining Frus in what I hope will be a fruitful dialogue with her "poetics and politics of journalistic narrative," this book will honor an invitation made by media scholar John J. Pauly in an essay on the politics of 1960s-era New Journalism. Pauly suggests a standard of communications research that merges close textual as well as close social analysis: "We might . . . interpret a work of reporting as a *social behavior*, without precluding close textual analysis," Pauly says. "We could study the *venues of publication* (i.e. the institutional sites at which the story was written, printed, disseminated, and discussed). We could then analyze the research and writing of a work as *social acts*, noting the way the reporting process implicates writer, subjects, and readers in relationships beyond a text" (112, Pauly's emphases). In response to Pauly's invitation, and with particular attention to his sense of nonfiction as a socially implicating act, the present study offers a way to read nonfiction that will account for the specific manner by which nonfictional narrative draws in its writers and readers as both historical agents and producers and consumers of texts.

Underlying the study are several assumptions: (1) any literary text, whether fiction or nonfiction, even one's own memory of events, is arbitrated or "crafted" in important ways, rendering impossible the simple equation of "actuality" with nonfiction; (2) even if that equation were possible, a standard based solely on the verifiability of nonfiction's claims would be inadequate because narratives, as both Frus and Tompkins note, operate in an intertextual milieu wherein actuality and its reproduction in story often are virtually indistinguishable; (3) the decision by either the author or the publisher to term a product "nonfiction" nonetheless remains an important key to how it is written and read and is much more socially constructed and negotiated by both author and reader than derived by some empirical standard of truth; (4) the decision to engage a nonfictional text triggers a powerful and ongoing dilemma for the author (who implicates herself as a creator of, and as a character in, the text she fashions) and for the reader (who implicates himself as a character in, and as a consumer of, the text he encounters).

The Power of the Body in Nonfictional Narrative

Teasing out the significance of that assertion for nonfiction might be enhanced by imagining how the author-subject-reader relationship would be different if, say, a novel such as Vladimir Nabokov's *Lolita* were written or marketed as nonfiction. Never would I argue—as did many formalist critics during the 1950s and 1960s who saluted its technical brilliance and professed indifference to its subject matter—that because it is fiction *Lolita* lacks the power to reach outside its text and disturb competent readers by the specter of a pedophile stalking a prepubescent twelve-year-old girl ("she was in my arms, her innocent mouth melting under the ferocious pressure of dark male jaws" [63]). Indeed, the novel's subject matter and realistic underpinnings create so powerful an effect that some readers who have experienced sexual abuse (and some who haven't) will be and should be deeply implicated by the representation of Humbert Humbert's statutory rape of Delores Haze.[2] But that reaction—strong and mimetically engaged though it may be—is not precisely the same as it would be were this a nonfictional text and were

Humbert Humbert a living pedophile whose meticulously crafted journal revealed to the reader his sexual abuse of a living twelve-year-old girl.

As a reporter I covered such a case, in which a man bribed and seduced young boys and girls (one was his daughter) into posing as unclothed corpses in an elaborately contrived "examination room" at his house so he could fondle and photograph their bodies. He composed meticulously illustrated and artfully written annals of his exploits (indeed, he later won yearly creative-writing contests in prison before dying there) that formed the centerpiece of the Commonwealth of Virginia's case against him. The nonfictional texts that the police seized from the man's home not only implicated their author but also produced a profound response from readers rightly concerned by both the text's exploitation of its subjects and its referentiality—the sense that it contained an intelligible account of specific historical events, even if that account was not objective, transparent, exhaustive, or exclusive.

The contrast of Nabokov's *Lolita* to the documentary evidence in a rape case might seem ludicrously obvious, but the critical framework that makes such distinctions possible is almost routinely erased in the current critical climate. Naomi Jacobs summarizes the collapse of meaningful fact/fiction distinctions quite succinctly in her recent study of historical fiction, *The Character of Truth:* "Facts not only can be manipulated but are inherently futile and false; any testimony about the past is a lie because nothing anyone can remember about the past is equal to the totality of the past," she says. "Even honest attempts to tell the truth will fail, because all knowledge is incomplete, all perceptions slanted. And even if we could know 'what really happened,' we would only know events that were shaped by specific perceptions, sometimes irrational, sometimes subconscious, of History itself" (179–80).

While such assertions are intended to subvert the putative equation of historical text with truth and fictional text with falsity, they set up other sorts of absolutes that seem equally ill advised. New binary oppositions pit unequivocal truth against unequivocal falsity, assuming the latter because the former is impossible. Yet not all manipulated facts are equally false; not all testimony about the past is equally futile; not all honest attempts to tell the truth are identically failed; some knowledge is more incomplete than other knowledge; some perceptions are more slanted than others. Certainly there is no "objective" stance outside history and culture from which we can sort these confusing claims with certainty. My readings will be flawed and culturally produced, as will be others. But paying specific attention to specific types of assertions and nonfictional narrative power relationships can teach us about the way truth matters, about the similarities and differences between *Lolita* and an actual pedophile's diary as well as the differing responses that authors, subjects, and readers might have to those texts.

James Agee spoke of this power in *Let Us Now Praise Famous Men*, a book that, while highly subjective and constructed, blended artful narrative with the reproduction of actual lives in both Agee's prose and in Walker Evans's powerful photographs. "The one deeply exciting thing to me about Gudger is that he is actual, he is living, at this instant," Agee writes of his protagonist. "He is not some artist's or journalist's or propagandist's invention; he is a human being: and to what degree I am able it is my business to reproduce him as the human being he is; not just to amalgamate him into some invented literary imitation of a human being" (240).

Before I turn my attention to a more general contrast between the generic conventions of nonfiction and realistic fiction, I want to look quite closely at one of the most specific differences suggested by the *Lolita* example: the sense that nonfiction signifies narrational operations on an actual body or bodies rather than on imaginary characters. A contrast of two sets of photographs published by tabloid newspapers during the O. J. Simpson trial might lend a way to understand some of these important distinctions. The first set was published by the *National Examiner* in April 1995 (Case 12) and shows a model with a strong resemblance to Nicole Brown Simpson lying open-eyed and face up in a pool of red liquid. A black bar, such as the ones that used to obscure the eyes of bystanders in true crime magazines, is superimposed over the model's throat. An accompanying photograph shows the same model lying barefooted in a near-fetal position over a red slick on a square-tiled floor. Headlines scream: "Exclusive Nicole Murder Photos: Crime Scene You Couldn't See on TV," "The Innocents," "Not for the Squeamish."

The second set was published by the competing tabloid *Globe* in September 1995 (Giobbe, "Supermarket" 10) with an identical "Not for the Squeamish" tag line. On the left side of a double-truck inside spread, headlined "World Exclusive: Nicole and Ron's heartsick family and friends beg jury: Don't Free O. J. To Kill Again," Nicole Brown Simpson lies with eyes closed and so much blood on her face and torso that her features virtually are unrecognizable. A much thicker black band obscures her throat. On the right side of the spread, Ron Goldman lies on his side, his lower body twisted toward the camera. Blood obscures his left pant leg and is spattered throughout the picture. It is not easy to recognize his head as that of a human being.

Two wallet-sized color photos of Nicole Brown Simpson and Ron Goldman are positioned in the corners of the crime scene shots, depicting the victims in life. Above a courtroom snapshot in which a surly-seeming O. J. Simpson eyes the camera, a relatively subdued typewriter font in reverse ink over a black background spills down the left side of the spread: "Chilling crime scene photos prove beyond doubt that murderer is cruel & savage monster."

Both photo sets are elaborate and obviously contrived narratives in which photographs and text are arranged to stimulate the simultaneously voyeuristic thrill and horrified recoil common to the tabloid medium. The text and design of the two tabloids deliver classic "hard sell" to the body photos, foregrounding their "exclusive" and forbidden nature ("not for the squeamish") at the same time that their positioning makes them impossible to ignore. Both tabloid spreads become parts of larger narratives in the magazines themselves and then parts of even larger and more complex narratives when "respectable" industry magazines like *Editor and Publisher,* national television networks, or even narrative series published by university presses respond to the tabloid depictions. Ultimately, however, none of the bloodied corpses is the "real" body of either Ron Goldman or Nicole Brown Simpson; all are photographs reprinted on pulp newsprint and propped in wire slots near the checkout stands of a hundred thousand neon supermarkets.

Yet to call these differing depictions obviously staged narratives is not to declare them equal. The first set uses a combination of model stand-ins, fake blood, stage sets, and computer enhancement to depict the crime scene, while the second set is pulled from courtroom evidence photographs explicitly sealed by Judge Lance Ito and apparently smuggled from the L. A. Police Department evidence unit to the editors of the *Globe* (Giobbe, "Supermarket" 11). Part of the power of the second set undoubtedly comes from the recognition that the "real-life" crime scene was far more gory than the computer enhancement the *National Examiner* staged; another part comes from a resistant and forbidden cachet to the extent that the reader understands the *Globe* photographs were leaked and published in direct defiance of a court order. But I want to insist that the greatest part of the power comes from a recognition that we are seeing a direct depiction (even though obviously filtered through photographic narrative) of two bodies that were once breathing human beings, not paid actors playing a part only to stand and walk away from the set. For all the billions of words and untold hours of expert rehashing on endless talk shows, for most viewers the sight of Nicole Brown Simpson and Ron Goldman's photographed bodies has startling and deeply implicating power (so much so that *Editor and Publisher* called the publication of the photos "the biggest coup of all" in the frenzied scramble for Simpson exclusives [Giobbe, "Supermarket" 10]).[3]

Los Angeles art critic Ralph Rugoff suggests some of the reasons for this power of nonfictional depiction in a recent article describing his visit to the Los Angeles County coroner's office. He is not allowed to peruse the department's archive, which adds 150,000 photographs a year and dates back to 1937, so he waits until the forensic photographer is called out of his office to examine a group of photos on his desk.

> Hidden among various images of bullet wounds (known as "locator" shots) is a full-figure photograph of a young black man laid out on a specimen table like a languorous male odalisque. . . . Though the average TV viewer takes in 13,000 dramatized killings by age eighteen, few if any of these images bear the least resemblance to this photograph. . . . The property of a public agency, it's essentially a private image, meant for exhibition only in court, and my looking at it is an intrusion, a rupture of its limited intentions. Since I'm not seeing it through bureaucratic filters, it hits me with a power it was never meant to have. . . . Rather than perusing color prints, I feel like I'm handling a dead man's belongings. (183–84)

Later, Rugoff sees a cadaver, a male child's corpse being washed down on a coroner's slab, and recognizes that his encounter with the photographs has not prepared him for the shock of an actual corpse. Again, despite its widespread fictional depiction on television and in film, "evidence of death is pretty much banished from our daily life, its management entrusted to specialists," Rugoff reflects, "and the physical presence of this tiny body seems like a violent intrusion from a foreign reality" (184). He nearly is overtaken by the power of the actual encounter with death, for which its repeated mechanical and digital reproduction has obviously not prepared him. "I keep staring, eyes locked like magnets in the foolish hope that if I look long and hard enough," he says, "it will begin to seem familiar, and no more threatening than a snapshot" (184–85).

If contemporary literary theory is slow to grant an essential difference between life and imagined life in the late twentieth century, the profit-making media certainly recognize and exploit the power that many sorts of audiences invest in the depiction of the "real." Several dozen reality-based television shows and tabloid-news shows market highly scripted versions of the "real" embedded within even more highly scripted frames. And although "snuff" films, depictions in which actors or actresses actually are murdered in the commission of their dramatic roles, remain taboo despite the hundreds of fictional deaths depicted during each evening's prime-time hours, unscripted or unplanned actual death has become a rapidly growing media industry. As recently as the 1980s the gunshot suicide of a Pennsylvania State treasurer during a taped news conference threw network news executives into self-described deep reflection as they decided whether or not to air the footage.

Actual death depictions were primarily relegated to such underground (but widely rented and viewed) videotapes as the *Faces of Death* series. A decade later, however, the depiction of actual death scenes on television "reality" shows has become routine. For example, while I was preparing a unit on the videotaped Rodney King beating and its aftermath for an advanced mass communications course during the spring of 1996, news broke of the videotaped beating of a truckload of Mexican nationals who had led San Diego–area police on a high-speed freeway chase. I set my videocassette recorder to tape the day's offerings of *Hard Copy, Inside Edition,* and *Extra* while I taught a night class, certain that at least one of the shows would have the footage of the latest freeway beatings. When I returned late that night and checked the tapes, I found that not only had all three used that footage—repeatedly showing a patrolman slam a Mexican woman's head into the hood of a police car, as well as replaying the Rodney King and Reginald Denny beatings—but the shows televised three scenes of actual physical death as well. As it happened, that night in the world of tabloid television Major League umpire John McSherry repeatedly walked away from home plate, pitched forward, and lay twitching from a fatal heart attack; a Los Angeles–area man cornered by police after a high-speed chase was shot and killed as he was about to pin a police officer between his car's bumper and a concrete wall; and a mentally disturbed woman who had entered a police station, gun drawn, was shot point-blank in the head as she rounded a counter in search of the police officer who had served the order that had committed her to a mental hospital. The death toll that evening was not that far out of line with any day's yield on the tabloid television shows.

Although I am insisting that the depiction of actual bodies explains part of the representational power of nonfiction in late-twentieth-century culture, I won't assert some sort of essentializing difference. Repeated popu-lar media depictions of actual deaths will desensitize audiences to the power of the body that I am tracing, even as developments in genetic engineering and artificial personality certainly will alter current perceptions of subjectiv-ity. The construction of virtual personalities in such media as computer bul-letin boards and user groups already makes it possible for browsers to converse in real time with fictional characters, some of whom they believe are actual persons and some of whom they assume are send-ups. Sherry Turkle's *Life on the Screen* details the creation of an unauthorized on-line alter ego in a multiuser domain (MUD) named "Dr. Sherry" that "was a derivative of me, but she was not mine. I experienced her as a little piece of my history spinning out of control" (38). When people power up their com-puters and step through what Turkle calls "the looking glass," they encounter other people or programs that blur fact and fiction. "As the boundaries erode between the real and the virtual," Turkle contends, "the animate and the inanimate, the unitary and the multiple self, the question becomes: Are we living life on the screen or *in* the screen" (39, Turkle's emphasis).

In one recent case a virtual personality named "Kyle Krittan" from Nebraska achieved celebrity status on Prodigy's gay and lesbian bulletin board for "offering downhome advice to other teens taking baby steps out of the closet, and sheepishly confessing to voguing on a John Deere tractor out on his farm while Madonna blasted through his Walkman" (Hannaham 32). When Krittan's death in a traffic accident on the way home from a football road trip was announced on-line by his grieving parents, a heated discussion ensued as to whether Krittan had been real, a pseudonym, or the whole-cloth invention of an unknown bulletin-board surfer.

Krittan's status would seem a particularly postmodern dilemma, but *Village Voice* cyberspace reporter James Hannaham outlines the stakes that even sophisticated Prodigy bulletin-board users invest in the distinction of fact and fiction and the manner by which the discussion centered on docu-mentary evidence to ascertain Krittan's identity and the reality of his body. The bulletin board users' greatest fear "was that Kyle had hoodwinked all his cyberfriends by inventing an 'identity' that didn't match his identity at all, and that they'd wasted their love and admiration on a lie," according to Han-naham. "Internauts, who tend not to connect well in RL [real life], find the managed interaction of cyberspace much easier to navigate and have a ten-dency to get taken in by the illusion of connection it brings" (32). Eventually the case was mostly solved by some rather old-fashioned documentary fact-checking: matching traffic-accident records near Krittan's home in Kearney,

Nebraska, to his reported time of death (no link shown); checking accounts of a football road trip on which the fatality was said to have occurred (his high school turned out to be playing a home game); and tracing the payments of Kyle's account with Prodigy (narrowed to two computer users in Lincoln, Nebraska, both of whom denied knowledge of Kyle [Hannaham 32]). In other words, Krittan's identity inside the conversational text that the bulletin-board users had constructed was read against what could be determined from other narratives outside the text.

What is interesting is that even as the concept of personality wavers at the end of the twentieth century, human beings—as the case of "Kyle Krittan" demonstrates—still tend to grope for some outside referentiality to arbitrate the "truth" about characters. And although this book will explore many sorts of distinctions between fact and fiction, the sense of human life and personality, it seems to me, remains a central way of classifying narrative. When characters die in fiction, characters die; when characters die in non-fiction, people die. If one grants no difference between Nicole Brown Simpson's bloodied body in photographs taken as evidence at Bundy Drive and the depiction of an actress playing her part in a staged and computer-enhanced mock-up of Bundy Drive, then few—if any—of the distinctions this book attempts to draw will be persuasive. But if one does care about the difference between real and imagined birth, death, and suffering, then these distinctions, while infinitely complicated and always threatening to reverse field, will be worth exploring.

Wendy Lesser's *Pictures at an Execution,* a compelling analysis of a San Francisco–area public television station's efforts to televise the execution of Robert Alton Harris, develops some of this same line of reasoning. Her research convinces her that an execution, whether re-created or "real-life," forms one of the most deeply staged and scripted narratives imaginable. Certainly it makes use of many almost-fictional devices of characterization (the executioner, the priest, the condemned) and rising tension (the last meal, the countdown, the prisoner's last walk, the midnight deadline). Yet in a central way Lesser finds the execution to be relentlessly real, no matter how scripted. She quotes New Orleans reporter Jonathan Eig, who witnessed an electrocution in the Louisiana State Penitentiary and speaks of the "unreal" quality of an execution "'as if it were a performance put on for the benefit of an audience'" (186). But in ways that reverberate with my own analysis, Lesser insists on a threshold difference. "The problem is that *this* performance, *this* exemplary moral tale of justice wrought, is also a real event," she says, "and the Villain who dies before the audience's expectant gaze (expectant even if anguished, as in Turgenev's case) is not just acting" (186, Lesser's emphases). And Lesser finds that the distinction between fact and fiction is just as compelling—in fact more so—in written narrative as it is in visual television or film narrative. An example even more recent than Lesser's book can be drawn from *Delaware State News* reporter Carlos Holmes's description of the hanging of killer Billy Bailey in Smyrna, Delaware:

> At about 12:01 A.M., the guards walked Bailey to the trap-door of the gallows. They bound his legs, put a black hood over his head and fitted a noose around his neck. . . . One of Bailey's fists was repeatedly flexing and balling. Then they moved away from him and to our surprise the warden walked over and pulled the lever, and Bailey went. There was no sound of his neck snapping. He dropped down, his body turned clockwise a few times and then counterclock-wise a few times, then swung back and forth like a pen-dulum, and then stopped. (qtd. in Giobbe, "Covering Executions" 9)

Of such narratives Lesser asks her reader: "Have you been spared the horror of this by being spared the actual sight of it? I think not. Reading also brings things in through the eyes, and words enable us to create sickening mental pictures. . . . Visual artifacts are not just props in a book, as they can be in a movie, where everything is visual; when they are highlighted in words, we are forced to pay attention to them" (55). I believe that the power to which Lesser refers begins with the presence of material bodies and their interaction in history. Even though truth is slippery and none of these presences can be experienced outside narrative, truth is always at issue when the text's referentiality intersects material bodies. Our goal, then, is to explore the ways in which truth matters even in deeply narrative representations of historical events and to examine nonfictional narrative over the edge of text and experience.

The Problem of Truth in the Construction of Genre

If I am to argue that there is no purpose in collapsing all fact-fiction boundaries—and that all nonfictional narratives to varying degrees (as well as some fictional stories, for that matter) throw readers and writers into this sort of multi-referential reading—it seems I can hardly avoid at least some discussion of nonfiction as genre. Although this book is not intended primarily to be a genre study, one can hardly insist on nonfiction's important power to implicate its writers and readers without considering some sort of "classifying statements" about it. I shall adopt, however, the sorts of genre guidelines proffered by Adena Rosmarin and Peter Rabinowitz in separate analyses of narrative classification. Rosmarin reminds us that genre must consider difference as well as resemblance. "[O]nce genre is defined as pragmatic rather than natural, as defined rather than found, and as used rather than described," Rosmarin explains, "then there are precisely as many genres as we need" (25). Rabinowitz extends that pragmatic approach to grant to readers the power to engage the politics of interpretation. "Genre is best understood not as a group of texts that share textual features, but, rather, as a collection of texts that appear to invite similar interpretive strategies," Rabinowitz argues. "Regardless of the text, regardless of the particular choices that a given reader makes as he or she processes it, those interpretive procedures always bring with them some kind of political edge" (137).[4]

Traditionally, attempts to draw the line between fact and fiction have been based on three sorts of arguments: empirical, cognitive, and intentional. The first assumption relies on a belief that "what actually happened" can be discovered and demonstrated and that nonfiction sticks to that realm, whereas fiction trades primarily in the realm of imagination. Aristotle's *Poetics* builds the classical distinction between poetry (fiction) and history (nonfiction) and assigns a hierarchy that privileges the fictive or mimetic as more significant:

> [I]t is not the function of the poet to narrate events that have actually happened, but rather, events such as might occur and have the capability of occurring in accordance with the laws of probability or necessity. . . . [T]he historian narrates events that have *actually happened*, whereas the poet writes about things as they might possibly occur. Poetry, therefore, is more philosophical and more significant than history, for poetry is more concerned with the universal, and history more with the individual. (48–49, emphasis added)

Elsewhere, in what has become a widely cited maxim, Aristotle states his preference for the "persuasive impossibility to an unpersuasive possibility"

(64), thus reaffirming the ascendancy of mimetic imagination over historical narrative. Similarly, Erich Auerbach's *Mimesis* contrasts the biblical authors who believe they are imparting true narratives to Homeric literature and suggests an important problem that he believes arises in biblical literature. "Far from seeking, like Homer, merely to make us forget their own reality for a few hours," says Auerbach of the story of the patriarchs, "it seeks to overcome our reality: we are to fit our own life into its world, feel ourselves to be elements in its structure of universal history. This becomes increasingly difficult the further our historical environment is removed from that of the biblical books" (12). In their 1995 study of the history of mimesis Gunter Gebauer and Christoph Wulf attempt to place Auerbach's analysis within a historical progression and to suggest that Aristotle's important recognition in the *Poetics* was that mimesis relieves fictional narrative from the obligation to refer to a given reality: "mimesis produces *fiction;* whatever reference to reality remains is shed entirely of immediacy" (55).

For my purposes Aristotle's accompanying contention is equally important (and problematic). Enfolded into his distinction between poetry and history is the assumption that history "happens" and can be discovered as a first cause; therefore, it can be discovered outside of the narratives that describe it. Although such classical binaries have been under attack for several decades now in English and linguistic studies, they continue to rule the dominant methodology within the journalism and publishing industries. As I will point out in subsequent chapters, the journalism textbooks distributed by all the major publishing companies as well as handbooks disseminated by major-media news organizations assume that a reporter can determine what the truth is in most cases and write about it accurately. The industry, for example, did not hesitate to discipline a writer like Janet Cooke, whose 1981 Pulitzer Prize was withdrawn when she admitted to having penned a composite character (see chapter 3). And even so recent a literary critic as Barbara Lounsberry, in her *The Art of Fact: Contemporary Artists of Nonfiction* (1990), concludes that the proper stuff of nonfiction is "documentable subject matter chosen from the real world as opposed to 'invented' from the writer's mind" (xiii). The rigidity of that binary, for Lounsberry, is enforced by banishment. "[W]hen the factual accuracy of a work is questioned, or when authorial promises are violated," she insists, "a work of literary nonfiction is either discredited or transferred out of the category" (xiv).

One can easily see how such rigid police work has convinced critics like Frus to throw out the binary altogether and to collapse distinctions between fact and fiction. Their (and my own) argument is that no objective platform exists outside of politics and culture wherein the narrative's "factual accuracy" can be putatively determined. As Roland Barthes's influential 1970 essay "Historical Discourse" declared, "Historical discourse does not follow reality, it only signifies it; it asserts at every moment: *this happened*, but the meaning conveyed is only that someone is making that assertion . . . once we achieve the insight that reality is nothing but a meaning, and so can be changed to meet the needs of history, when history demands the subversion of the foundations of civilization 'as we know it'" (154–55, Barthes's emphasis).

Current literary theory in large part agrees that it is difficult indeed to separate "what happened" from how it is told or experienced. Paul Virilio suggests that even science has a difficult time asserting an empirical truth since the recognition of quantum physics and Einstein's theory of relativity. He contrasts photographic narrative, which claims to present the world as it is in an instant, with the human eye, which experiences movement over time, and argues that either can be true or false depending on what presumptions the observer brings to the observation. "[F]or the human eye, the essential is invisible," Virilio asserts, and "since everything is an illusion, it follows that scientific theory, like art, is merely a way of manipulating our illusions" (23). Moreover, the deeply and increasingly mediated nature of our experience sets up a circle of presumptions that will become interdependent on other equally mediated and intangible assumptions. Gebauer and Wulf trace out the stakes of that recognition, which subverts Aristotle's assumption of a sharp distinction between empirical reality and mimetic representation:

> When the gap between the empirical and mimetic worlds narrows, empirical reality loses its autonomy over against interpretive mimetic worlds: it comes increasingly to approximate itself to them; events become indistinguishable from interpretations and quotations. There is then no reality beyond interpreted and quoted worlds; mimesis no longer represents any other world. It becomes a self-illustration, a self-presentation. . . . Different images, because they are flat, because they are electronic and miniaturizable, become similar to each other across their substantive differences. They are all part of the fundamental transformation of contemporary image worlds; they dissolve things and transpose them into a world of appearance. Moreover,

increasing numbers of images are produced which have only themselves as a point of reference. The ultimate result is that everything becomes art, becomes a play of images that no longer refer to anything, that no longer function as models, but are equivalent to nothing but themselves. The distance between the mimetic and the prior world, the intermediary spaces, ceases to exist once mimesis has become all-encompassing, and the mimetic and the other world collapse into each other. (320)

The implications of such reasoning are obvious. If there is no empirical standard, no objective place, from which we can agree on facts, then there is no way that we can judge narrative to be truthful solely by its adherence to independently evaluated facts. A clear distinction between narrative that is factual and that which is fictional has therefore been lost.

These sorts of issues have engaged historiography and narrative theory for decades and even centuries. In the present context I will restrict my discussion of previous approaches to several that have been advanced to address the specific problem of twentieth-century nonfictional reportage that plays across the boundary of fact and fiction. From that critical tradition two efforts to maintain a clear division between fact and fiction in the face of decreasing reliance on empiricism are the intentional and cognitive standards. One of the most articulate exponents of a genre standard based on the intentions of an author is Eric Heyne, who offers a way to recognize the special power of nonfiction and to make the reader an important partner in the negotiation of truth, while forcing perhaps too simple a wedge between the actual effects of fiction and nonfiction. In a 1987 article in *Modern Fiction Studies* Heyne uses speech-act theorist John Searle's *The Logical Status of Fictional Discourse* to build a case for literary nonfiction that distinguishes between the text's "factual status" (determined by the author's intent) and its "factual adequacy" (judged by an empirical standard whereby the author's version of the facts is compared and contrasted to the facts themselves). When a speaker or writer claims that something is a "true story," Heyne argues:

We mean either that it is to be taken in a certain way or that it can serve as an adequate representation of real events. The madman's tale is "true" in the first sense, but

> not in the second. The first distinction is between fact and
> fiction, the second between good and bad fact. The differ-
> ence is important because . . . different sorts of responses
> are appropriate for fiction and nonfiction. If Searle's dis-
> tinction makes sense, it follows that the author is sole de-
> terminant of whether a text is fact or fiction, whereas the
> reader must decide for herself whether a work is good or
> bad fact. (480)

Heyne insists that a fictional text (that is, one whose author has not asserted
it to be true) has neither factual status nor factual adequacy; a nonfictional
text, he asserts, has factual status, but readers would have to resolve individu-
ally or by debate the question of its factual adequacy. Status is either/or, a
binary matter determined by the illocutionary intentions of an author (Searle
325), whereas adequacy is a relative matter open to debate among readers
(480–81).

The value of Heyne's distinction of "status" and "adequacy" is that
it begins to account for the differing effects produced by many fictional and
nonfictional texts and it creates room for author-reader negotiation at the
factual-adequacy stage without erasing the unique status of the nonfictional
narrative. Heyne's analysis also allows the reader to negotiate factual adequacy on a sliding scale without denying the power of a nonfiction claim that
makes the analysis possible. "When we are challenged by a narrative that
presents itself as fact, but includes dialogue or events that we may doubt,
our response is usually to challenge the text and determine its worth, not
throw up our hands and surrender," Heyne asserts. "We will continue to
maintain the fact/fiction distinction at least as long as we find it worthwhile
to conduct a collective search for the truths of our past" (484). Heyne's for-
mations complicate a rigidly binary empiricism by addressing fact-fiction issues on two levels: intent and adequacy. But, while very helpful, Heyne's
model does not appear to account for the sorts of texts—like those by Don
DeLillo, O'Brien, and Didion that I will address in some detail during the
latter half of this study—in which the text's referentiality grows from its depiction of actual bodies (Lee Harvey Oswald, William Calley, Roberto
D'Aubisson, and many lesser-known characters) even though authors or
publishers deliberately blur their generic intent. Heyne believes his model
is adequate because the texts it won't account for, by his very definition, are
fiction and thus not to be submitted to analyses of factual adequacy.[5]

I agree with Heyne that there is no reason to abolish the discussion of fact-fiction boundaries. Indeed, they may be of invaluable assistance in explaining how many of the texts marketed as nonfiction implicate their authors and readers. But basing binary classification solely on the author's intent confuses those instances in which the reading audience believes that it is reading factual (or even fictional) discourse when it is mistaken about the author's intention. And I doubt that blurred authorial intent is as experimental or marginalized as Heyne thinks. Our increasing confrontation with just this sort of blurred reality/textuality in our extra-literary lives accounts for some of the disturbing power of contemporary nonfiction. We turn on our televisions to see a fictional character respond in narrative "real" time to the taped account of an "actual" vice presidential speech six months earlier while the vice president is filmed watching the "actual" television show in an elaborately staged (nonfiction?) media photo opportunity. Moreover, to my mind it serves little purpose to dismiss all concerns about the interaction of story and events when a text is presented as fiction. Several of O'Brien's Vietnam narratives (which I shall discuss in detail in this book's last chapter) as well as many other fictional narratives refuse that essentialization.

Finally, even if the work's factual status can be determined, the second stage of Heyne's analysis asks us to negotiate factual adequacy by deciding whether "it can serve as an adequate representation of real events" (480). Heyne's formation, while adjusting the equation in valuable ways, thus also assumes a truth standard not far removed from classical empiricism. It assumes both that the audience can determine what is real and that it can establish a standard by which it can judge an adequate representation of the real. In the matrix of history and culture, however, any audience will bring its preconceptions to these issues. What one sort of audience believes to be real may be flatly rejected by another, so the standard of factual adequacy remains slippery at best, if not impossible. I would join Heyne in the effort to consider the factual adequacy of nonfiction narrative (it is in fact that which most distinguishes my approach from those who would collapse all distinctions), but I don't believe factual adequacy can be proven with the generic certainty he envisions, nor do I believe it is relevant only to such texts as the author has specifically asserted to be true.

A genre standard that relies on the cognitive powers of the reader rather than the intent of the author is advanced by narrative theorist Barbara Foley. Writing as a Marxist critic, primarily about documentary fiction, Foley offers a socially grounded theory to describe the way that historical details affect readers cognitively. In *Telling the Truth: The Theory and Practice of Documentary Fiction* Foley contends that documentary narrative is distinguished by its claim to verifiable links to the historical world. To investigate truth claims, Foley argues, is to illuminate the assertive capacities of narrative, whether in fiction or in nonfiction (26). I like the way Foley concentrates on narrative power as assertion and recognizes that it can take place in a variety of texts; her study's influence on my notion of narrative implication is important.

Foley's analysis, however, in my judgment, finally is marred by its rather doctrinaire insistence that fiction and nonfiction can be read only through "totalizing frames." Writing during the mid-1980s, when Marxist critics felt the attack of "ahistorical" poststructuralism, Foley wants to save a strictly material analysis, which requires the ability to distinguish history from the narratives that contain it. "I would not therefore conclude," Foley writes, "that all inherited cognitive oppositions are equally ideological and equally fallacious. Some oppositions—between fact and fiction, for instance—describe very real (and, I believe, necessary) cognitive operations, in which actual historical people engage and have engaged" (35). Therefore, Foley ultimately argues that all narrative must be read as fiction or nonfiction, like the Gestalt rabbit/duck drawing, "because any given particular must be understood as part of a larger scheme" (36). The strands that make up its narrative, she argues, must be read in "totalizing frames," must be "scanned and interpreted as either factual or fictive in order to be read and understood" (40).

Even if we grant Foley her metaphor, are there not those moments when the vision blurs as the reader (or even the writer) abandons one Gestalt for another? Is there not a sensation of dizziness when the rabbit is lost but the duck has not yet emerged? Sometimes the eye gropes for patterns that will not impose themselves. The twentieth century might be described as one such moment.[6] In contradistinction to intentionalist theories such as Heyne's, Foley explicitly rejects any grounding for her "Gestalt" theory in the intent of the author—exemplified by "speech-act" theories of discourse. Not surprisingly she believes that a theory driven by authorial intent leaves little room for the explicitly social power she carves out for documentary fiction and, therefore, must rest her case for the essential difference between fiction and nonfiction not on intent but on an insistent cognitive certainty wherein concepts "with blurred edges" are not necessarily concepts that lack a principle of unity (18). Foley rather intriguingly lumps John Searle with

Louis Althusser, the poststructural Marxist, and suggests that both would "dehistoricize" the text: "Searle's stipulation that fiction suspends illocutionary force resembles in some ways Althusser's view that literature 'alludes' to reality," Foley says. "By consigning all fictive discourse to an epistemological region midway between ideology and science, moreover, the Althussarian definition makes it impossible to judge whether one representation of historical activity possesses more legitimacy than another" (83).

One can easily see the ways in which Heyne's and Foley's separate analyses intersect with mine: like Heyne, I believe that the intent of the author plays a powerful (but not all-determining) role in its interaction with an audience; like Foley, I believe that representations of material bodies and historical activity are equally intriguing, despite the intent of the author to present them within a fictional or nonfictional contract. Yet unlike either of their differing analyses, I believe our minds are capable of comprehending a blurred genre status as the reader negotiates texts. Ultimately I am much more interested in concentrating on the relationships among author, written text, reader, and character in nonfictional texts (and some texts normally classified as fictional) than I am in determining their generic status with precision. Therefore, the readings I value are those that recognize that fact-based narratives can affect and challenge actual human beings through the process of representing the history of material human bodies.

The move I am arguing for here is the sort of close reading that grows from the rhetorical tradition of narrative theory into readings that examine a text within culture. James Phelan has suggested a fruitful path into this approach in *Narrative as Rhetoric: Technique, Audiences, Ethics, Ideology*, a recent volume of the Theory and Interpretation of Narrative series in which he responds to the challenges of poststructural theory. "With the point that there are no facts outside of some framework for describing them I am in complete agreement," Phelan concedes in posing what he calls a new kind of antifoundationalism. "It is the next step of the pragmatist logic, the conclusion that truth is constituted by our discourse about it, that gives me pause. That our facts change as our discursive frameworks change does not prove that there are no facts; it proves rather that there are multiple facts and multiple ways of construing facts" (17).

I want to propose that for most forms of nonfiction, the trio of author, text, and reader that Phelan admits into the rhetorical framework must be expanded to admit a fourth player: the actual living or lived beings that make up the subjects of nonfictional narrative. The young boys and girls who were the characters in the criminal narrative uncovered by rape investigators should be able to crowd their way into our rhetorical considerations in even more insistent ways than will the characters in a text like *Lolita*. The author may try to hide, or even escape, that recursive relationship with his subject by changing the names, hiding his own identity as a narrator, or inventing details about characters, but the resisting reader will bring her powers of interpretation precisely to bear on that evasiveness. The reverberations set in motion by the contradiction of a nonfictional text—an artificial construction of memory as well as a compelling representation of history that draws a reader into the life of the text—are what separate nonfiction from many forms of fiction and explain much of its affective power. Both writer and reader are implicated by their socially constructed memory of events in a clash of varying stimuli and responses, many of which echo the intertextuality of everyday life and the uneasy feeling that it has become increasingly difficult to distinguish the narrative of one's own memory from what is mediated or constructed by others.

The Power of Referentiality and the "Shame" of Nonfiction

Two decades ago, during the era of Yale school high deconstruction, J. Hillis Miller argued that a work of fiction is "a chain of displacements," in which an author assumes the invented role of narrator, which in turn displaces itself into the lives of imaginary characters who are represented in the language of indirect discourse as if they were real. The fictional text, Miller continues, attempts to hide (and inadvertently reveals) the contradictions entailed by this displacement.

> [A] work of fiction is conventionally presented not as a work of fiction but as some other form of language. This is almost always some "representational" form rooted in history and in the direct report of "real" human experience. It seems as if works of fiction are ashamed to present themselves as what they are but must always present themselves as what they are not, as some non-fictional germ of language. A novel must pretend to be some kind of language

validated by its one-to-one correspondence to psychological or historical reality. (456)

Whatever the merits of Miller's approach to fiction, I want to look at this
equation from the other direction. I want to examine the way that nonfiction—despite the suggestive differences we have begun to outline between
the materiality of the human body in fiction and in nonfiction—is treated by
much contemporary literary theory as if it were in fact a work of fiction.
Echoing and reversing Miller, I would argue that it seems "as if works of
nonfiction [or at least their critics] are ashamed to present themselves as
what they are but must always present themselves as what they are not, as
some *fictional* germ of language." By this I mean not so much the sense of
"literariness" or "creativity" (the usual proofs to which literary journalism is
subjected in order to gain its admittance to the literary canon) or even its
facticity, but that the issues of access to knowledge, to events, and to the
minds of characters are granted as given when in fact such questions lie at
the very heart of what is most challenging about reportage and nonfictional
representation.

For example, in commenting on Don DeLillo's *Libra* (a sometimes
fictional, sometimes factual biography of Lee Harvey Oswald that blurs the
boundaries of fact and fiction in ways that would defeat Foley and Heyne's
classifications and convince theorists like Frus to abandon the distinction
altogether), *New York Review of Books* critic Robert Towers offers a note of
warning to readers who recall the Kennedy assassination. "Readers over 35
[now almost 45] will remember not only the major events narrated but their
own reactions and thoughts concerning them. Some will want to compare DeLillo's fictional account with the other countless published speculations, and that way madness lies, as well as contamination of the critical
process" (13).

Towers wants to warn his readers away from the edge of *Libra*'s
history, counseling us to read the book safely inside its covers, where *Libra*'s
plot matters more than the Kennedy assassination plot, which stirred actual
"reactions and thoughts" from actual readers. Towers's concluding metaphor
suggests that such reactions introduce the germs of human experience (always messy, usually emotional, hard to classify and control) into the sterile
operating room of the fictional text and its critical reception (detached, cere-
bral, uninvolved). One can imagine how that concern might now be com-
pounded by the subsequent release of Oliver Stone's *JFK* or by Mailer's

book-length narrative on Oswald, two more contaminating entries in the Os-wald/Kennedy germ pool.

Towers's response to *Libra* serves to clarify the ways in which the approach to nonfiction offered by this study differs both from the critical tradition in which generic boundaries are safely maintained and from more recent approaches that would collapse all distinctions between fictional and nonfictional discourse. Towers's stated desire to maintain a safe ahistorical boundary around the fictional text would bother Frus (as it does me). She, after all, "want[s] fiction to take on some of the intellectual and political power of nonfiction—its propositionality, or ability to make statements that influence the way we frame and interpret our experience" (xiv). But Frus, it seems, would agree with Towers's desire to avoid the "madness" of trying to sort through competing discourses to explore their factual interaction and what each teaches the reader about the narrative in question and the facts that underlie it. Not only does Frus call such work "hopeless" in the quote I've already cited, but on other occasions terms it a "common misplaced emphasis on the error and falsity of a narrative account" (193) or a "tedious recital of error [with] a long and dreary history" (257n). Her objection certainly is framed in what she believes is the impossibility of such an agenda rather than in the traditional belief that such extratextual tasks ruin the purity of "art," but the final effect seems much the same. The "madness" of facing history over the edge, of sorting through "competing speculations," can, and perhaps should, be avoided by the contemporary critic, Frus seems to suggest.

The upshot of this approach is that the experience of reading fiction and nonfiction is virtually the same, although the reader may (somewhat na-ively, one gathers) presume that what he is reading is verifiable. "The events reported are *presumed* to be verifiable by other means, although it is not expected that the same story told by another person from a different view-point would be narrated in exactly the same way," Frus contends. "In other respects the experience of reading an invented tale is *identical* to that of reading a historical one. . . . The *text's* materiality is the same, whether the events outlined have externally attested counterparts or not, and whether or not the characters have historical referents" (160–61, first and second em-phases added).

My objection is that this analysis is based on a notion of text that is, ironically, just as "germfree" as the one that Towers proposes, one that col-lapses actual readers into ideal readers and gives all power to the words on the page over the reader who helps to create the text. Actual readers are less manageable. A reader with specific experience of events off the page (in Towers's example, a reader with actual memories of the Kennedy assassination) will bring a thick and sometimes unmanageable response to the nonfiction text because she recognizes its ability to construe her experience off the page. In ways less applicable to most fiction she becomes an actual character in the very document she is reading. The reaction, though certainly unpredictable, makes a material difference in the text. To that reader (a class that becomes quite large when the event is as public as a presidential assassination or a war waged by one's nation), rather more is at stake than reading about the fictional lives of invented characters.

Many realistic novels, of course, also have made use of actual characters or public events such as the Kennedy assassination to draw readers into the mimetic life of the text, a process that can produce reactions that are similar to, but not identical with, the process of implication that I am attempting to describe in nonfiction. As I move toward a more specific discussion of genre questions surrounding nonfiction, I want to explore what sorts of assistance that contemporary literary theory, as well as my own experience as a writer and reporter, can bring to this problem. What is it, exactly, that might be said to distinguish nonfictional reportage from the sort of realistic fictional narrative that also can implicate its readers through memories of actual events or people?

Although the boundary is never absolute, I want to suggest some differences by looking first at what I believe is the most articulate of the recent readings of realistic fiction, Lillian R. Furst's 1995 book, *All Is True: The Claims and Strategies of Realist Fiction.* Furst's provocative study traces the history and practice of realistic fictional narrative from the deeply mimetic *aletheia* (the merging of illusion and imitation in the early history of the novel) to the *adequatio,* a sense of the narrative as a self-conscious illusion "invested with truth through belief in the power of representation" (7–8). The nineteenth-century realists' equation of truth with illusion means they could achieve their ends "only at the level of pretense," Furst argues, "by prevailing upon their readers" to accept the validity of their contentions and to accept the reality of the fictive worlds created in the narrative.

> They were remarkably successful in doing so because they were able largely to conceal the literariness of their practices [the impulse Miller identifies]. In a sense, therefore,

the realistic novel can be seen as a prodigious cover-up. Translated into more affirmative terms, the realist endeavor can be taken as an ambitious exercise in bringing the novel to terms or at least to a truce with the essential artificiality of art, through an act of repudiation that takes the form of the defiant assertion *"All is true."* (9–10, Furst's emphasis)

Subsequently, the concept of *adequatio* realism came under the attack of structuralism and poststructuralism, which exposed realism's deep dependence on "the authenticity of its illusion" (17), rather than its sense of mimesis or imitation. Furst shows how Wolfgang Iser, following the philosopher Hans Gadamer, first set free the notion of representation from its yoke of mimesis and how Barthes then foregrounded the textual rather than referential, the semiotic rather than the mimetic. Ultimately, however, Furst finds such distinctions limiting, arguing for a middle course between "the referential fallacy" that the novel "is simply a faithful mirror of everyday life" and the "linguistic fallacy" that it "is simply a web of words" (22). Rather, she argues, realistic fiction should be read for "the appearance of truthfulness inherent in the illusion" that "derive[s] primarily from the effect of the words printed on the page, even while they seem to refer to an external world" (25). According to Furst, realistic fiction lives in a "slippery, ill-definable," (25) uncomfortable middle situation that is not wholly fact, or lie, or truth.

The "conviction," the appearance of truth projected by the artifact, resides not in its relationship to an anterior model but in the response it evokes, through its artifice, in viewers/readers. So, in order to explore how realist fiction achieves its "air of reality," the focus of analysis must be shifted from the author to the readers, from the novel's origins to its reception, from the putative sources onto the text itself. For to read a realistic narrative is to submit to an act of persuasion, the aim of which is to convert readers to the belief that *"all is true."* (26, Furst's emphasis)

One can readily see the similarities between Furst's project and my own as well as the one signal difference that I believe demonstrates the contrast—no matter how blurred their edges—in the genres that interest us. Both Furst and I are interested in the relationship between truth and illu-

sion, the way that the facts of a text rub up against their expression in narrative, most especially in the "slippery, middle situations." Both of us grant
readers an important role in the equation and recognize that it will be the
responsibility of the competent reader to uncover the stakes of the text's
persuasion. But what separates our two approaches is our starting point. Because she is concerned with realistic fiction, Furst can start with the assumption that it is not the "anterior model" but the response that counts (even if
that response makes use of historical facts and characters); but because I am
concerned with events and characters that *always* have a presence outside
the text as well, I do not have the luxury of disregarding the text's relationship
(even though it always will be intertextual) to its anterior models. This is the
sense in which I open up Phelan's interrelation of authorial agency, textual
phenomena, and reader response (*Narrative* 19) to admit the fourth player:
the subject of the narrative across the edge of its boundaries. Nonfiction, in
my judgment, forces negotiation with its referentiality. And in my judgment
literary theorists too often read nonfiction as if they are embarrassed (no
doubt a holdover from our worship of artistic creativity) by the aims of referentiality or by the actual labor it takes and will take to gain access to the
materials of nonfiction.

 Perhaps an example drawn from my life as a writer would make
some of these distinctions more clear. When I was a reporter in Charlottesville, Virginia, I covered the case of a woman whose bloodied car was found
on an exit ramp from the nearby interstate highway. Medical records con-
firmed the blood to be hers and of sufficient amount that her wound surely
would have been fatal. The woman's body was never found. On the first anni-
versary of her disappearance I spent a weekend in her small home community about 150 miles to the southwest near the West Virginia border, talking
to her mother, her mother-in-law, her employer, and her best friends. I
checked court records from several assault cases she had filed against her
estranged husband (who was a suspect in the case but later was cleared by
police), interviewed state police investigators, was given her personal scrapbooks to examine by her mother, and visited several key locations that fig-
ured in her life and subsequent disappearance. My research was no secret
in the small community (indeed, I could not have kept it a secret had I
wanted to), and many people, including the woman's mother, wanted to be
sure that I sent them copies of my articles about the woman's life and
disappearance.

 During the writing and subsequent publication of the articles, which ran as a series and were structured as New Journalistic narrative rather than in the traditional inverted pyramid news style, I was keenly aware that I was in the position to control much about the way the woman might be remembered. And, as I've noted before, my account certainly had all the indeterminacy of text: I had to decide which quotes to use, how to arrange them, what details to add from the hundreds in my notebook. But the woman's presence in her home town before her disappearance and the memories that people had of her also formed a powerful part of the equation, as did the court narratives, the medical records, the scrapbooks, the police evidence, and our newspaper's claim to be factual. The centerpiece of that equation was the woman's name, Kimberly Jane Britts, a name that (then and now) signifies something outside the boundaries of the articles as well as inside their narratives. Although as a writer I could control a lot of her history, I had no power to control everything, nor did I covet that control.

Five years later, for an advanced creative-writing workshop taken in connection with my graduate studies, I wrote a short story based on the disappearance. I tried to imagine what had happened among the woman, her husband, and a man whom she had been dating (and whom I also had interviewed in connection with my stories) before her disappearance. As realistic fiction the story had many details of place and character that either were taken from life or mirrored life: a cafe in the small town, the road entering the town, even a statue on the town square of Confederate General Harry Heth, who had defeated the Union troops commanded by Colonel Rutherford B. Hayes in May 1862. From research on an unrelated story I drew details that I tried to make significant in this narrative: how the silver-finished nine-millimeter automatic handguns manufactured for police departments by the Italian firm Beretta had room for one less bullet in their clips and more complex safeties (one officer had told me it was a "fussy" safety) than the black-finished, nine-millimeter Beretta automatic then favored by drug dealers in that part of Virginia and elsewhere. Although the narrative was fiction, I was scrupulous about these realistic details, checking historical facts as well as gun-manufacturing specifications so as to build the story's factual credibility and so as not to offend anyone who knew guns or Civil War history better than I did. But I also changed the name of the shooting victim (indeed made her no longer a victim), imagined her and other characters' thoughts, and perhaps most importantly, gained imaginative access to conversations and scenes that would have been impossible to observe or at the very least would have been altered profoundly by the presence of an observer/intruder.

My graduate workshop readers challenged me briskly on both factual details and technique. They issued such challenges as "She never would have said that" or "You don't have the cafe right," but they never challenged the name I granted her nor questioned the facts of the characters' lives in the story against the life of Kimberly Jane Britts. Although it was nominated for a writing award, I have not attempted to publish the story, so I had no opportunity to gauge its reception other than in the workshop. But I doubt that the story would have gained the intense interest that the woman's hometown community had shown in the nonfictional series. Other than a few details of scene, I doubt they would have recognized the woman at all or felt much sense of ownership over her character. For by the time the fictional story was finished it was about some other woman and some other life. The few readers of my fictional story cared deeply about the *character* but not her propositionality to real life; by contrast, even those readers of the newspaper series who had never before heard of Kimberly Jane Britts seemed strongly affected by the sense that the population of the world had been reduced by one and that the loss mattered because she had begun to live for them in the story that represented her history in her small southwestern Virginia community.

From my experience, my work on the fictional version of the disappearance narrative is almost precisely described by Furst's analysis of realistic *fiction* and its relationships with writer, reader, and fact: "The appearance of truth . . . resides not in its relationship to an anterior model but in the response it evokes" (26). And had the story traded on even more public events—say, by evoking the histories of those in the community who had been scarred by the Vietnam War or by local civil rights conflicts—its use of realistic detail might have drawn even more complex reactions from readers. On the other hand Frus's description of nonfiction in her *Politics and Poetics of Journalistic Narrative*, provocative though it is, seems inadequate to the nonfictional version of the story, to my experience of writing the newspaper series, and to the response it gained from readers. Frus claims that "fictional narrative cannot be distinguished from nonfictional narrative on the basis of the fictivity of any of its elements, for even fictivity must be represented in language. Rhetorically, no state or condition is more imaginary than any other: all characters and personae are created; the world is constituted after the fact by texts" (11). She also later contends that "our experience of reading stories about characters and events that we know (from other sources) actually existed or have happened" is identical "to reading about invented ones (including narrators)" (36).

I do not believe the experiences of writing and reading the two narratives to be identical. Certainly, the writer of realistic (or even quasi-realistic) fiction ignores the power of facts at her own risk. I could have changed the facts of Italian gun production or even rearranged the statue on the town square, but, theoretically at least, that would only have compromised my complicity in what Miller rightly identifies as its pretense to a kind of language validated by its "one-to-one correspondence to psychological or historical reality" (456). Moreover, resistant readings have taught us to question the narrative stance of fiction as well as nonfiction, especially when a male writer presumes to relay the thoughts of a central female character, and to expose the way that omniscient realistic fiction naturalizes and often effaces the ideology of a central (and gendered male) consciousness.

Despite Frus's contentions, these are not precisely the same questions that might arise regarding the nonfiction author's control over an extra-textual identity, her power to gain access to scenes and conversation, or her ability to read minds and arrange factual representations. My depiction of Kimberly Jane Britts's life and death in the nonfictional series was intertwined with the fact of her body: my access to her thoughts was circumscribed by the words in her diary, her scrapbook, her sworn statements in her spousal-abuse complaints. By contrast, I could access (or create) any thought or scene I wanted to access (or create) in the fictional narrative. To say, as Frus and others do, that fiction and nonfiction cannot be distinguished on these levels by either writer or reader is to ignore both the ideology and the power of narratives that purport to construe lives, overhear conversations, attend events, and read minds outside those narratives.

Autobiographer and essayist Annie Dillard certainly seems aware of this difference in her recent description of the anxiety of writing her memoirs about growing up in Pittsburgh. Despite her recognition that she writes a "coherent and crafted" (56) narrative with all the artistry of a fictional piece, she understands that the experience of both creator and reader is different because the characters spill outside the book. "I tried to leave out anything that might trouble my family," she recalls of her autobiography, *An American Childhood*. "My parents are quite young. My sisters are watching this book carefully. Everybody I'm writing about is alive and well, in full possession of his faculties, and possibly willing to sue." She concludes, perhaps a trifle ruefully, "Things were simpler when I wrote about muskrats" (53).

Similarly, Ian Frazier describes the ramifications of writing about actual characters in his recently published memoir/biography, *Family*. Frazier believes that factual writing is by definition a guilt-drenched "psychic jujitsu" because of the way the narrative construes actual characters, even those who are no longer living.

> [Y]ou have plain old survivor's guilt; you're writing about the dead. If somebody had said to my great-grandfather, pointing to me, "this little kid with his baseball cap on backwards is going to tell a lot of people what your life meant, he's going to be the sole repository of your good name," he might have been outraged. I also felt uneasy writing about the Civil War veterans, because of how much that war was a part of their life and how much they cared about it. I knew I wasn't going to get it completely right, and I felt the weight of their invisible displeasure. . . . I just kept dosing my guilt with one thing or another to reduce it to a size I could live with. I recommend that to memoir writers. (138–39)

But are Dillard's or Frazier's experiences unique to nonfiction? The novelist Toni Morrison feels something of that same link with and responsibility for the dead when she writes fictional narratives such as *Song of Solomon* or *Beloved* because she is attempting to be "deadly serious about fidelity to the milieu out of which I write and in which my ancestors actually lived" (92). That milieu is racism and slavery, which, Morrison says, creates "the absence of the interior life, the deliberate excising of it from the records that the slaves themselves told" (92). As Furst recommends, Morrison wants to evoke "the appearance of truthfulness inherent in the illusion" (25). Morrison means her narratives to reimagine the interior life of her ancestors, to restore their lost voices; she wants her narratives to spill off the page into the truth of her ancestors and their past. Morrison says,

> the crucial distinction for me is not the difference between fact and fiction, but the distinction between fact and truth. Because facts can exist without human intelligence, but truth cannot. So if I'm looking to find and expose a truth about the interior life of people who didn't write it (which doesn't mean they didn't have it); if I'm trying to fill in the blanks that the slave narratives left—to part the veil that

was so frequently drawn, to implement the stories that I heard—then the approach that's most productive and most trustworthy for me is the recollection that moves from the image to the text. Not from the text to the image. (93–94)

I have no quarrel with Morrison and her project, nor with the deep similarities between fiction and nonfiction and their engagement in history that both Frus and Furst eloquently describe. But Morrison's project in *Beloved* or *Song of Solomon* is not precisely the same as it would be were the narratives nonfiction, were they the depiction of actual lives such as the memoirs written by Dillard or Frazier. Following Morrison's description of her creative work a bit further will make some of those most important distinctions more clear. In telling the story of her ancestors Morrison says she creates a narrator who can imagine herself into the interior lives of her characters. She recommends that the narrator maintain the illusion that she speaks from the characters' point of view, when in reality the telling, of course, remains under direct control of the author. "I like the feeling of a *told* story," says Morrison, where the reader begins to identify the narrator as the reader's own voice, comforting, guiding, "alarmed by the same things that the reader is alarmed by" and unsure of what action is to happen next:

> So you have this sort of guide. But that guide can't have a personality; it can only have a sound, and you have to feel comfortable with this voice, and then this voice can easily abandon itself and reveal the interior dialogue of a character. So it's a combination of using the point of view of various characters but still retaining the power to slide in and out, providing that when I'm "out" the reader doesn't see little fingers pointing to what's in the text. (100)

My contention is that the power "to slide in and out of the interior dialogue" of characters that Morrison rightly reserves for her narrator in fiction is a deeply complicated notion when it is applied to nonfiction. I doubt that the nonfictional characters who concern Annie Dillard would grant such license to slide in and out of their minds unless, perhaps, they are muskrats. Although the stylistic innovations of what came to be called New Journalism certainly explored interior-dialogue and point-of-view narrative, the issue of access to character by author always remains critical in the sorts of readings I am advocating.

My next chapter will begin with a detailed look at the ideology of such an invasive narrative stance, arguing that the nonfictional status of a text, in this case Jane Kramer's *The Last Cowboy*, can force its author into ideological (and logical) contradictions that the author would not face were the narrative presented as fiction. The ability to read minds, to gain access to scenes, to name names, I will argue, is never an innocent enterprise in nonfiction. Those negotiations, in which experience and manuscript interact, even more than the text's truthfulness, are what explain the power and problems of nonfiction. As this study will show, particularly in the chapter that engages the Vietnam writing of O'Brien, that power can be extended to the sort of historical fiction that trades on actual characters and events, but in general builds from such sources as the reader's encounter in nonfiction with characters and events that also live outside the text. Other important factors are the reader's belief that he is reading a text linked to outside experience, the author's implication as a reporter as well as a creator, and the reader's understanding that the author and/or publisher has made some sort of truth claim about the work. In sum, the notion of experience operating on the manuscript even as the manuscript operates on experience is, in my judgment, the source of nonfiction's special power.

This unmanageable power derives from a textual interchange, one that was perhaps best explained by Mas'ud Zavarzadeh in *The Mythopoeic Reality*, a 1976 study that too often is overlooked, perhaps because of Zavarzadeh's complicated structuralist-era typology and his mistaken belief that adventurous nonfiction offers "zero degree interpretation" on the part of its authors (89).[7] But beyond that claim, Zavarzadeh asserts in *The Mythopoeic Reality* that the nonfiction texts that interest him are composed of a bireferential dialogue between inner and outer reference. He says, adjusting Northrop Frye, that these texts combine an in-referential creation of a world "mapped out within the book" as well as an out-referential "external configuration of facts verifiable outside the book" (55). The enduring, and largely unrecognized, value of Zavarzadeh's bireferential approach is that it subverts the possibility of a reading in a world removed from the actual (of either the sort Towers or Frus proposes) as well as forecloses the comfort level that might result from believing that the nonfiction text is unambiguously "true."

Zavarzadeh's bireferential narratives unleash readers and writers to form open, dynamic systems in active tension with the experiential world

outside the book. The dialectical quality of these systems is partly derived
from their attitude toward facts. Reading nonfiction narrative in its full bireferential complexity, Zavarzadeh argues in a line of reasoning I will explore
more deeply in the next chapter, requires a reexamination of the question of
the function of fact in nonfiction (58). The nonfictional narrative—one that
purports to recreate for the reader an experience that is at least potentially
also available outside the text—forces the reader into a multireferential
reading, not simply, as Zavarzadeh has argued, because of the bizarre nature
of contemporary fact (humans have for thousands of years faced war or other
disorienting experiences) but because the reader now experiences the original event both within and without the story. Several strands of potentially
complicated relationships are established: writer (outside text) to event;
writer (through text) to event; reader (outside text) to event; reader (through
text) to event; event arbitrated by text; text arbitrated by event and interpreted by writer and reader.

Reading over the Edge of Ritual and Rhetoric

The force of this study, as perhaps already is apparent, intentionally blurs
and reworks several rhetorical and social traditions in criticism. The study
recognizes that nonfiction narratives normally are born and marketed as
mass mediations and thus are produced and read as reportage: representations of public knowledge and history. The study, therefore, examines nonfiction's determinative effects as a form of written communication as well as
artistic expression and examines such effects in culture rather than as discrete, ahistorical cases. But within communication studies, what has been
the valuable rhetorical emphasis on a text as a communication device has
too often been restricted to an intentional encoding/decoding model. That
encoding/decoding model (a strategy that, ironically, is not unlike Heyne's)
would read texts solely for the author's "intent" to present "truth" and would
assess her success from an empirical standard of whether the reader appre-
hends that "truth" effectively. Such methodology still is the paradigm for
many quantitative studies in journalism schools that stem from reader sur-
veys and message effectiveness and is related to what media theorist James
Carey critiques as "the nineteenth-century desire to use communication and
transportation to extend influence, control, and power over wider distances
and greater populations" (43).

I believe such a formulation is simply too narrow. I want to read nonfiction's rhetorical effects as communications rituals, concerned "with how messages, or texts, interact with people in order to produce meanings" (Fiske 2) or what Carey identifies as centering "on the sacred ceremony that draws people together in fellowship and ceremony" even if such ceremony is only "characterized by domination and [is] therefore illegitimate" (43). That method of reading, which I will outline in more detail at the beginning of the next chapter, necessarily raises questions of subjectivity and how subjectivity is forged by communication rituals in social situations. Examining the ritual of social communication forces the subject to understand the manner by which life implicates us, the manner by which our actions implicate others, and the manner by which others attempt to "author" us and to interpret our existence (Davis 212–13).

If we grant the assertion that culture is both that which defines us and that which is the site for our struggles for liberation, then I believe we will read literature (particularly nonfictional literature) over a dialectical edge. Nonfiction is literature whose historical assertions and representational intentions are by definition an effort to fix our identity within the world around us. Nonfiction's claim begins with an either-or invitation to the reader (either this is true for you or else you are wrong; either this is your history or your history is inauthentic) that is then negotiated as the reader engages the text. That negotiation in turn creates readers who examine history over the boundary between reader and writer, history and discourse—dialectical concepts that Walter A. Davis calls "mutually determining and vitally in need of one another, a *union* grounded [by] the tension between them [that] *defines* each" (328, Davis's emphases).

But at the same time, work in cultural studies and media theory such as I am using—with its traditional emphasis on the textuality and narrative organization of meaning—has much to gain from the sort of close readings at which narrative theorists working in the rhetorical tradition have excelled as well as from their practice of being as specific as possible about what kinds of narrative strategies might tend to produce what kinds of effects. I am particularly persuaded by contemporary narrative theory that can recognize the differing and interrelated ways that texts can engage readers mimetically, synthetically, and thematically (Phelan, *Reading* 10–14) and that read the complexities of narrative presence against authorial strategy. For this reason, I will take several occasions to test my theories of nonfiction against the theories offered by Phelan's *Narrative as Rhetoric*. Rhetorical theory, though it has tended to be limited primarily to fiction, offers an alternative to the current critical climate that sometimes seems both ashamed of the concept of close reading and anxious to erase all distinctions between such literary concepts as fact and fiction.

Finally, then, an implicated reading of nonfiction over the edge of history is served by an active contest of readings and referentiality, not by a collapse of all distinctions between fiction and nonfiction nor by a binary approach, whether it be empirically, intentionally, or cognitively grounded. In the pages that follow I want to look at that "active contest" from four angles: first I examine the way that writers of nonfiction implicate themselves within the text, how their narrative presence reveals the ideology of their projects. I will begin in the chapter titled "Writing Inside Out" with a close exploration of what it means for a narrator to negotiate access to scenes and to the thoughts of other characters. And through an extended analysis of a Freudian case study I will show how a close reading of Freud's presence inside the text reveals an agenda special to the nonfictional case study: an effort to "fix" the historical character outside as well as inside the text. In that regard the decision to present speech verbatim, to construct scenes, and to comment on speech and action provides critical clues to the presence the narrator assumes in the text as well as his desire to construct the identity of subordinated characters.

In chapter 3, "Writing Outside In," I approach the nonfictional author from the other direction, reading the facts of the author's life, the events he has covered, and the circumstances of publication against what we can determine of the author's self-created presence inside the text. Primarily from examples drawn from the nonfictional writings of John Reed and Tom Wolfe, I want to demonstrate how holding flesh-and-blood authors accountable for their work opens up the propositional nature of nonfiction and illuminates its writing.

The final two chapters will explore how readers are positioned inside and outside of nonfictional narratives. Chapter 4, "Reading Inside Out," traces the inside construction: the way a text can position its readers by its narrative strategy and the way in which a reader can be encouraged to identify with or against the position of power that the text's narrative strategy creates. I contend, primarily through an analysis of the writings of Didion, that nonfiction gains particular power to manipulate and/or release the anxieties of its readers because the reader of this historical document becomes in one way or another an actual character in the very text she is reading.

Finally, the fifth chapter, "Reading Outside In," will argue that non-fiction properly is read by examining outside knowledge from other historical narratives that we can gain of the author and the events covered by the writing. I argue that the text reveals itself when outside knowledge is pitted against the text's internal references. Moreover, I choose a set of texts—O'Brien's narratives about My Lai and surrounding areas of Vietnam—that push against the boundaries of fiction and nonfiction and that deliberately create an intertextual milieu that mirrors the deeply mediated and intertextual experience of our daily lives. I hope to show, however, that reading the facts of O'Brien and My Lai from the outside in can create a text that engages its readers, a text in which truth matters because of the materiality of its referents. Even if it is difficult to know with certainty what always happens in those referential and created worlds, O'Brien's texts, despite (and because) of their challenge to generic certainty, build a body of deeply implicating writing for their author, a body of writing whose sum is far greater and more unsettling than its parts. Read from the outside in, each text that the author and reader create together about the history of Vietnam, I will contend, leads toward a critical lesson for the power of nonfiction that hovers over my entire study. If you ask if the story is true, and if the answer matters, you've got your answer.

2.

WRITING INSIDE OUT:

The Nonfiction Narrator in Scripted and Conscripted History

READING NONFICTION OVER THE EDGE as implicated text calls for examining its narrator against the possibilities and limitations of an actual reportorial presence as well as against the grain of what we know of its author in history. The first of these two concepts I will cover under the present chapter's exploration of writing inside out, and the latter I will cover in the following chapter's examination of writing outside in. Both operations have as their purpose an effort to implicate the author of nonfictional narrative, in which attempt I adopt John J. Pauly's concept analyzing "the way the reporting process implicates writer, subjects, and readers in relationships beyond a text" (112). I also extend Pauly's notion of implicated author to expand Wayne Booth's famous notion of "implied author" outlined in *The Rhetoric of Fiction* (1961) and adjusted in that volume's revised edition (1983) and in Booth's *The Company We Keep: An Ethics of Fiction* (1988). In *The Rhetoric of Fiction,* Booth says the implied author occasions "the intuitive apprehension of a completed artistic whole" (73) and is implied by the book's total form "regardless of what party his creator belongs to in real life" (73–74). By the revised edition of *Rhetoric of Fiction,* and in *The Company We Keep,* Booth had blurred that distinction somewhat, now defining the implied author as a presence "who knows that the telling is in one sense an artificial construct but who takes responsibility for it, for whatever values or norms it implies" as well as the illusion that "in responding to *me* you respond to a real person" (*Company* 125, Booth's emphasis). My notion of implicated author, of course, refuses to distance that "real-life creator" and her affiliations from the book's narrative work. Those reportorial and analytical methods are always open to scrutiny because the nonfiction narrator is measured against a human presence that must gain access to the other presences that become part of the narrative. Because she deals with characters whose presence extends outside the text, the author must negotiate such issues as whether she can read minds, be omnipresent, give "voice" to characters, and the like. We will not transfer nonfiction narrative out of the category if we find moments of constructedness, for all narratives are constructed. Rather, readers can learn about the author and the narrative from the way the author constructs (his)story.

A more specific example from Booth's *The Company We Keep* might help to make the distinction between his and my approach more clear.[1] There, Booth contrasts Norman Mailer's *Executioner's Song* to Anne Tyler's *Dinner at the Homesick Restaurant*—a novel whose plot imagines the moment of death in a way that reminds Booth somewhat of Mailer's history of the Gary Gilmore execution:

> Imagining herself into a situation [Tyler] could hardly know at first hand, one that involves characters she had had to "make up," she immediately asks us to begin inferring the meaning, for character and event, of such a wrenching death wish. Instead of two cliched kids . . . we have a puzzling wish, a promise of complexity, and of course a direct oath of office sworn by the implied author: "I shall imagine a complex world with you; I shall resist the easy way of simply reporting a world that you are to accept as actual without having to work much at it." It would seem that simply on the scales of quantity, reciprocity, and range, Tyler will prove the better friend. (208)

In part, Booth simply is repeating Aristotle's preference in the *Poetics* for a "persuasive impossibility to an unpersuasive possibility" (48) as Booth salutes Tyler for "resist[ing] the easy way of simply reporting a world that you are to accept without having to work much at it." But Booth at least proves to be more honest than a strictly formalist critic would be in detailing his objections to Mailer. He admits that part of his problem is with the "public image 'Norman Mailer,'" most of whose books Booth has read and who, Booth says, "is simply playing games with me; he does not care a hill of beans for my welfare" (209). Booth thus at least indirectly suggests that a narrative intended to be read as nonfiction positions an actual authorial presence and implicates its author much more readily than does fiction. The "real" Tyler, Booth seems to recognize and, indeed, virtually to celebrate, is neither a character in her novel nor a physical presence that hovers over the novel in quite the same way as does Mailer. He admires her (as do I) for her ability to imagine herself into the thoughts and ambiguities of a character facing death. But Booth's second—and in my view even more significant—objection is banished to a footnote that, ironically, insists on evoking, then discounting, its own force:

> *I have deliberately ruled out of my discussion an additional motive* I have for mistrusting "my" Mailer. I am from the area of Utah in which his "novel" is set; I know how misleading some of his portraits of the area and the people will be to readers who live elsewhere. And I fear the harm that his book will do to many of those who are caricatured in it, including Gilmore's wife, children, and relatives. Though such objections make me think less of Mailer the man, they are in large part irrelevant to my appraisal of the book as a narrative that I might recommend to one of my own friends. (210n, emphasis added)

Why should Booth—who after all is posing an *ethics* of criticism here—dismiss as largely irrelevant his reactions to Mailer's reworking of history and culture? The effect of a nonfictional narrative on its characters as well as the relatives and community of the characters always is germane, because both the author and characters live outside the text as well as inside. Considerations of characterization and its effects, in my judgment, lie at the root of its implication in history and are never "irrelevant" to an appraisal of the practices of nonfictional communication.

I am thus proposing a model for reading nonfiction that would first locate the author inside and outside the text, examine these intertwined and differing presences and explore their relationships in both historical and artistic terms. We might examine specifically the author's positioning vis-à-vis the subject, not only what the author *acknowledges* (the intention) but also what the author *reveals* and thus communicates through cultural signs in the production and exchange of meaning. The emphasis in these sorts of readings is on the relationship of the writer to his subject and to his reader within a literary and social text.

A brief analogy will make this distinction more clear. An employer summons a new employee to his office. "You will find that we are all treated as equals here at the Acme Widget family," he says with a welcoming smile. "I want you to make yourself at home and think of me as your friend, rather than as your employer." The traditional analysis of communications transmission, one based on empirical considerations, would concentrate on the intent and effectiveness of the statement, taking the employer's statement on its face value and examining it against the text of the employee's subsequent experience at the company and the message's ability to produce the behavior that the speaker desired. In other words, the effectiveness of the communication would be evaluated from the premise of the speaker's intent, even if that intent might be fairly ironic or complex. But those readers who are interested in evaluating a nonfictional claim within a ritual view of communication already would be exploring not only the speaker's intent and the listener's specific response, but the symbolic, cultural exchange. I am using the term "ritual" here in the sense that James Carey adjusted it from Clifford Geertz's *The Interpretation of Cultures:* "A ritual view conceives communication as a process through which a shared culture is created, modified, and transformed" (43).

The ritual of communication can play across its stated intent by revealing itself symbolically as well as directly—that is through differing, often subtly nuanced, details of power and relationships that assume meaning beyond themselves as symbols will—as well as by direct statements (Gagnier 6). In the present analogy is the interview scheduled at the employer's convenience or at the employee's? Does the employer sit on a plush chair behind an imposing desk while the employee sits on a stationary chair facing his boss? In the universe of the Acme Widget family does the employer have a communications system at his fingertips (phone, intercom, computer terminal, fax machine, television remote) while the employee receives and transmits his messages second-hand? Is the employer allowed a range of expression in clothing (tailored suits, hand-painted ties, even T-shirts and jeans) while the employee is expected to dress in a uniform, formal or otherwise, largely selected by someone else? The cultural relationship between the author and receptor of the message, therefore, becomes as important as the words that make up the message.

Applied to nonfictional texts, this cultural view of communications will pay close attention to the author's relationship to the reader: to her word use and scene construction, to her tone and theme. A close (even a resisting) analysis alive to the intent and symbolic rituals of communication will measure not only what the author *crafts* but also what the author *reveals*, even as it locates the author as a presence inside and outside the text. Even a nonfiction text that largely represents "private" events will bring its author's discursive properties into question. And although this sort of resisting reading is also possible for fiction, the depiction of characters with material bodies outside the written document, as the previous chapter attempted to demonstrate, will produce a response that intersects more directly with actual life.

The Problem of the Nonfiction Narrator Who Knows Too Much

Jane Kramer's *The Last Cowboy*, a nonfiction narrative about Texas ranch life, provides an opportunity for me to demonstrate the value of reading the author both at the level of intent and for its communication rituals. Although its characters and exact location are not readily known to the general reader, its publication history (originally as "Cowboy" in *The New Yorker*, later published in book form as *The Last Cowboy*, and still later reprinted in Norman Sims's collection *The Literary Journalists*) asserts that *The Last Cowboy* is nonfiction. Kramer adds to the narrative's claim and reveals her stated intent of authenticity by publicly crediting the *New Yorker* researcher "who checked 'Cowboy' so thoroughly that he started dreaming about the grain sorghum price index and differentials in the Ogallala water table" (*Last Cowboy* ix). The reader only interested in reading the narrative for its stated intent and empirical veracity would therefore take *The Last Cowboy* as truth unless there were some specific facts that emerged that would provide reason to doubt its authenticity. The reader who believes there is no important distinction between fiction and nonfiction would read *The Last Cowboy* as a text in which specific truth claims and their construction largely are irrelevant. But my approach is to read for the author "inside out," to argue that there is a tremendous value to reading the narrative specifically as a *nonfiction* narrative that implicates its author, in this case Kramer, as an important if unnamed and unacknowledged character in the text.

In *The Last Cowboy* Kramer presents the story of a ranch foreman whom she names Henry Blanton. Her decision not to provide Blanton's actual name is critical, as I shall demonstrate in this chapter's subsequent consideration of the Freudian case study. But for now, I am more interested in what the text reveals about Kramer's ritual of communication. Blanton is alienated from his labor on a shrinking and increasingly mechanized ranch, drinks too much, and finds himself unable to make any meaningful connections either with his wife or with any other female. In one of the narrative's pivotal scenes Blanton and his brother drive their pickup truck out for a night on the eve of Henry's fortieth birthday. Kramer presents verbatim their brief but bitterly ironic conversation in the pickup cab, building authenticity by evoking their language usage and pronunciation and by entering first one and then the other's thoughts. I will quote the passage at some length so I can demonstrate the potential of specific textual analysis to my agenda of reading nonfiction narrative from the inside out:

> "It's like this, Tom," [Henry] said after they had driven in silence for half an hour, passing Henry's pickup bottle back and forth. "Here I'm getting a certain age, and I find I ain't accumulated nothing. I find . . ."
>
> Tom nodded.
>
> "I mean, it was different with Daddy," Henry said. "Those old men like Daddy—they turned forty and they was just glad if they had a job. But nowadays, you turn forty—you figure you got ten, fifteen years left to really do something." Henry thought for a while. "So that's what I'm figuring to do," he said finally. "Do something."
>
> "Shoot, Henry, we're just peons, you and me," Tom said. Tom was known for his way of putting things. He was nearly thirty-seven, but he was still all bones and joints and bashful blushes, like a boy, and when he talked, with his Adam's apple jumping around above his T-shirt collar, even his brother half expected that his voice would crack.
>
> "Peons," Tom repeated. It was his favorite word for himself, and he liked to stretch it out in a long drawl— "peeeeons." But the fact was that Tom had been thinking about doing something, too. He had just bought an old jukebox for twenty-five dollars, and he was planning to fix it up, sell it, and, with his profit, buy two old jukeboxes, and then four, until he bought and sold his way to a used-jukebox fortune. (24–25)

The scene achieves immediacy and poignancy by silences as well as by verbatim conversation, capturing the pacing of real speech, particularly that of two men unaccustomed to voicing their fears. Silences are interpreted omnisciently ("Henry thought for a while"), which implies that the narrator can know the difference between mere silence and rumination. Tom's physical and verbal mannerisms as well as his thoughts about his jukebox scheme are presented as if the narrator were able to hear and observe the conversation as well as to read the participants' thoughts, even though there is no evidence that anyone (least of all a non-Texan female reporter from the *New Yorker*) was seated on the truck seat between the two cowboys.

Read specifically as nonfiction—as a piece that cuts its narrator against the grain of the possibilities and limitations of an actual author—the episode presents a theoretical impossibility. The entire thrust of the scene (which ends with Henry and Tom Blanton slashed and beaten in a meaningless fight with two city slickers) and of *The Last Cowboy* as a whole (which ends with Henry Blanton emasculating three "black stud" bulls [147] in an act of vengeance to which Kramer attaches enormous symbolic value) is that neither brother really has been able to articulate his pain and humiliation, let alone relay those thoughts to a woman. Strictly speaking, the only way Kramer could have gained her story is if the thematic underpinning of her narrative were false: that is if Blanton or his brother *could* speak frankly and self-perceptively during a pickup truck ride in front of a sophisticated, educated, and presumably articulate woman about their feelings of political, social, economic, and perhaps physical, impotence. But if that were true they would no longer fill the role that the narrative prepares for them.

Of course it is quite plausible that Kramer might have learned of Tom's jukebox dreams ("he had been thinking about doing something, too") and assessed his physical and speech characteristics ("he was still all bones and joints and bashful blushes, like a boy") through separate research. If so, no modern reader would object to her making use of such research to add immediacy and detail to a crucial scene. Moreover, if the two cowboys had separately reenacted the conversation for Kramer, all but the most obsessively literal reader would have granted Kramer permission to cast the scene in the "exact" words of the men.

But the evidence throughout the narrative is that neither Blanton would ever cooperate in such a way even if he wished to. For the cowboy code that Kramer is demonstrating throughout her characterization would forbid it. And even if we suppose that Blanton relayed his thoughts to Kramer through his wife, Betsy, it would undermine the narrative's overall point that Blanton no longer is capable of any meaningful conversation with his own wife. In fact Henry's emotional remoteness from Betsy is dramatized repeatedly as one of the book's most compelling themes. Betsy cries in bed at night, hoping to no avail that Henry will wake and comfort her (124). She reads him Kahlil Gibran's "The Prophet," hoping that the words will make him tender, but they make him "bored and fidgety instead" (125).

One could surmise that Henry might be more comfortable talking to Kramer than to his own wife, except that he also clams up around Bay Robinson, a "shrewd and maternal" (27) ranch wife from Dallas who clearly has the men's grudging respect and to whom Kramer appears to have gained access. But Robinson learns no more specifics about Henry and Tom's feelings than do the other women. Throughout the book Henry's inability to talk to women frankly or to handle conflict without violence is consistent. For example, confronted with daughter Melinda's wish to dance at the Friday-night social at the Catholic parish hall, "Henry refused to discuss it and had whipped her soundly with his belt the one time she tried to argue with him about going" (122).

For her part, Betsy clearly seems free to confide in Kramer when she and the reporter are alone, and although Kramer never dramatizes her own character, she presents a long statement from Betsy (131–37) that is filled with the vernacular of kitchen-table conversation ("But now I figure that Henry maybe couldn't *face* Christmas. Here he was, fixing to be forty years old. I mean, he always thought . . . " [131]) that presumably was tape recorded by Kramer. Betsy's statement, laced with examples of her husband's remoteness and its psychological toll on her, ends with the poignant recognition that the wife will never be granted access to the thoughts of her husband that matter:

> He's a good man—and all the drinking and stunts, that's because of his disappointment. He sees me going to work,   · so tired all the time, and he knows it's to help him out, and he gets ashamed. I mean, he knows if we didn't need the money I'd be free for driving Melinda to her track meets or cheerleading practice. So he takes that bottle of bourbon from the chuck wagon. I used to empty those bottles fast as I found them, but I gave it up. I figure he's better off at the wagon than most places, *and there's no point talking, 'cause that's not the sort of thing he'd feel comfortable talking to me about.* (136, emphasis added)

Why then should the reader believe that Blanton would choose to talk about those very things with the reporter? Does Kramer mean to imply that she seduced Henry Blanton to reveal himself in a way that his wife could not? Is the subtext of the narrative that a professional woman of privilege can always rope a naive cowboy into unwilling compliance while his working-class wife cannot?

Were *The Last Cowboy* written or marketed as fiction Kramer would not be expected to answer those questions. Her narrator could assume access to her fictional characters' thoughts and speech, although nothing would preclude a critical reader from attacking those characterizations for their aesthetic, social, or political content. But in reading a nonfiction narrative inside out for the manner by which it implicates its author, the narrator or author will need to account for that access. If there's "no point talking" because Henry Blanton is not comfortable revealing his pain to anyone, how then do we hear him? By what channel do we read his thoughts or hear him speak in the book's final scene when, after a long lonely night of drinking in his pickup because "he did not have the heart to face Betsy" (147), Henry explodes in impotent violence against three runaway bulls. "The taste in his mouth was foul. His head was pounding. A kind of helpless fury came over him as he sat smoking, and made his hand shake. . . . Henry took his knife out. 'The way I see it, it's like you had a daughter and she was raped,' he said, and then he cut. For a minute, he felt better. By the time he had roped and thrown the next bull, he knew that he was not expressing right—not expressing right at all—but by then there was nothing he could do about it" (148).

This reading may be unusually literal to make a point, but one cannot readily imagine such an analysis of *The Last Cowboy* were it a fictional text, which it resembles in every sense except for its marketing as nonfiction. My argument is that the nonfiction claim of *The Last Cowboy* thrusts it inevitably into the world of social and historical discourse. While nonfiction authors, at least since the social convention of New Journalism entered the publishing marketplace, normally are expected to take advantage of leeway in omniscient and omnipresent narration, the issue here is that Kramer is implicated directly by her decision to present a narrative strategy that seems to contradict her story's characterization, plot, and theme. We might ultimately grant a nonfiction author such extended powers, but a reader alive to nonfiction's communication ritual will not grant those powers unexamined. Were the narrative presented as fiction, we would not concern ourselves with how Kramer's narrator came to know her characters' thoughts and speech, and that specific objection would disappear, although others might emerge.

In the introduction to *The Last Cowboy* not included in the narrative's initial *New Yorker* version Kramer offers the one insight into her direct relationship with her subjects, saying that Betsy and Henry Blanton "never once flinched or reconsidered at the sight of a stack of notebooks, growing bigger every day, on the bench by the kitchen door" in their home. But if the two subjects of the piece actually were comfortable talking about their problems or had changed significantly during the research of the narrative so that they became able to talk to each other honestly, that growth is contradicted by the narrative itself. The piece's overall theme is that Henry Blanton—like the cowboy way that Kramer means to celebrate and critique—is incapable of change. In fact it is this very inflexibility, she suggests, that eventually will undermine him and the way of life that his stoic strength has made possible.

The inside out reading of a narrative like Kramer's *The Last Cowboy* demonstrates how reading nonfiction in the way I am proposing works to analyze the ritual of communication among author, textual phenomena, subjects, and reader. Kramer's stated intent to present truthful narrative is one part of the equation, but its communication can also be assessed by what her cultural communication reveals: the way she "dresses" the text symbolically through her unstated narrative decisions. Because *The Last Cowboy* does not report widely known events or have characters who are recognizable as actual human beings by most readers, Kramer's claim to factual status as well as the work's marketing as real-life narrative by the *New Yorker* and its subsequent book publisher assumes increasing importance in the way it is read. If *The Last Cowboy* did depict widely known actual characters and events, it might cast the same sort of implication outside the text, even if it happened not to feature an overt nonfictional claim by either author or publisher, because the material bodies of its characters and their interactions in events would assume a presence that would be less manageable by text.

Another way to analyze the problems posed by *The Last Cowboy* is to examine its rhetorical work. In *Narrative as Rhetoric* James Phelan establishes the ability of F. Scott Fitzgerald to employ Nick Carraway as a character narrator who knows more than he should know, particularly when Nick narrates the events that occur in George Wilson's garage the night after Myrtle Wilson is killed. Here Nick reports facial expressions on an occasion when he could not have been present and reads omniscient significance into those expressions at the time of the events. Phelan calls Nick "a New Journalist *avant le lettre* as he not only gives a verbatim report of a conversation he did not overhear but also includes numerous small dramatic details" (106). The phenomenon Phelan traces in the fictional account, then, raises the same sorts of rhetorical problems that I have raised about the nonfictional *The Last Cowboy* and will enable me to examine more clearly the ways that the conventions of fiction and nonfiction differ when read from the inside out.

Phelan argues persuasively that a homodiegetic or characterized narrator in fiction can be rhetorically effective even when (and perhaps even because) the narrator violates narrow mimetic logic. That is, the reader will grant license to a fictional homodiegetic narrator because the reader agrees to "a set of conventions for representing what we provisionally and temporarily agree to be real" (110). Phelan's argument about Nick's omnipresence and omnipotence raises two important issues for me when applied to the reading of nonfiction: (1) In a sense, all nonfiction narrators are homodiegetic in that their access to characters and information has to be negotiated within the boundaries of previously occurring events, thus making them characters (even if unnamed) in the stories they tell. (2) The reader should be more aware, and perhaps less forgiving, of mimetic lapses, such as when the narrator tells more than he can know (paralepsis), if these lapses are found in nonfiction. While such lapses won't signal a removal of the text from the nonfiction domain, they will reveal the author's work and underlying ideology.

A signal difference between nonfiction and most forms of fiction is that the narrator assumes a tangible presence that is circumscribed by the possibilities and limitations of an actual human being. Within the boundaries of the narrative proper, Kramer does not characterize herself, but when she makes claims in the introduction to the book about her rigorous fact checking or about her pile of notebooks, she has raised the issue of her access to the events of her material and the thoughts of her characters. While no one expects that any story will be unambiguously true, nonfiction pits the teller and its subjects in a contest over facts and interpretation that plays out across the text. The subject cannot be contained within the imagination of the author; thus the author confronts a living subject as one character to another.

If this assertion is true, then it follows that rhetorical dilemmas in nonfiction assume a theoretical importance somewhat more tangled than what Phelan describes as the potential ability of fictions to be "more rhetorically effective as a result of their violations of narrow mimetic logic" (110). For example, a well-publicized dilemma of paralepsis occurred when the journalist Joe McGinniss attempted to explain how he could write omniscient narration from Senator Edward Kennedy's point of view in *The Last*

Brother when he had not interviewed the senator about specific events that made up the narrative. The technique, McGinniss says, "represents my best effort at trying to engender in the reader not merely sympathy for Teddy Kennedy, but empathy with him. . . . I have quite consciously written portions as if from inside his mind" (621). McGinniss seems to rely on two explanations for this decision: it is permissible because "truth is elusive . . . and not necessarily attainable by conventional methods" (623) and even if the technique is wrong, everyone else is doing it. The three examples that McGinniss cites of everyone else doing it, however, are drawn from biographies of Mozart and Samuel Johnson as well as from a history of the French Revolution. In these cases all the subjects of the narratives are rather safely dead and thus not able to compete with the author for possession of their thoughts. Moreover, Kennedy, as a public figure of immense notoriety, is virtually libel proof and thus is likely to subscribe to the view that the less he engages McGinniss's competing accounts, the sooner reader interest will die and the better off he will be. On the subject of truth, McGinniss sounds as antifoundationalist as any contemporary critic while at the same time he seems anxious to cash in on the rhetorical power of factual narrative: the illusion that he has created the "real story" about the youngest Kennedy brother as well as an exclusive account of the senator's thoughts during, for instance, the night of the accident at Chappaquiddick. "My view is," says McGinniss,

> let the writers write, let the readers read, let books stand or fall on their merits. Either there is an internal logic and an inherent plausibility to the presentation of a real-life figure in a book or there is not. If not, all the footnotes in the world cannot breathe truth and life into a misshapen portrait. If there is, I would suggest that a book then be accepted for what it is: in the case of *The Last Brother*, an author's highly personal and interpretive view of his subject. . . . In seeking first to develop and then convey the deepest possible understanding of the subject, [the author] not only can but must go beyond the traditional and universally accepted approaches, not only can but must take certain risks with technique. (622–23)

We have come a long way here from the fictional Nick Carraway's account of an event that he did not see to McGinniss's argument that the possession of another living being's thoughts merely represents "a certain risk with technique." As Phelan points out in ways that are suggestive for McGinniss's rhetorical strategy, "the relation of the narrator's governing ideology to that of the author is always a part of the narrative's meaning" ("Present Tense" 230). My contention is that both the cultural rituals of nonfictional communication (reading the narrative for the way McGinniss positions himself vis-à-vis Kennedy and the way he uses that positioning to build a desire in the reader for the "inside truth" of the Kennedy experience) and its rhetoric (tracing the presence and impossibilities of nonfictional paralepsis) will produce a rich reading of nonfiction wherein its very differences from many forms of fiction will emerge.

The Problem of the Nonfiction Narrator Who Knows Too Little

A nonfictional narrative that poses similar problems from a different direction is Tom Wolfe's *The Electric Kool-Aid Acid Test*, his account of the psychedelic hipsters who surrounded novelist Ken Kesey during the mid-1960s. Unlike Kramer's *The Last Cowboy*, many of the characters in *Acid Test* have commented on Kesey's depictions of their lives, which will form part of my analysis when I turn my attention in the next chapter to examining the author's work from the outside in. Although Wolfe never fully develops himself as a character in *Acid Test*, he does devote most of the few pages between his two meetings with Kesey, which open the book, to chronicle his deepening recognition of the implications of entering the Pranksters' "scary, scary stuff out on the raggedy, raggedy edge . . ."[2] (29) world. In fiction an author can more easily create a narrative presence (usually a character who tells the story or even a "voice" that clearly is distinguished from the author's voice) separated from the author's presence and thus permanently naive while the author is wise. But read against the grain of its historical author, Wolfe's characterized presence in the opening scenes—while he is pretending to be in the sway of Kesey and the Pranksters: "we can't stop here, next rest area 40 miles" (14)—is at work on more subtle cultural and aesthetic tasks. For example, Wolfe is forced, like Kesey's followers, to use a service station bathroom near the Harriet Street garage, and when he does so, he gets "the look" from its proprietor along with a "bladder totem" restroom key attached to a Shell Oil can. Wolfe thus symbolically, if only temporarily, crosses the boundary between acceptable class (the credit card elite "tanking up and stretching their legs and tweezing their undershorts out of the aging waxy folds of their scrota") and unacceptable social class.

To be a fugitive from American class hegemony, it seems, carries a cost. "Suddenly it hits me that for the Pranksters this is *permanent*. This is the way they live. Men, women, boys, girls, most from middle-class upbringings, men and women and boys and girls and children and babies, this is the way they have been living for months, for years, some of them, across America and back" (16). Wolfe tells us he begins to develop "a strange feeling about the whole thing," a feeling that deepens when he hears the Pranksters refer to Kesey as The Chief and that bears witness to the inevitable synchronicity that seems to determine their actions. The feeling deepens and turns to "*mysto,* as the general mysto steam began rising in my head. This steam, I can actually hear it inside my head, a great sssssssssss, like what you hear if you take too much quinine. I don't know if this happens to anybody else or not. But if there is something startling enough, fearful, awesome, strange, or just weird enough, something I sense I can't cope with, it is as if I go on Red Alert and the fogging steam starts. . . ." (16–17).

Having established his own "Red Alert" fog, like some creeping rash of roseola, Wolfe summons all his verbal pyrotechnics as he introduces his book-length theme of Kesey and the Pranksters as protoreligious mystics come to shake late-1960s America by its sizzling teeth. Wolfe, as a characterized narrator, confesses that he has almost begun to buy into the metaphors, to slide into the group-think of Kesey's parables, and he portrays himself (and, by association, any readers who have identified with him as the central consciousness of the text so far) as teetering on the brink of surrender. A quote of some length is required to gain the full flavor of Wolfe's strategy and language:

> Faith! Further! And it is an exceedingly strange feeling to be sitting here in the Day-Glo, on poor abscessed Harriet Street, and realize suddenly that in this improbable, ex-pie factory Warehouse garage I am in the midst of Tsong-Isha-pa and the sangha communion, Mani and the wan persecuted at The Gate, Zoroaster, Maidhyoimaongha and the five faithful before Vishtapu, Mohammad and Abu Bekr and the disciples amid the pharisaical Koreish or Mecca, Guatama and the brethren in the wilderness leaving the blood-and-kin families of their pasts for the one

true family of the sangha inner circle—in short, true mystic brotherhood—only in poor old Formica polyethylene
1960s American without a grain of desert sand or a shred
of palm leaf or a morsel of manna wilderness breadfruit
overhead, picking up vibrations from Ampex tapes and a
juggled Williams Lok-Hed sledge hammer, hooking down
mathematical lab drugs, LSD-25, IT-290. DMT, instead of
soma water, heading out in American flag airport coveralls
and an International Harvester bus—yet for real!—amid
the marshmallow shiny black shoe masses— (27–28)

The passage reads like a rap by Neal Cassady, Jack Kerouac's legendary companion who by 1966 is a full-blown Prankster and methedrine addict: Wolfe
is on the edge, chanting religious references like mantras, riffing them off
late-capitalism brand names and a mish-mash of alpha-numerical drugs for
the "marshmallow shiny black shoe masses" (at least some of whom are his
readers) who somehow don't quite yet get the connection.

Of course the Tom Wolfe outside the narrative, the one who was
writing *The Electric Kool-Aid Acid Test* more than a year later, had long since
divested himself, at least on the surface, of any true personal dread that he
might get sucked into the Prankster *mysto.* By the next time the book's chronological structure loops back to the moment of time that opens the book
(late October 1966, a few days before the Acid Graduation), Wolfe will be
depicting the psychedelic movement as some sort of over-the-hill compen-
dium of Marxist splinter groups in the 1920s, which for him is a testament
not of their power, but of their ineffectuality. Thus his narrative presence
(the naïf almost persuaded) played off against his historical presence (but
sufficient to have stood) allows him an extended fantasy of escape and recapture. We know, at least on second reading if not the first, that he, along with
Kesey, believes the Pranksters "blew it" by allowing their religious vision to
slide into an institutional morass of power and control. Moreover, Wolfe believes that the Pranksters' religious icons have been seized by "secular" pro-
moters like Bill Graham and that the group no longer serves to attract even
the fringe believers it once did.

As such, Wolfe's narrative stance is disingenuous in that he presents
himself in radically differing ways at the same historical moment even
though that moment is separated by some 250 pages in the book's looping
structure. I will examine this problem first from a rhetorical perspective and
later extend my analysis to examine the ritual of communication posed by the

passages. Phelan points out in an extended discussion of Frederic Henry's narration in *A Farewell to Arms* and Joe Butler's narration in "My Old Man" how Hemingway makes rhetorical use of a naive narrator even though the governing logic of the narrative would insist that the character can no longer be naive at the time of the story's telling. In ways that reverberate for my discussion of the nonfictional *Acid Test,* the narrator is engaged in paralipsis, a device in which he discloses less than he should know. Phelan asserts that fictional narrative allows its teller this leeway when the author takes advantage of what Booth has called distance. "When we detect a discrepancy between an author's values and those expressed in a narrator's voice," Phelan reasons, "we have a situation of a double-voiced discourse: the narrator's voice is contained within—and its communication thereby complicated by—the author" (*Narrative* 61).

Phelan shows how in *A Farewell to Arms,* Hemingway can limit Frederic's vision and voice to the time of the action, even though as a character Frederic will later come to understand the ways in which his initial perspectives were mistaken. Similarly, in the story "My Old Man," Hemingway's narrator, Joe Butler, illustrates a paradox of fictional paralipsis in that he narrates his disillusionment with the world of horse racing—and his sorrow for his father's place in it—from an unspecified point after he has become disillusioned. Yet the narrative itself presents Joe's voice as naive until the very end of the story. "Logically, his new attitude toward his father should permeate his narration," Phelan points out. "But it does not. If Joe's new attitude did permeate his narration, the ending would lose all its power. Yet we feel neither that Joe is being insincere nor that he is deliberately withholding his knowledge from us for his own artistic purposes (if he were, then, he would not be a naive character but a highly sophisticated narrator). In this respect, the story exposes the inescapably synthetic nature of apparently mimetic naive narration" (103).

Wolfe's narrator in *The Electric Kool-Aid Acid Test* allows me to engage this problem more completely and to use it as a springboard toward a fuller discussion of the cultural communication rituals at work in the book. What Wolfe's narrative poses is a historical figure narrating a book in which he professes to have two differing responses to the same key events at the same moment in October 1966. First: "Despite the skepticism I brought here *I* am suddenly experiencing *their* feeling. I am sure of it. I feel like I am in on something the outside world, the world I came from, could not possibly comprehend, and it *is* a metaphor, the whole scene, ancient and vast, vaster than . . ." (25). Now, the same moment in time about three hundred pages later: "It's a little like the socialist movement in New York after World War I—the Revolution is imminent, as all know and agree, and yet . . . they're all cranking away like mad and fuming over each other's translations of the message" (337).

Although nonfictional narration often defies strict mimetic logic with strongly positive results (such as when a scene that the author cannot have witnessed is presented at the time of action with speech and details legitimately researched from subsequent interviews), the careful reader of nonfiction, in my judgment, will always test those violations to explore what they reveal about the narrative. In the present instance Wolfe's efforts to portray himself in radically differing ways at the same moment expose an underlying contradiction that cannot be overcome by granting him this sort of technical leeway. Hemingway's Joe Butler could be contained within "My Old Man" and manipulated within the fiction in a way that he could not were he a flesh-and-blood presence available to readers outside the text. In the same way that the characters of *Acid Test* live both inside and outside Wolfe's book, so does its author and narrator. The Tom Wolfe who meets Ken Kesey returning from jail to Harriet Street is a human presence as well as a narrator. In contrast to his analysis of fiction, Phelan summarizes the two possibilities open to a human presence in nonfiction: either his knowledge (Wolfe's disillusionment with the Prankster experiment) must inform his narration or he cannot portray himself as believing at a moment in time when he has already ceased to believe (103). Even as Kramer almost certainly could not have gained access to a scene that defies the very theme and logic of her book, Tom Wolfe almost certainly could not draw an exactly opposite conclusion about his main character at the same historical moment in October 1966.

Perhaps aware of these contradictions, Wolfe deftly separates that moment by some three hundred pages and progressively effaces his characterized presence during those pages. Readers who encounter *Acid Test* as fiction or believe there is little difference between fact and fiction will no doubt grant Wolfe the same sort of leeway that Phelan traces for such fictional narrators as Frederic Henry or Joe Butler, but readers exploring the book carefully in the light of its explicit nonfictional claim will unearth its contradictions.

My contention is that Wolfe progressively effaces his own characterized presence to conceal the underlying ideology of his project from the reader, even as he insists that his reporting is impersonal and objective. *The*

Right Stuff and *Acid Test,* Wolfe said in 1983, are "completely about the lives of other people, with myself hardly intruding into the narratives at all. They were based on reporting, so a lot of it is impersonal and objective. It can be discouraging to see it described as implausible, personal, and unbelievable. I very seldom use the first person anymore. I think it's a very tricky thing because whether you know it or not, if you use the first person you've turned yourself into a character" (qtd. in McLeod 178). Here, Wolfe seems anxious to hide his own historical presence so as to deny the sort of reading that, as I have argued earlier, would treat all nonfiction narrators as homodiegetic or characterized. Wolfe's move here is not unlike the decision by an author to change the names of nonfictional characters so as to gain more control over their presence in the text, as I will trace in some detail in my discussion of a Freudian case study that will conclude this chapter. Careful reading will uncover that presence and the communication rituals that the narrative reveals.

After the first few chapters of the book and once the narrative enters its long flashback into the origins and mission of the Merry Pranksters, Wolfe virtually disappears as a physical character other than in his role of researcher and commentator of new religious movements. But Wolfe's narrative presence suffuses the book nonetheless, primarily through a sometimes subtle and sometimes not-so-subtle dialogic in which that presence provisionally assumes the voices and values of a variety of characters—sometimes actual people, sometimes a whole race or class. On occasion Wolfe takes pains to document his sources for this language, which is lifted from diaries, other written records, recordings, or films and is presented as actual thoughts. Most notably in "The Fugitive" chapter, Wolfe informs the reader that he uses Kesey's letters to novelist Larry McMurtry as a source for some of Kesey's internal monologue in that chapter (371). Other justly celebrated point-of-view writing is found in such sections as those where Sandy Lehmann-Haupt slides into paranoic delusions, which, Wolfe tells the reader, Lehmann-Haupt later recounted to him in "especially full and penetrating detail" (371).

But despite all of the exacting work already produced on the particularities of Wolfe's style, no commentator has yet written in detail about its social positioning and what we have come to describe as its ritual of communication. Yet we know from Wolfe's own words that these considerations are crucial to him, that he believes that cultural tastes "become established in a political fashion" (Zelenko 173) and that "perfect journalism would deal constantly with one subject: Status" (Dundy 9). Subtly and not so subtly

Wolfe assigns a class and rank to virtually every person and group of people in the book. A ready example comes early when he comments on the "head" world's assessment of shoes: "The heads have a thing about shoes. The worst are shiny black shoes with shoelaces in them. The hierarchy ascends from there, although practically all lowcut shoes are unhip, from there on up to the boots the heads like, light fanciful boots, English boots of the mod variety, if that is all they can get, but better something like hand-tooled Mexican boots with Caliente Dude Triple A toes on them" (2). Indeed on many occasions Wolfe's narrator (sometimes in his hectoring mode) reinforces those rankings by purporting to give voice to the values and beliefs of an entire racial or social classification. At these moments Wolfe is far from the "impersonal and objective" (McLeod 178) narrator that he purports to be. He is working from no written or electronically reproduced records for this voiced but never quoted material and is thus far less certain of the "relatively assured credibility of his factual contract" (Hellmann 106) than he would like to project.

I shall explore in some detail several examples of this sort of Wolfeian narrative presence and the largely covert social and political ramifications that its use triggers. Initially, of course, Wolfe deftly voices the sensibilities of "shiny shoes" squares, so as to play off the Pranksters against the people who "just don't get it" and to align himself clearly as one who does. For example, in the following passage Wolfe not only describes the reaction of San Francisco police to Haight-Ashbury but slides in and out of their voice:

> The cops are busy trying to figure out these new *longhairs*, these *beatniks*—these crazies are somehow weirder than the North Beach beatniks ever were. They glow blue like a TV tube. The hippie-dippies . . . their Jesus hair, men with hair falling down to the shoulders and limp like . . . *lungers!* Sergeant, they're lollygagging up against the storefronts on Haight Street up near that Psychedelic Shop like somebody hocked a bunch of T. B. lungers up against windows and they've oozed down to the sidewalks, staring at you with these huge zombie eyes, just staring. And a lot of weird American Indian and Indian from India shit, beaded headbands and donkey beads and temple bells—and the *live* ones, promenading up and down Haight Street in cos-

tumes, or half-costumes, like some kind of a doorman's coat with piping and crap but with blue jeans for pants and Mod boots . . . *The cops!*—oh, how it messed up their minds. (315)

The passage begins and ends in conventional third-person if somewhat omniscient description but slides into words like "Jesus hair," "crap," "hocked a bunch of T. B. lungers," and "weird American Indian and Indian from India shit" meant to evoke some sort of yahoo (if metaphorically creative) police officer running his mouth to the sergeant back at the cop shop. In dialogical narrative Wolfe deftly constructs both the subject/escapee (Haight denizens) and the observer/captor (shiny-shoes cops) as well as the conflict between them. In interviews Wolfe likens this narrative technique to method acting. "Instead of using the approach of the man dissecting rather tawdry little specimens down there on a plate—like Orwell, whom I admire very much, looking down on the art of Donald McGill and his seaside postcards," Wolfe explains, "I tried to get the opposite approach, a kind of Method acting, trying to get inside of some of these manifestations: discotheque life in New York, or the stock car racing in the moonshine foothills of North Carolina, or London debutantes" (qtd. in Dean 24).

One of the most revealing uses of "method acting" narration in *Acid Test* is Wolfe's evocation of the Vietnam Day Committee leftists who have organized a protest at Berkeley and have invited Kesey to be one of the "shock workers of the tongue" who will rouse the protesters until "they are ready to march and take billy clubs upside the head and all the rest of it" (195). Wolfe, who was quoted in 1987 by *Rolling Stone* as saying "ninety-five percent of the young people in the United States in the Sixties didn't give a damn about Vietnam" (Mewborn 234), initially can't resist an opinion stripped of dialogical camouflage. "There had been about forty [speakers]," he reports in his own voice, "all roaring or fulminating or arguing cogently, *which was always worse*" (195, emphasis added).

But with that exception, Wolfe chooses to ridicule the organizers of the demonstration, not directly, but from inside their own heads. Never does Wolfe tell us that he extended his "saturation reporting" to the Vietnam Day Committee or any other group that purported to be New Left, nor was he at the rally, yet he seamlessly shifts inside the New Left group think ("he's ruining the goddamn thing") as they watch Kesey and the Pranksters cavort on stage to the strains of a harmonica-honking "Home on the Range":

> If they had had one of those big hooks like they had on
> amateur night in the vaudeville days, they would have
> pulled Kesey off the podium right then. Well, then, why
> doesn't somebody just go up there and edge him off! He's
> ruining the goddamn thing. But then they see all the Day-
> Glo crazies, men and women and children all weaving and
> electrified, clawing at guitars, blowing horns, all grazed
> aglow at sundown. . . . And the picture of the greatest anti-
> war rally in the history of America ending in a Day-Glo
> brawl to the tune of Home, home on the range. . . . (199)

Kesey eventually tells the crowd to "look at the war, and turn your backs and
say . . . Fuck it . . ." (199), and Wolfe reports with evident satisfaction that
although no one could prove Kesey had done it, "something was gone out of
the anti-war rally" (200).

Wolfe enters the New Left's group head for a second time in a
rather astonishing verbal critique of Martin Luther King Jr.'s nonviolent tac-
tics and their relevance to a potentially "physical confrontation" with police.
Although it is not entirely clear from the narrative, apparently Wolfe is reporting that someone (because of Kesey's performance) had suggested that
the police were not worth challenging directly that day, and a second person
may have called that someone a Martin Luther King. Wolfe unleashes a rac-
ist "hectoring narrator" in the sensibility of the imaginary New Left agitator:

> That was about the worst thing you could call anybody on
> the New Left at that time . . . big solemn preachery Uncle
> Tom. Yah! yuh Tuskegee-headed Uncle Tom, yuh, yuh
> Booker T. Washington peanut-butter lecture-podium No-
> bel Prize medal head, yuh—*Uncle Tom*—by the time it
> was all over, Martin Luther King was a stupid music-hall
> Handkerchief Head on the New Left—and here they were
> calling each other Martin Luther Kings and other incredi-
> ble things—but nobody had any good smashing iron zeal
> to carry the day—O where is our Zealot, who Day-glowed
> and fucked up our heads—and there was nothing to do but
> grouse at the National Guard and turn back, which they
> did. What the hell has happened to us? Who did this? Why,
> it was the Masked Man— (200–201, ellipsis added)

Here, again, Wolfe constructs a verbal lens of one social group (the New Left) by which to critique another (nonviolent blacks), meanwhile escaping the fray except for the initial, almost off-handed, personal opinion delivered early in the scene.

This sort of analysis, like the one of Kramer's *The Last Cowboy*, will show how reading nonfiction inside out for traces of the author in narrative differs significantly from that of fiction. First, by admitting that he is almost, but never quite, seduced by the Kesey aura, Wolfe's narration gains the sort of capital boasted by a revivalist preacher who enthralls the flock by evoking previously unimagined sins along with an exhortation to resist the thrills. Because he is an actual character in the text, Wolfe's confession that he is sliding into the freak life of the other Merry Pranksters near the beginning of the book ultimately reveals itself as a sham. Since Wolfe in his nonfiction presents himself as a historical figure, not some sort of fictional narrator, his duplicity in the linked scenes reveals his strategy in the book both from a rhetorical perspective such as Phelan proposes and as a cultural communication.

The capital established in the opening passages works to establish Wolfe as an experienced but ostensibly reliable guide on this long strange trip to Edge City. Throughout *Acid Test*, he suggests to his readers that he certainly understands Kesey's movie better than "Mom&Dad&Buddy&Sis," or the "White Smocks," or the "Sport Shirts," or any one of a number of the other synecdochic squares and has-beens who are summoned to play off the Pranksters' (and Wolfe's) sensibilities. Nonetheless, so as not to surrender fully to the escape fantasy, he won't enter the movie even though he leads the reader to believe he does. Reading outside in for the implicated writer—testing Wolfe's narrative against what we can determine of his history outside the book—adds even more strength to the sense of narrative presence that I have been outlining, as I will show in the next chapter. But for now I want to look much more closely at the efforts of a nonfiction author and narrator to close off his subject from the engagement of authorial agency, textual phenomena, reader response, and character presence that I have been arguing for in nonfiction. That engagement, as I hope my discussion so far has shown, cannot ignore the referentiality of the body in nonfictional narrative. A close consideration of Sigmund Freud's case study *Dora* will reveal the ways in which Freud attempts to cut off access from his reader to the subject of his study even at the same time Freud wishes to trade on the referential power of nonfiction's truth claims.

The Nonfiction Narrator and the Effaced Subject

Michel Foucault sets the stage for such an analysis by showing the way in which scientific discourse assumes properties that we might assign to such narratives as "literary journalism" even as their authors insist on their scientific claims. "It is no longer a question of simply saying what was done—the sexual act—and how it was done; but of *reconstructing*, in and around the act, the thoughts that recapitulated it, the obsessions that accompanied it, the images, desires, modulations, and quality of the pleasure that animated it" (*History* 59, emphasis added).

Dora: An Analysis of a Case of Hysteria is Freud's first case study and is still a canonical text for psychoanalytic training (Marcus 56). While for some readers it remains an instruction manual, for others it offers compelling, though perhaps unwitting, representation of the power struggle its methodology encodes and seeks to contain.[3] Freud's methodology, according to Toril Moi's study of sexuality and epistemology in the case study, assumes that Dora's fragmentary case can be completed by the work of the author (187) and that "[p]ossession of knowledge means possession of power" (194).

While my reading can add little to the wealth of post-Freudian psychoanalytical reconsideration already produced on the subject of Freud and *Dora,* it means to explore specifically how Freud implicated himself as a nonfiction writer through his development and adjustment of the case-study style. For it is in that nonfiction contract and its accompanying style that Freud seeks to exert textual power over both Dora and his readers. Reading *Dora* as a text that implicates its author both as a narrative presence in the text and as one whose author intends his case history to be consumed as fact reveals a type of truth claim particular to the Freudian case study. In *Dora* Freud presents what he claims is actuality within a highly constructed text (not unlike the strategy of a docudrama or nonfiction novel) while at the same moment he exerts all the rights and privileges of a factual contract in which the scientist-psychoanalyst attempts to hold the powers of interpretation and to exclude both his subject and his readers from meaning formation. In that context I want to explore from the inside out the relationship between the all-interpreting writer-subject (Freud as author-character) and the progressively effaced written object (Dora) that underlies the case study's narrative style. Freud's rewriting of history as case study finally consumes virtually all traces of Dora's extratextual and intratextual identity until all that remains is his own voice. And because this power relationship is encoded within a document that makes a direct extratextual truth claim, what emerges is a text in which Freud not only dominates Dora as the female "other" but, finally, seeks to dominate his reader as well.

We can quickly see how reading *Dora* as nonfiction creates problems for Freud's methodology that would not be so sharply drawn were his narrative presented as fiction. One key arena of conflict is his granting or not granting a voice to his subject. A narrator who purports to analyze within the text the "exact words" of a character who, inexplicably and against all evidence, speaks just like him has raised in fact the sorts of questions about his methodology that implicate him, that cut against the grain of his voiced intent and reveal his ideology. At stake are many of the properties and powers we routinely grant to a narrator in fiction: an ability to read minds, to foretell the future, to be omnipresent, to reproduce speech verbatim, and the like. These conventions of fiction are purchased at great price in nonfiction and must be socially negotiated because the characters and events of nonfiction cast a shadow outside the narrative as well. We may ultimately grant a non-fiction author extended powers, for as Hayden White has shown in *The Content of the Form*, all historical narratives are inevitably contrived [21], but a reader alive to nonfiction's social construction will not grant those powers unexamined. A reading for the implicated author, then, opens to scrutiny the author's methodology and style, not only (or even primarily) to determine the "truth" of the text, but to uncover the author's communication rituals.

Although Freudian case studies rarely have been discussed in the context of nonfiction theory, their threshold contract is their claim to tell truth; otherwise, they collapse into entertainment and are insufficient to meet Freud's stated production goal of "intelligible, consistent, and unbroken case history" (32). Recent studies that explore *Dora* as a fictional text (Marcus 64; Sprengnether 272n) certainly demonstrate its moments of artificiality and constructedness but ultimately miss the implications of Freud's contract with his readers. In *Discipline and Punish* Foucault exposes the terms of the case study. He found that "scientific" discourses, particularly those of the nineteenth century, gained control over deviance by fixing the identity of others within the norms of "objective" research and constituting individuals as "describable and analyzable" objects (190). In a way that seems distinctly true for nonfiction, where presumably actual subjects are the sources of written records, "the child, the patient, the madman, the prisoner, were to become ... the object of individual descriptions and biographical accounts. This turning of real lives into writing is no longer a procedure of heroization; it functions as a procedure of objectification and subjection" (192).

Philip Rieff's introduction to the Collier paperback edition of *Dora* endorses just that sort of "objectification and subjection" formation in his enthusiastic tribute to Freud's methodology. Rieff salutes a project that seems to be nothing less than the rewriting of a woman's life in Freud's own terms. "By any practical test, Freud's insight was superior to Dora's," Rieff contends. "Hers had not helped her win more than pyrrhic victories over life, while Freud's, engaged as he was in the therapeutic re-creation of her life, demonstrated its capacity to make Dora superior to some of the symptomatic expressions of her rejection of life. Her own understanding of life had in no way given her any power to change it; precisely that power to change life was Freud's test of truth. His truth, therefore, was superior to Dora's" (11–12).

Freud's overtaking of Dora's story reveals the stakes of his project and its intimate connection to nonfiction discourse; there is no correlative in traditional fiction, no fictional contract that presents a writer with so much control over an extratextual life. It is difficult to imagine a critic making a statement like Rieff's about, say, the relationship of George Eliot to Dorothea Brooke, a critic who would claim that Eliot's writing of Dorothea's life "demonstrated its capacity to make [some real-life Dorothea] superior to some of [her] symptomatic expressions."[4]

This crucial distinction may be illuminated by further teasing out Mas'ud Zavarzadeh's "typology of prose styles" to which I referred in the first chapter. Zavarzadeh builds on a system of classification first posed by Northrop Frye in *Anatomy of Criticism* to distinguish between "in-referential" and "out-referential" truth claims (55). While *Dora* and *Middlemarch* can in differing senses both claim "true" representation of their female characters, Freud's claim is that the "truth" of the *Dora* text has an external configuration, some sense of an external "Dora" by which readers must arbitrate the written Dora. Analyses that insist on reading fiction and nonfiction only as similarly constructed texts will miss Freud's deep implication in Dora's history and the ramifications of his purpose in constructing Dora's life as a written text. In fact if the extratextual Dora herself were to read *Dora*, Freud says, "she will learn nothing from it that she does not already know" (23). By this he means not so much that Dora accepts his analysis but that he explicitly claims that he has presented accurately the facts of her life and of the analytical sessions.

Freud thus asserts a direct one-to-one correlation between the truth of his text and its external configuration. By contrast, Dorothea Brooke's life is in-referential, and although her characterization is rendered according to the conventions of nineteenth-century realism, it does not depend for its truth claims on what Lillian R. Furst calls an "anterior model" (26), as would the depiction of a character with a material presence outside the book, even if the book claimed to be fiction. The reader assumes that Dorothea's identity (even if it is based on Eliot's notion of some sort of external life) is, in Zavarzadeh's terms, "mapped out within the book" (55). If that were not so, we might have to give serious attention to articles written by people who would claim to have met later the "real" Dorothea Brooke and who would bring that professed knowledge to bear on Eliot's representation. We can, of course, read such an article about "Dora," by Felix Deutsch. He claims to have met Ida Bauer (the real name of the subject that Freud named "Dora" in the case history) and reports that the encounter was enough to convince him of the essential correctness of Freud's original analysis. Moreover, Deutsch reports, the Ida Bauer who had broken off Freud's analysis turned out to be a "repulsive hysteric" (43).

This chapter's insistence on the threshold importance of the nonfiction claim that Freud's narrative poses with *Dora,* of course, places it partly at odds with Steven Marcus, the Freudian scholar whose landmark essay "Freud and Dora: Story, History, Case History" makes a compelling case for reading *Dora* as modernist fiction.[5] Marcus finds a Proustian enterprise in the narrative, in which Freud plays the auteur sifting the fragmentary nature of modern experience to build a compelling though ultimately failed fictional coherence to Dora. There is much to recommend Marcus's reading, but ultimately it never confronts the specific power formation encoded by Freud's claim to write nonfiction. For despite the brilliance of his argument that "what Freud has written bears certain suggestive resemblances to a modern novel," Marcus finally returns to a point very similar to that made by Deutsch and Rieff. At the same time that he insists he reads *Dora* as fiction he relies on the irreducibly out-referential nature of the *Dora* text to grant Freud's superior interpretation of a person in history. "She refused to be a character in the story that Freud was composing for her, and wanted to finish it for herself. As we now know, the ending she wrote was very bad indeed" (88).

Zavarzadeh's analysis in *The Mythopoeic Reality*—beyond illuminating the essential difference between in-referential and out-referential narrative in a way we can explicitly apply to *Dora*—surpasses Frye's in its recognition that both in-referential and out-referential narratives, while moving in opposite directions, share a monoreferential contract that evidences the author's desire to construct a singular meaning in the text. Freud lessens the possibility that reality could impinge on the text at the same time the text organizes reality by making Dora both "real" (an extratextual truth claim) and anonymous. While he perhaps partly is motivated by compassion for her privacy (which seems, after all, not to have worked [Deutsch 38]), his subject's anonymity ensures that Freud's interpretation of her history is the controlling one, because it tries to cut out the ability of the reader to move beyond the text directly toward its subject. In his postscript to *Dora* Freud admits that his methodology "brings with it the disadvantage of the reader being given no opportunity of testing the correctness of my procedure" (134) but declares that "the material for my hypotheses was collected by the most extensive and laborious series of observations" (134). This "truthful" but unverifiable strategy seems to be an enduring quality of the case-study narrative form, because it precisely inscribes the power relationship that underlies its monoreferential intentions. As Foucault similarly demonstrates by his analysis of Jeremy Bentham's panopticon, the sideways glance is prohibited within this narrative strategy. No reader—at least as revealed by Freud's stated intentions—can approach Dora except through Freud.[6] The subject of analysis is thereby repositioned as object. Centralized power is the only power, at least until it is breached by someone who "discovers" the extratextual Ida Bauer at the heart of Dora's representation.

Freud explicitly asserts his right as psychoanalyst and writer to construct all textual power at the formation and consumption levels. Moreover, he asserts both his and other professionals' rights over the dissemination and reception of the representation: "Needless to say, I have allowed no name to stand which could put a non-medical reader upon the scent; and the publication of the case in a purely scientific and technical periodical should, further, afford a guarantee against unauthorized readers of this sort" (23).

By contrast, some nonfiction texts deliberately air out this closed discourse system by revealing sources and naming names, thereby subjecting truth claims to external verification and ongoing negotiation. Even when Wolfe writes about Kesey's drug-induced paranoia in *The Electric Kool-Aid Acid Test* (a text that in some senses is also a document of both historical and hysterical experience), Kesey's experience is presented bireferentially, open to a complex negotiation in which Wolfe, Kesey, Wolfe's writings, Kesey's writings (both those inside and outside Wolfe's text), supporting written documents, taped messages and film, recalled and re-created fantasies, verbatim testimony, memory, and so on, all are at least theoretically open to reader scrutiny. Wolfe makes this task easier—although he is not above some duplicity, as this study reveals—because he names the names of subjects and reveals information about the sources of his knowledge. Zavarzadeh argues that bireferential nonfiction narratives tend to present facts phenomenalistically, "post-mimetic, non-verisimilar, anti-symbolic," while monoreferential nonfiction narratives tend to present facts comprehensionally in an effort "to discover the significance [always under direct authorial control] behind the random facts" (63).

Freud not only routinely treats the facts of Dora's body and history comprehensionally, but he explicitly organizes their comprehensional significance so as to lay the very foundation of case-study narrative methodology. The relationships stack up this way:

sign—signification
Dora—Freud's reading of Dora
case study—psychoanalytical generalization

The initial relationship between Dora and Freud may be demonstrated by Freud's oft-quoted passage in *Dora* in which he reserves for the psychoanalytically trained observer the final power to read the significance of human signs:

> There is a great deal of symbolism of this kind [Dora's fingering of her reticule as a symbol of masturbation desire] in life, but as a rule we pass by it without heeding it. When I set myself the task of bringing to light what human beings keep hidden within them, not by the compelling power of hypnosis, but by observing what they say and what they show, I thought the task was a harder one than it really is. He that has eyes to see and ears to hear may convince himself that no mortal can keep a secret. If his lips are silent, he chatters with his finger-tips; betrayal oozes out of him at every pore. And thus the task of making conscious the most hidden recesses of the mind is one which it is quite possible to accomplish. (96)

At the level of case study leading to psychoanalytical generalization, Freud's formation of significance from sign is demonstrated by the unstated argument of Freud's narrative contract, which assumes that Dora's experiences, particularly her dreams, are significant only to the extent that they prove the theories that he is exploring. Everything pales before that task; Freud tells us that he will not burden us with messy details or technical explanations if they get in the way of the streamlined equation between sign and significance that illuminates the neurotic disorder:

> I have as a rule not reproduced the process of interpretation to which the patient's associations and communications had to be subjected, but only the results of that process. Apart from the dreams, therefore, the technique of the analytic work has been revealed in only a very few places. My object in this case history was to demonstrate the intimate structure of a neurotic disorder and the determination of its symptoms; and it would have led to nothing but hopeless confusion if I had tried to complete the other task at the same time. (27)

Not only, then, is the sideways glance precluded by Dora's anonymity, not only is her ability to read the significance of her own actions precluded by privileged, centralized power, but Freud informs the reader that the case study will efface its "analytic work" or power apparatus so as to avoid "hopeless confusion." His refusal to reveal that apparatus—although it has been breached in contemporary readings—virtually precludes his readers' ability to construct a different interpretation of the raw data than that of the master's, which is just the sort of "unauthorized reading" that Freud seems anxious to deny by making Dora anonymous. Therefore, we are presented with a unique nonfiction style—the case study—tailored to undergird Freud's psychoanalytic theory. It emerges as the central surveillance tower with no backlighting, its power visible but unilluminated, unexplained, and therefore unverifiable. As Foucault explains in *Discipline and Punish:* "Visible: the inmate will constantly have before his eyes the tall outline of the central tower from which he is spied upon. Unverifiable: the inmate must never know whether he is being looked on at any one moment; but he must be sure that he may always be so" (201).

If the overall narrative strategy of the case study, as we have shown, is to objectify its subject in the scientific project, we might expect to find through an inside out reading of narrative that Freud's strategy is revealed in his style, particularly in the voice he constructs for the narrative's central character, Dora. What a close reading of *Dora* reveals is that Freud never quotes Dora directly unless her speech supports his psychoanalytic assertions. Because Freud took no notes at the time of the conversations (24), any direct quotes are suspect, so the writer's decision to quote directly may be regarded as more than the ordinary desire to take advantage of what a direct quote can inscribe in any narrative: immediacy, credibility, interest, the creation of voice, the ability to relate opinion without its specifically being seen as the writer's own opinion.

In this context we can look first at how Freud's quoting addresses the moment of conflict between his and Dora's interpretation of a significant event: his analysis of Herr K.'s kiss in the office. Freud believes that the pressure of Herr K.'s erection (Freud's own supposition) is displaced by Dora into repressed oral desire, which in turn becomes the hysterical cough and proves that her sublimated memory of the kiss (sexual desire) contradicts her conscious memory (powerlessness and disgust). Many writers have examined the weaknesses and strengths of this diagnosis, but none has examined how Freud's nonfiction style reveals itself when he disagrees with his patient. It is my contention that although Freud was aware that withholding Ida Bauer's name and publishing his case study in a medical journal would short-circuit the work's bireferentiality, his denial of a voice to the subject of his case study was not an overtly intentional act. Rather, Freud unintentionally reveals by his methodology his anxiety about his power to "rewrite" his patient's life through the analysis and narrative control.

Freud registers Dora's disagreement in oblique, evasive terms: "did not find it easy, however, to direct the patient's attention to her relations with Herr K. *She declared that she had done with him* (47; emphasis added).[7] In the German, Freud chooses the infinitive "zu lenken" to show that he needed to "turn" the patient's attention in the direction of his analysis. Moreover, her response, indirectly quoted, is framed by the subjunctive "sie behauptete," which indicates that she insists on an interpretation that to Freud is not necessarily true: "Sie behauptete, mit dieser Person abgeschlossen zu haben" (190). Freud has already shown the careful reader that he will not hesitate to quote a long conversation directly even when he has no written record of it. So why would Dora not be given a direct voice on this most pivotal point? Even the indirect quote itself is not permitted to be more than reactive. The analyst's movement ("zu lenken" or "direct the patient's attention") is privileged and controlling; Dora's responding declaration can only try to deflect its directive force.

Because Dora's supposed repression of her love for Herr K. is central to the entire case study, one would expect more immediacy if Freud's project truly were creating a fictionlike style rather than a monoreferential inevitability to his own interpretation of Dora's history. What is more, Dora's absence of a voice contrasts vividly to the immediately preceding 216-word direct quote of Herr K., which is filled with just the sort of idiomatic expressions—"ubrigens" (184), or "by the by" (41), and "nicht zu versichern" (184), or "need scarcely assure you" (41)—that establish both immediacy and a sure sense of voice, a status Dora does not receive. That this quotation also contains the "I get nothing out of my wife" (42) line that Dora is supposed to have recalled from her second encounter with Herr K. not only underscores Freud's underlying control of the case study, as Marcus points out (81), but questions its credibility. If Freud wants to invest so much meaning in Dora's "slips" of speech, in her exact words, it might be more convincing were more of those "exact words" presented.

Instead, until the discussion of the first dream Dora's voice is limited to such interjections as "'three to six weeks, too,' she was obliged to admit" (55), whose force do nothing more than inscribe Freud's authority. The second-hand comment of an unnamed seven-year-old companion of Dora's ("You can't think how I hate that person . . . and when she's dead I shall marry papa" [74]) is the longest sentence to pass Dora's lips during the first two thirds of a narrative that constructs her own life, and even then she is not permitted to impart her own words. During the dream discussions, Freud introduces a colloquy form that does provide Dora with a directly quoted voice. But is it her own? What is remarkable here is how much the eighteen-year-old girl resembles her therapist in word choice and sentence formation. When recalling the moment she challenged Herr K.'s unauthorized presence in her bedroom, she says, "By way of reply he said he was not going to be prevented from coming into his own bedroom when he wanted" (84).

Would a moment with such clear emotional impact for Dora likely to have been recounted in such a formal, dispassionate manner? Whose words are "by way of reply" or "Er gab zur Antwort" (228)? Freud's or Dora's? The reader obviously cannot know for sure, but the qualifying introductory clause sounds more like the style of Freud the writer than that of a

teenager recalling the moment when she awoke to find an adult man standing by her bed. The narrative strategy that Freud reveals here seems to be
more concerned with monoreferential control than with the fictionlike artistry that Marcus celebrates. M. M. Bakhtin examines the difference in *The
Dialogic Imagination*. A writer, Bakhtin says,

> may, of course, create an artistic work that compositionally
> and thematically will be similar to a novel, will be "made"
> exactly as a novel is made, but he will not thereby have
> created a novel. The style will always give him away. We
> will recognize the naively self-confident or obtusely stub-
> born unity of a smooth, pure single-voiced language (per-
> haps accompanied by a primitive, artificial, worked-up
> double-voicedness). We quickly sense that such an author
> finds it easy to purge his work of speech diversity: he simply
> does not listen to the fundamental heteroglossia inherent
> in actual language. (327)

Although Freud tells us he wrote Dora's account of the dreams immediately after the sessions (24), he does not say that he attempted to create
a word-for-word transcription of the conversation during the sessions and in
fact admits it is "not absolutely—phonographically—exact" though "it can
claim to possess a high degree of trustworthiness" (24). What, then, is the
careful reader to make of this: "[Dora:] He says it will not do: something
might happen in the night so that it might be necessary to leave the room. . . .
[Freud:] Now, I should like you to pay close attention to the *exact words* you
used. We may have to make use of them. You said that 'something might
happen in the night so that it might be necessary to leave the room'" (82;
emphasis added). While it might seem reasonable that the careful scientist
would want to pay close attention to Dora's exact words, the exactness of her
words is anything but certain. Thus, the movement from "exact words *you*
used" to the "*we* may have to make use of them," from "irher eigenen Aus-
drucke" to "Wir werden sie vielleicht brauchen" (226), seems to reveal the
manner in which Freud's entire case-study narration displaces the voice of
his subject and implicates his motivations in the project. And, because the
case-study convention maintains Dora's anonymity, no reader could check
her recollection of this conversation. Her voice is effaced both within the

text and by the underlying theory that has produced *Dora* as a "truthful" but unverifiable narrative.

What is clear in the case study *Dora* is that Freud uses the conversational mode only so long as the constructed conversation makes his point. He interrupts it to demonstrate the correlation between the case study and psychoanalytic generalization and terminates it when Dora's interpretation differs from his own:

"[Freud:] In short, these efforts prove once more how deeply you loved him. . . . [Dora: silence] [Commentary:] Naturally Dora would not follow me in this part of the interpretation. I, myself, however, had been able to arrive at a further step . . ." (88). Throughout, Freud's commentary is laced with a rhetorical style that appears to give his conclusions inevitable scientific force: "naturlich" ("naturally"), "unentbehrlich schien" ("seemed to me indispensable") (232) even if they sometimes spring from circular reasoning: "*I could not help supposing* [mußte Ich (218)] in the first instance that what was suppressed was her love of Herr K. *I could not avoid the assumption* [Ich mußte annehmen (218)] that she was still in love with him. . . . *In this way I gained an insight* [bekam Ich auch Einsicht (218)] into a conflict which was well calculated to unhinge the girl's mind" (75, emphasis added).

Ultimately, Freud's voice consumes Dora's. Dreams are first told in Dora's voice, but as the force of Freud's interpretation builds, the narrative shifts the "I" of her voice to the "she" locked within his point of view until the text at last relates the dream addenda unlocked by, and inseparable from, his analysis: "I informed Dora of the conclusions I had reached. The impression made upon her mind must have been forcible, for there immediately appeared a piece of the dream which had been forgotten: '*she went calmly to her room, and began reading a big book that lay on her writing table*'" (120, italics in Strachey translation) and "she herself helped me along it by producing her last addendum to the dream: '*she saw herself particularly distinctly going up the stairs*'" (122, italics in Strachey translation). Why did James Strachey use both direct quotes and the third-person pronoun in the standard English translation? Perhaps because Freud's own use of quotation marks in the German text is unusual and reveals that voices are blurred and contested in the case study. Freud chooses in his colloquy with Dora on the dreams to enclose only Dora's speech in quotation marks, while he reserves for himself the opportunity to speak (unencumbered by the apparatus of direct quotes) variously as a character, as a narrator, or as a commentator.

For example, when Dora recalls the first night she dreamed about

the house fire, Freud's standard German text introduces a conversation between Dora and Freud. Freud encloses in quotes Dora's speech: "Der Papa
will nicht, daβ der Bruder bei Nacht so abgesperrt sein soll. Er hat gesagt,
das ginge nicht; es konnte doch bei Nacht etwas passieren, daβ man hinaus
muβ" (226; "Father does not want my brother to be locked in like that at
night. He says it will not do: something might happen in the night so that it
might be necessary to leave the room" [82]). But Freud does not use quotation marks for his direct response: "Das haben sie nun aug Feuersgefahr
bezogen?" (226; "And that made you think of the risk of fire?" [82]).

   As Dora continues to speak (her voice always circumscribed by quotation marks), Freud's responses drift in and out of direct speech in a pattern
that is more revelatory than intentional. At times, as in the example above,
he speaks directly to Dora. Other times he summarizes the drift of their
conversation: "Dora hat nun aber die Verbindung zwischen dem rezenten
und den damaligen Anlassen fur den Traum gefunden" (226; "But Dora had
now discovered the connecting link between the recent exciting cause of the
dream and the original one" [82]). And still other times, he reveals his scientific agenda: "Es light mir nun daran, die Beziehung zwischen den Ereignis-
sen in L. und den demaligen gleichlautenden Traumen zu ergrunden" (227;
"What I now had to do was to establish the relation between the events at
L—— and the recurrent dreams which she had had there" [83]). Throughout these interjections Freud continues to present Dora in directly quoted
speech as if the two are having a conversation.

   Strachey's translation attempts to rectify this quoting practice
(which is also nonstandard in German) by enclosing Freud's obvious remarks
to Dora in quotation marks and reserving free of quotation marks Freud's
comments as an after-the-fact first-person narrator or as an analyst. But because Freud's own German makes no such distinction, his methodology reveals that he wished to fix Dora as a character bound in the history of
verbatim speech and constructed scene while at the same time he would be
free either to speak to her within that scene or to turn directly to his audience
and command the stage while she remains suspended in the moment.[8]

   This blurring suggests less the emotional force of an intense psychoanalytic session than it does a narrative strategy and style that has entirely
consumed its subject. Ultimately, at the end of the last visit, the force of
Freud's voice reduces the Dora of the narrative to silence and acceptance:
"Dora had listened to me without any of her usual contradictions. She
seemed to be moved; she said good-bye to me very warmly, with the hardiest

wishes for the New Year, and—came no more" (130) (Sie hatte zugehort, ohne wie sonst zu widersprechen. Sie schien ergriffen, nahm auf die liebens-wurdigste Weise mit warmen Wunschen zum Jahreswechsel Abschied und—kam nicht wieder [272]).

If the "came no more," or "kam nicht wieder," clause encodes Dora's final resistance in a surprise ending, Freud, of course, again and again will reserve the last word for himself: writing an epilogue, revisions, foot-notes, and commentaries on the text. He declines to treat the actual "Dora" again, insisting, "I have always avoided acting a part, and have contented myself with practicing the humbler arts of psychology. In spite of every theo-retical interest and of every endeavor to be of assistance as a physician, I keep the fact in mind that there must be some limits set to the extent to which psychological influence may be used, and I respect as one of these limits the patient's own will and understanding" (131). And so it seems Freud forges his special brand of truth claim, the case study, so that he can trans-gress those patient limits of "will and understanding" in prose if not in life: the truth claim without possibility of verification, the perfect patient who never talks back.

Reading nonfiction narrative for the manner by which it cuts across the limits of history, by contrast, will reopen that dialogue between the au-thor and subject. It will examine the narrator of the text (the unseen listener-teller-organizer of dialogue and events) against what we know of the limita-tions and possibilities of a nonfiction author (the Freud who silenced Dora by the methodology of his case study as well as by the apparatus of his analy-sis). Far from consigning nonfiction to some sort of inferior plane in the scale of reading experiences, as critics since Aristotle have assumed, such methods open up nonfiction to dynamic, resisting readings. The intent of these read-ings is not to transfer a narrative into the category of "fiction" as soon as discrepancies are found but to examine it for what it reveals of its ritual of communication and of the cultural relationships among author, subject, and reader. How does the author position himself against his subject? What does he reveal of his methodology? Does he seek to dominate his subjects and readers, or does he open the process so that subjects and readers more readily can join the author in a complex process of negotiation?

Some discrepancies revealed by this sort of close stylistic analysis, certainly, might be so large as to cause us to shut the book or to read it as fiction. But more often a reading of nonfiction that is alive to the way it implicates its author will bring a wider understanding of, and possibly even a deeper appreciation for, the style of the text and its history. In the chapter that follows I will approach the nonfictional text and its author from the other direction: reading the author's historical presence and what we can determine of the characters' materiality over the edge of the text itself. My attempt is to show how a nonfictional narrative is always in contest with the material lives that it cannot quite contain.

3.

WRITING OUTSIDE IN:

Implicating the Author in the Narratives of Tom Wolfe and John Reed

IF EXAMINING THE WRITER OF THE NONFICTION TEXT inside out means that we read the narrator's communication rituals inside the story against the limitations of an actual author, then examining the writer of nonfiction outside in will require that we read what we can discover about the author's outside presence in history against the narrative stance that she constructs for herself inside the text. In either case the goal is to read nonfiction narrative over the edge of text and of experience and to search for the ways that authors and readers are implicated by the stories that construe their lives. The boundaries of an inside out reading and an outside in reading are never fixed; in many cases both operations reflect on the other even as the analysis of the implicated writer is in many ways inseparable from the way that writer implicates the reader. Still, there are useful distinctions among these concepts, and I will continue my consideration of Tom Wolfe's *The Electric Kool-Aid Acid Test* from the perspective of what I can learn of Wolfe's life and the events that he used as the basis for his text. Similarly, I will bring historical research to bear on the work of American journalist John Reed, whose work both predicts and contradicts Wolfe's in intriguing ways.

Reading both Wolfe's and Reed's nonfiction for the manner in which they implicate themselves (overtly, covertly, or inadvertently) as historical presences will help to show us the ways by which they draw many of their readers into their projects. For his part, Wolfe was to promise in his writing a new frontier by which his subjects (and, by extension, his readers) could redefine and free themselves through everyday social choices and broadly defined political acts. Reed, in his coverage of revolutions in Mexico and Russia, promised an even more thoroughgoing opportunity for change. Careful analysis of the histories of both writers, however, particularly when read against the narratives each constructs, reveals contradictions between their messages and communication rituals. Reed had overcome many of these contradictions by the end of his career—even if that resolution in some ways cost him his life—while Wolfe never has resolved his narrative presence in a text like *The Electric Kool-Aid Acid Test* against what we can determine of his historical presence.

Tom Wolfe and the Writing of Recapture

As I began to demonstrate in the previous chapter, time and again the escape fantasies that Wolfe writes for his late-1960s-era characters (and even readers) are circumscribed by the recapture of those characters. Similarly, Wolfe's own stylistic experimentation seems to be circumscribed by his unwillingness to grant full permission to himself and to other writers to challenge fully the way that the journalistic industry marketed "facts" to readers. Published in 1968 at the height of New Journalism's impact and controversy, Wolfe's *Acid Test* promises to take its readers on a no-holds-barred trip to the frontier of cultural struggle that is so much the source (and occasionally the product) of New Journalism.

Reading what we know of the historical Wolfe against his narrator—as well as what we know of the historical record of the Merry Pranksters against the record that Wolfe builds in the book—reveals Wolfe's efforts to evoke and then arrest the social and political breakout represented by his deep challenge to the journalistic conventions of the 1960s. Ultimately, Wolfe's brand of New Journalism transforms itself, moving toward a literary realism that more and more has become synonymous with social and cultural conservatism. Wolfe offers a fascinating subject for this sort of investigation because he has been so outspoken and so articulate, if often evasive and contradictory, on so many occasions.[1] Wolfe says he believes that literary and aesthetic tastes "become established in a political fashion" (qtd. in Zelenko 173), but takes pains to exclude himself from the implications of that assertion by insisting that his own cultural reporting and writing can be "impersonal and objective" (qtd. in McLeod 178). It seems that if Wolfe were really to open himself as a character in his nonfiction it would be that much more difficult to maintain the illusion of the impersonal objectivity he wishes to claim. But a reading against the grain—an outside in reading for the implicated writer—will aim to uncover the very presence that the author wishes to conceal.

While questioning Wolfe for an interview that subsequently was published in the April 1966 edition of *Vogue,* writer Elaine Dundy asked Wolfe—who was only to become the nation's most famous author of "truthful" narrative during the next two decades—about his habitual practice of lying. Wolfe, it seems, had told Dundy that he had lots of brothers and sisters, only to retract the tale as Dundy's research deepened. "Tell about the lying," Dundy prodded. "For instance you told me you had eight brothers and sisters and then later retracted it." Wolfe replied:

> That one began in Sunday school when I was about five. The teacher asked each of us in a kind of getting-to-know-one-another way if we had any brothers and sisters, and I said I had eight. She knew I hadn't and spoke to my mother about it, but it still persists. I don't understand it. I've always had a fantasy of lots of brothers and sisters. I have a fantasy brother named Harris who runs a hotel in Cuba and he leads to a fantasy of the F.B.I. being on my trail because of him. I think there must be some symbolic truth underneath the lies. (17)

Only a few months after the publication of the interview Wolfe gained an opportunity to open the doors of perception toward the "symbolic truth" of his fugitive fantasy. It was during the summer of 1966, Wolfe tells his readers in the initial pages of *The Electric Kool-Aid Acid Test,* that he first became interested in Ken Kesey, a "Young Novelist Real-Life Fugitive" (5), the author of *One Flew over the Cuckoo's Nest* and *Sometimes a Great Notion* and a celebrated escapee from two marijuana indictments. Then a writer for *New York Magazine,* the Sunday supplement of the New York *Herald-Tribune,* Wolfe flew to California in October 1966, shortly after Kesey's arrest, and opens his narrative a few days shy of the Halloween Night Acid Test Graduation of Kesey's Merry Pranksters. Wolfe first comes face-to-face with his fugitive double through a twenty-four-inch glass partition in the visiting room of the San Mateo jail. While Wolfe scribbles shorthand notes, he and Kesey shout at each other over a raspy telephone. "I don't want to be rude to you fellows from the city," Wolfe recounts Kesey's unspoken thought, "but there's been things going on out here that you would never guess in your wildest million years old buddy . . ." (8).

As were many of the New Journalists of the mid-1960s, Wolfe was rebelling against a news establishment that, like his former employer the *Washington Post,* forced him to go on deadline to the parents of a dead crime victim and convince them "that it was in the best interests of humanity that they surrender a picture of this girl." The *Post's* motive, Wolfe recalls almost three decades later, was "'sheer prurience, the way every other newspaper's is'" (Sellers 268). His ongoing critique of the news business, then and now, goes far beyond its prurient deadline competition. In an interview with Chet Flippo published in *Rolling Stone* Wolfe takes dead aim at newspaper monopoly economics and, despite the fact that Wolfe no longer had to worry much about his own next meal, accurately describes the exploitative habits of the news industry:

> I doubt if there are five cities where there is still newspaper competition. . . . When this happens, the monopoly newspaper cuts back on its staff—always happens. They just stop covering local events—too expensive. And they'll hire children from journalism schools at the lowest possible scale. They'll let them work for a couple of years, send them to the Statehouse, 'cause at the Statehouse they can pick up four or five stories a day handed out by public relations people. (101–2)

Within *Acid Test* itself Wolfe manages to critique the straight news business on several occasions, beginning with his "PALO ALTO, CALIF., July 21, 1963" dateline that ends the "What Do You Think of My Buddha" chapter and recounts the press's befuddlement at the last-night party on Bohemian Perry Lane. "[I]t was hard as hell to make the End of an Era story come out right in the papers . . . but they managed to go back with the story they came with, End of an Era, the cliche intact" (48). Wolfe's critique culminates at the Acid Graduation, when the TV crews press close to get Kesey's words to the multitudes and start ordering the Pranksters around. "The heads are disgusted. They just stare at them," Wolfe reports, adding that Kesey "shoots a few whammies their way." Then suddenly Wolfe is inside Kesey's head, but what is revealed, predictably, sounds a lot like Wolfe. "These bastards and their . . . *positioning* . . . They're punctures in the dirigible, flatulent murmurs in the heart" (353).

Wolfe, of course, was prepared to search for alternatives to pack journalism. And like Kesey he doesn't mind a little self-promotion if that is what it takes to spread the word. Of "The Kandy-Kolored Tangerine-Flake Streamline Baby," the magazine piece that gave its name to Wolfe's first collection of articles, Wolfe wrote in his 1973 manifesto "The New Journalism": "It was hard to say what it was like. It was a garage sale, that piece . . . vignettes, odds and ends of scholarship, bits of memoir, short bursts of sociology, apostrophes, epithets, means, cackles, anything that came into my head, much of it thrown together in a rough and awkward way. That was its virtue. It showed me the possibility of there being something 'new' in journalism" (15). Imagine, then, Wolfe's fascination with Kesey's Pranksters, out on the Edge, huddled in the glow, "starting to *rap,* a form of free association conversation, like a jazz conversation, or even a monologue, with everyone, or whoever, catching hold of words, symbols, ideas, sounds, and winging them back and forth and beyond . . . the walls of conventional logic" (*Acid Test* 53).

But like his reconstruction of Kesey's Pranksters—or at least the many examples of unspoken language attributed to them in the passages that form the first part of this chapter's discussion—Wolfe at the same time was fending off another more politically engaged form of New Journalism. From the New Left of the 1960s had arisen the challenge of a committed form of writing that, while it differed from Wolfe's, represented just as deep a rupture in the mid-century American practice of corporate, "objective," inverted-pyramid journalism. Most subsequent scholarly studies of the creative nonfiction loosely grouped as New Journalism have not examined the political and social struggles that lie at its core and instead have confined themselves to considerations of genre and canon: New Journalism's peculiar truth status and the question of whether or not it deserves to be studied as serious literature. But at least two theoretical articles written between 1965 and 1974 by a pair of the form's leading practitioners—reprinted in Ronald Weber's anthology *The Reporter as Artist: A Look at the New Journalism Controversy* (1974)—offer a direct challenge to Wolfe's own poetics.[2]

Nat Hentoff, in his essay "Behold the New Journalism—It's Coming after You!" called for reporting that breaks down the barriers between reporter/reader/history by eliminating the reporter as "faceless note taking onlooker." Hentoff asks for engagement between writer and reader: "It's I who am there; it's I telling you where I've been, what I've seen, how I felt about it, what changes it made and did not make to me" (53). Such engagement, Hentoff argues, would disclose journalism's dirty little secret, the idea that somehow subjective judgments don't come into play in the creation and consumption of news product. Though Hentoff is rebelling from the same sort of corporate media power as is Wolfe, his belief that any reporting necessarily is deeply subjective strikes at the heart of Wolfe's contention that he can present "impersonal and objective" reporting in *The Electric Kool-Aid Acid Test*. "I can get in the mind of Ken Kesey . . . ," Wolfe told interviewer Joe David Bellamy the same year that Hentoff's essay was published in Weber's anthology, "get completely inside Kesey's mind, based on interviews, tapes that he made, or letters he wrote, diaries, and so on. It's still a controversial thing to do but I was not at all interested in presenting *my* subjective state" (qtd. in Bellamy 45, emphasis in original).

That promise of objectivity squares with Wolfe's belief, expressed elsewhere in the interview, that there "are certain things that are objectively known," even if different subjects experience those objective phenomena somewhat differently: "[Y]ou can't dismiss the common denominators in the external world and say there is no reality," Wolfe said (qtd. in Bellamy 45). Therefore, to Wolfe, New Journalism remains a revolution of *technique,* not of epistemology or politics. In the following exchange Wolfe's questioner summarizes Hentoff's position succinctly, and Wolfe's response is telling:

> BELLAMY: [I]sn't the real crux of the issue the question of the nature of reality itself? It seems to me that one argument that's been given in favor of the new journalism is that so-called outside reality doesn't really exist, that all you really have is subjective reality. So the reporter, instead of using the old rigid forms and formulas, which were supposedly a way of capturing outside reality, assumes now that he's being more honest by giving his subjective experience, which he sees as truer to reality. And isn't that really the argument that the new novelists are giving too—that there is no "outside reality"? So that leaves you open to go into fantasy—because that's part of what reality is, after all, because fantasy is part of reality. We're *always* having fantasies.

> WOLFE: I disagree with that totally. Because, for my money, the only thing new in this new journalism I'm talking about is the new *techniques* that nonfiction writers have discovered they can use. The subjectivity that I value in the good

examples of the new journalism is the use of *techniques.*
(44–45, emphasis added)

In another interview Wolfe describes those techniques with explicit reference to *Electric Kool-Aid Acid Test.* He says he would review his notes for
an upcoming chapter of the book, then try to envision himself as living those
events, "going crazy, for example . . . how it feels and what it's going to sound
like when you translate it into words—which was real writing by radar" (qtd.
in Thompson 212). But he insists that he was reporting objectively.

Hentoff and other more politically motivated journalists of the
1960s, however, were less willing to circumscribe the issue of subjectivity to
formal and technical limits. They preferred to critique the illusion of objective reporting as a matter of social and political control. Wondering aloud,
for example, how the New York *Times* "would look if it were edited and
written by the people from Bedford-Stuyvesant," Hentoff finds that "all the
news fit to print" is determined by social and cultural, not objective or even
formal, standards. Hentoff, therefore, defines the promise of New Journalism as follows:

> A new generation of young readers is being brought into
> the news in ways that make more and more of them realize
> that they need not remain only voyeurs in living history.
> The new journalism, because it is powered by feeling as
> well as intellect, can help break the glass between the
> reader and the world he lives in. A citizen has to be more
> than informed; he has to act if he is to have some say about
> what happens to him; and the new journalism can stimu-
> late active involvement. (52)

Hentoff's arguments are made even more forcefully by then-*Village
Voice* senior editor Jack Newfield in an essay, "Journalism: Old, New, and
Corporate," written shortly after the 1968 presidential election and also published in Weber's anthology. In that essay Newfield argues that his "gripe
against the respectable gray pillars" of American journalism is not simply
that "there is monopoly ownership in too many cities by publishers who care
little about professionalism, and everything about profits"; is not simply that
"the newspaper unions have become conservative" perpetuators of "a senior-
ity system that protects the lazy and punishes the imaginative"; is not simply

that "advertisers have a subtle say about what goes into a newspaper" (54–55). To Newfield,

> The disturbing reality is that the press censors itself, through superficiality, through bias, through incompetence, and through a desire to be the "responsible" fourth branch of government. . . . They have a mind-set. They have definite life styles and political values, which are concealed under a rhetoric of objectivity. But those values are organically institutionalized by the *Times*, by AP, by CBS, into their corporate bureaucracies. Among these unspoken, but organic, values are belief in welfare capitalism, God, the West, Puritanism, the Law, family, property, the two-party system, and perhaps most critically, in the notion that violence is only defensible when employed by the State. I can't think of any White House correspondent, or network television analyst, who doesn't share these values. And at the same time, who doesn't insist that he is totally objective. (55)

Read twenty-five years later, the particular historical thrust of Newfield's piece is that journalism, like radicalism, cinema, and music, has emerged "beyond the frozen frontiers of the older forms" (60). Adopting the term "participatory journalist," Newfield contends that new journalists will recognize along with Andrew Kopkind that "objectivity is the rationalization for moral disengagement, the classic cop-out from choice-making" (61). Interestingly, Newfield includes *Electric Kool-Aid Acid Test* among his examples of the new participatory journalism, though he complains elsewhere in his essay that Wolfe has "no politics" (63). Despite that, Newfield finds that a resistant streak creeps through Wolfe's reporting, because it is "written with intelligence from inside the drug subculture" (65). Ultimately, Newfield argues that engaged writers will be the cornerstone of the rebellion against old journalism. His argument is presented here at some length to retain the flavor of its 1960s-era faith in freedom and newness:

> Participation and advocacy remain the touchstones of the new insurgent journalism. The evidence now seems overwhelming that the closer a serious writer gets to his material, the more understanding he gets, the more under-

standing he gets, the more he is there to record those decisive moments of spontaneity and authenticity. He gets inside the context and sees scenes and details that distance and neutrality deny to the more conventional reporters. He does not have to write about impersonal public rituals like ghost-written speeches, well-rehearsed concerts, and staged and managed press conferences. He is there to see and react to the human reflexes exposed late at night that illuminate a man's character. The advocacy journalist breaks down the artificial barrier between work and leisure; between private and public knowledge. He can do this because he is writing, by choice, about subjects that excite his imagination, rather than fulfilling an assignment made by the city desk, and that needs to be approved and edited by the copy desk. He is a free man, relying on his instincts, intelligence and discipline. (65)

The struggle between Wolfe's and the Hentoff/Newfield brands of New Journalism, ironically, reverberated inside the world of unconventional New York journalism of the late 1960s, though it would be too reductive to consider the larger social and political rift only as some internecine dispute. Wolfe's early reporting was published in the Sunday *New York Magazine* section of the New York *Herald-Tribune,* a breeding ground of adventurous feature reporters that Wolfe sketches in the opening sections of his essay "The New Journalism." Under the editorship of Clay Felker, the Sunday supplement branched out as the prototypical "city" magazine in 1968, the same year *Electric Kool-Aid Acid Test* was published, and Wolfe was named a contributing editor. Ken McAuliffe's history of the *Village Voice* (1978), where both Newfield and Hentoff were editors, notes that the *Voice* and *New York Magazine* "competed for ads, especially after the *Voice* began seriously looking for national advertising, for readers—about one in three *Voice* readers also read *New York Magazine*—and on a purely prestige level for the bragging rights around town to having started the New Journalism" (377).

McAuliffe writes that declining circulation during its first years of independent publication forced *New York Magazine*'s Felker to shift the publication's emphasis away from politics and toward "lifestyle"—a direction that, coincidentally, had always been Wolfe's consuming interest. McAuliffe quotes Felker: "We as journalists looked too long and too lovingly at the hippies, yippies, protesters and rock groups. . . . They are no longer, to use the cliche, relevant. What *is* relevant is that you can go broke on $80,000 a year, that you can't get an apartment, that there are new pressures on marriage and new ways to make money" (369–70). For his part, Wolfe described the *Voice* and its editors, such as Hentoff and Newfield, as serving a role, along with the *New York Review of Books,* as the "pulpit-voice in the Church of Good Liberals" and said that reading it would "confirm you in your supposition that it is really not worth going below 48th Street—ever" (qtd. in McAuliffe 131). Wolfe more recently has insisted that the social rebellion of "style" overshadowed any of the tumultuous political upheavals of the decade (Mewborn 235).

The final irony of this sometimes intramural squabble (which should not overshadow the very real social, political, and epistemological rifts within New Journalism) was that by 1974 Felker had purchased a controlling interest in the *Village Voice* and thus was in a direct position to settle the future of the market, in both its uptown and downtown incarnations (McAuliffe 441). In an interview shortly after the purchase, Felker named Wolfe as the journalist he most admired, and suggested he might keep a tighter rein on the point of view expressed by *Village Voice* writers, if not their creative form: "I'm concerned with content here [at the *Voice*]. This is me, but even here, I give the writers—the essential thing that I do is come to an agreement with the writer as to *point of view,* but after that I don't interfere with what they have to *say.* I don't believe in that. And I think you will kill a writer's creativity by doing that" (qtd. in Frankfurt 263, emphasis added).

Wolfe's concept of "New Journalism" and the service it can do for the profit-making news industry is ironically summarized in an essay written by Thomas R. Kendrick, the editor who is credited with building the *Washington Post*'s feature section into a profitable and influential arbiter of daily newspaper feature style. Kendrick says he "demurs" when Newfield calls "participation and advocacy" the "touchstones" of New Journalism, then adopts Wolfe's (who is, after all, a *Post* alumnus) New Journalism forms as the ones the *Post* accepts. "There is nothing wrong in 'exploiting the factual authority of journalism' and no necessity to take license with fact," Kendrick argues, in terms that have become standard in feature textbooks. "And there is no reason that much information cannot be conveyed entertainingly [if] newspapers are to survive" (xi).

The *Washington Post*'s squeamishness about factual reporting was perhaps understandable, as it was that newspaper's *Style* section that lay at the heart of the Janet Cooke case, in which a *Post* reporter wrote the story of an eight-year-old heroin addict named "Jimmy." The case raises a number of fascinating issues for the discussion of fact and fiction. Recreated scenes and even composite characters are not that uncommon in the adventurous nonfiction often classified as New Journalism, but Cooke's greatest sin seemed to be publishing her story in the *Washington Post,* which under Kendrick's direction in the *Style* section, touted formal nonfictional experimentation but scrupulously avoided larger epistemological issues. The *Post* perhaps particularly was sensitive because of widespread criticism of its use of unnamed sources in its Watergate coverage and the pervasive. though unproven, belief that "Deep Throat" was a composite character. Interestingly, the editor Bob Woodward, the only reporter ever to have interviewed "Deep Throat," served as an interlocutor in the in-house questioning that ultimately led to Cooke's confession that she had made up "Jimmy." ("'If a just God were looking down,' said Woodward, 'what would he say is the truth?'" [Sager 210]).

Cooke's case also demonstrates a second theory central to this book, that of reader implication, which I will discuss in the next chapter. Because readers believed that the "Jimmy" in the story signified a material body, they were deeply implicated by Cooke's descriptions of his plight: "The needle slides into the boy's soft skin like a straw pushed into the center of a freshly baked cake. Liquid ebbs out of the syringe, replaced by bright red blood. . . . 'Pretty soon man,' Ron says, 'you got to learn to do this for yourself'" (qtd. in Sager 209). Prompted by thousands of concerned readers, the Washington, D.C., police launched a citywide search for "Jimmy," which ultimately determined that the eight year old did not exist. Such reactions are rarely excited by fictional narratives, though they have a different, and often equally strong, sort of power to implicate their readers. Finally, the Cooke case demonstrates the market value currently placed on "real-life" stories, even those that depict the author of one of the great journalism "hoaxes" in history. In 1996, fifteen years after her Pulitzer was withdrawn, Cooke signed a $1.6 million agreement with TriStar pictures for the story of her life, of which she will receive 55 percent and her biographer, former *Washington Post* reporter Mike Sager, will receive 45 percent (Dutka 12E). The $880,000 thus earned at least approximates the salary Cooke would have earned had she remained a *Post* employee for the intervening fifteen years. No wonder the *Washington Post* and its famous graduate Tom Wolfe believe in the power of facts and do little to question the epistemological entanglements that lie at the core of factual narrative.

It was within the specific social context of the political versus formal ruptures of New Journalism, then, that Wolfe, using his "method acting" technique of subjective objectivity, climbed on the psychic bus with Kesey and the Pranksters and tried to imagine how it would be to be a best-selling novelist and fugitive from justice. The bus's destination was "Further"; its warning sign, "Weird Load Ahead." Wolfe was on a tight deadline as he sat down to write *Acid Test* in two frenzied months while he attended to his seriously ill father in Richmond. It seems he wasn't so sure the counterculture that the Pranksters represented had much staying power. "See, there was a time problem in writing that book, too. It looked as if the whole psychedelic, hippie phenomenon was disappearing. So there was pressure just to get it done," he told Bellamy in 1974. "This was before Woodstock, and, you know, I *believed* people who said, 'Well, nobody wants to read about this anymore'" (qtd. in Bellamy 59).

In final preparation for his two-month writing blitz, Wolfe traveled to Buffalo, where a friend gave him a 125-milligram dose of LSD "for research." Wolfe described the experience as "tying yourself to the railroad track and seeing how big the train is, which is rather big" (qtd. in Reagan 196) and on a later occasion went into more detail:

> At first I thought I was having a gigantic heart attack—I felt like my heart was outside my body with these big veins. . . . As I began to calm down, I had the feeling that I had entered into the sheen of this bobbly twist carpet— a really *wretched* carpet, made of Acrilan—and somehow this represented the people of America, in their democratic glory. It was cheap and yet it had a certain glossy excitement to it—I even felt sentimental about it. Somehow I was *merging* with this carpet. At the time it seemed like a phenomenal insight, a breakthrough. (qtd. in Thompson 212)

Toby Thompson, in her *Vanity Fair* article, quotes Wolfe as saying that his carpet hallucination doesn't signify "a goddamn thing" (212), but Wolfe's contradictory sensations of community and catastrophe repeat the escape/recapture fantasy and are everywhere in *Electric Kool-Aid Acid Test*. For the promise of a new frontier by which Wolfe's subjects (and, by implication, his readers) could redefine and free themselves from the clutches of conventionality is soon circumscribed by their arrest and recapture, even as Wolfe sought in his theoretical writings of the early 1970s to apprehend the deep challenge to corporate journalism that his writing had helped to unleash.

In this respect it is worth examining one more scene in *Acid Test* in some detail: the Pranksters' visit to Timothy Leary's Millbrook estate. When events outside the book are read over the edge of the book's narrative, the discussion can illustrate how Wolfe dramatized the tensions that pervaded counterculture and the emerging New Journalism in the late 1960s and can serve as a transition toward a more specific exploration of Wolfe's attraction to and escape from the Prankster fantasy. Wolfe presents the Millbrook visit as a potential summit between Kesey's Edge City crazies and the Eastern psychedelic establishment represented by psychologists Leary and Richard Alpert. The reader is drawn into familiar turf here. Wolfe inhabits the heads of the Learyites (but does not report in his author's note that he ever interviewed any of them [371–72]) as they sniff their disapproval of Kesey's gang and thereby, ironically, forfeit their place on Wolfe's status ladder: "We have something deep and meditative going on here, and you California crazies are a sour note" (94). While the Pranksters cavort on the Millbrook grounds, coopting the Learyites' guided tour to poke fun at their pretensions, Wolfe relays the big question of the day: "Where was Leary? Everyone was waiting for the great meeting of Leary and Kesey. Well, word came down that Leary was upstairs in the mansion engaged in a very serious experiment, a three-day trip, and could not be disturbed. Kesey wasn't angry, but he was very disappointed, even hurt. It was unbelievable—this was Millbrook, one big piece of uptight constipation, after all this" (95).

Yet a photograph taken by poet Allen Ginsberg, who had boarded the Pranksters' bus after having set up a meeting between Kesey and Kerouac at a party in Manhattan, presents ready proof that Leary actually did leave his room. Here is Leary, tongue clasped between his lips, head leaned back against a window of the "Further" bus, wrapped in sweater and scarf, while a shirtless and blade-faced Neal Cassady looks on. Some twenty-five years later, before his death, Leary recalled that he soon left the Pranksters' bus and went upstairs, not for a three-day trip but to recover: "I had just fallen in love with a woman who later became my wife, so needless to say, that was number one on my consciousness. Not only was I lovesick, but I had also come down with a heavy flu. So I went right to my room and went to bed. Put yourself in my place. I didn't know this was history being made, a meeting of the acid tribes. I was preoccupied with other things" (qtd. in Perry 97).[3]

Although he later reveals that Sandy Lehmann-Haupt was given the dose of the powerful hallucinogen DMT at Millbrook—which, in fact, helps to trigger Lehmann-Haupt's later breakdown in the "Dream Wars" chapter—Wolfe in *Acid Test* portrays the Prankster-Learyite visit as quite brief, almost uneventful. Ginsberg's photo record, however, shows nurse/guide Susan Metzner, the wife of psychologist Ralph Metzner, injecting Cassady's bare bottom with DMT in an attic bedroom of the Millbrook mansion, as well as a beatific Alpert entertaining the Pranksters on the mansion's front porch. Alpert, now known as Baba Ram Dass, recalls:

> There was no forewarning whatsoever that the Pranksters were going to show up at Millbrook. Our situation was as follows: The night before, there were about twenty of us. We had all done acid and it turned out to be a very intense and profound trip. We sat by the fire, all of us huddled together. There was a lot of intimacy and profundity and it was a very deep trip that had gone on all night long. By seven or eight in the morning, everybody was in mellow, delicate, vulnerable space and drifting off to bed for the day. It was at this very moment that the bus drove up. (qtd. in Perry 93)

Wolfe tells us the bus "entered the twisty deep green Gothic grounds of Millbrook with flags flying, American flags all over the bus, and the speakers blaring rock 'n' roll" as Lehmann-Haupt tossed great green smoke bombs overboard (93–94). Ron "Hassler" Bivert now remembers "their house was kind of enveloped in green smoke. It was like the Huns coming to visit Camelot" (qtd. in Perry 93). While Wolfe recounts the Learyites' manner of greeting as "a couple of figures there on the lawn dart back into the house . . . finally a few souls materialize" (94, ellipses added), Ken Babbs, who as the "Intrepid Traveler" was Kesey's chief lieutenant, has written the following "flashback" of the arrival: "They emerge from the green smoke pulling to a stop in the turnaround in front of the mansion, greeted by Richard Alpert and the lovely lithe bikinied maidens; Pranksters tootling and fluting the arrival; Babbs and Cassady and Kesey and Ginsberg leading the handshaking charge; followed closely by the rest of the Merry Band" (qtd. in Perry 95).

By now, of course, the visit has been so mediated and remediated that everyone's memories are mostly of other accounts and other memories, not the least of which is Wolfe's book. In this way the transaction is reminiscent of what historian A. J. P. Taylor has to say about John Reed's *Ten Days That Shook the World:*

> As with most writers, Reed heightened the drama, and this drama sometimes took over from reality. Bolshevik participants, when they looked back, often based their recollections more on Reed's book than on their own memories. . . . In this sense, Reed's book founded a legend, one which has largely triumphed over the facts. Not that the legend was untrue. Most legends spring from facts. But the mood and emotions of the Bolshevik revolution would not stand out so clearly if Reed had not been there to record them. (ix)

The thrust of Wolfe's legend of the Prankster-Learyite summit, however, was to dramatize a gulf that, at least with the passage of time, does not seem so deep to many of its participants and that is directly controverted by the photographic record. Alpert/Baba Ram Dass, who seems to have stayed on friendly enough terms with the Pranksters—despite the Millbrook visit—to be a guest at Kesey's La Honda house the weekend of the first Hell's Angels party, finishes the story:

> I remember them staying around for the day. I remember sitting on the porch railing talking to them. We all went out to the little tennis house where people would go for a week of silent retreat and they did sort of a ceremony out there. Then they took a bath and ate and slept. They really did little more than that. It was fairly disappointing for them. They caught us about twelve hours too late; it was nothing more than that. If they had come the night before, it would have been an entirely different story for all of us for the rest of our lives. (qtd. in Perry 101–2)

The foregoing analysis is just the sort that Phyllis Frus ridicules as a "tedious recitation" of facts and that she recommends not be undertaken in nonfiction analysis because of the impossibility of ever reaching a final "truth" about events. I agree that the final truth can never be pinned down, but reading nonfiction narratives from the outside in after this manner will uncover the writer's cultural work as it interacts with the memories of characters who are also historical presences in the world. Although the initial Mill-brook incident is presented in one of the book's shortest chapters, Wolfe makes symbolic use of the aborted Kesey-Leary summit to build one of *Acid Test*'s most important and compelling themes: the manner in which Kesey's experiments represented a profound and indeed ecstatically religious chal-lenge to mid-1960s society. But it was a challenge mounted from the Left Coast electricity of neon shopping strips and freeways rather than the East-ern/Far Eastern establishment of meditation, Zen, Yoga, and inner contem-plation. Predictably, Wolfe's narrator, at least on the surface, chooses sides, although the passage also signals the beginning of the long downward spiral of the book (Hellmann 113) by which Wolfe can reject both alternatives and move toward Kesey's final conclusion: "We Blew It" (368).

Ironically, as was mentioned earlier, Wolfe discloses several chap-ters later, though without making an explicit link to the Millbrook episode, that Prankster Sandy Lehmann-Haupt had been injected with DMT at Leary's mansion, thereby lending more credence to the competing photo-graphic records than does Wolfe's own narrative. For both thematic and structural reasons Wolfe could not disclose this fact in the Millbrook chapter, because he was far more concerned then with painting the Learyites as up-tight Eastern acid mystics than as the authors of Sandy's demise. He saves that role for Kesey and the Pranksters in what is one of the book's best and most fully dramatized passages. Sandy is beginning to slide into paranoic delusions, particularly centered around his growing feeling that Kesey wants to control his thoughts and actions. He mentally "unpaints" the bus in a DMT flashback, disassociating himself from its "Further-Weird Load" agenda. On a group outing, sickened by the "violence" of a Tom and Jerry cartoon, Sandy leaves a movie theater, only to be confronted when he re-turns. "'Where the hell have you been? Kesey is looking all over for you.' Sandy runs back into the theater. *Kesey!* He looks up on the screen—and the mouse, Jerry, tricks the cat, Tom, and the cat goes off a cliff and *hits*, flattened in an explosion of eyeballs, thousands of eyeballs" (107–8).

Wolfe's writing is at its very best here, multi-leveled, compelling, rocketing, rocketing, "toward—what?" (104). Images of the edge become images of falling; Sandy's sense that Kesey wants to control him becomes an omen for later scenes in the book in which Kesey himself will demand more overt control over his followers:

> Sandy falls off the bed, dead, lying on the floor, and he
> leaves his body in astral projection and sails out over the

Pacific, out from the Esalen cliff, out for 40 or 50 miles, soaring and the wind goes in gusts, *huhhhhhhnnnhh, huhhhhhhhhhhnnh, huhhhhhhhhhhhnnh*, and he is the wind, not even a compact spirit flying but a totally diffuse being, dissolved in the upper ethers, and he can see the whole moonlit ocean and Esalen way back there. Then he comes to, and he is on the floor of the cabin, breathing hard, *huhhhhhhhhhnnnh, huhhhhhhhhhhhnnh, huhhhhhhhhnnnh.* (108)

In depicting a panicked Sandy picked up by police and turned over to the custody of his brother, Wolfe has implicated his readers in an effective but subtle way. By going so deeply inside Sandy's thoughts during the "Dream Wars" chapter, he has made most of his readers care deeply about Sandy's fate. From then on many of those readers will understand that the Pranksters' seductive fantasy extracts a potentially steep price. With that cautionary overlay, in the following chapter, "The Unspoken Thing," Wolfe introduces in a much more formal way his thesis that Kesey is in fact a religious mystic and that the Pranksters' experience is a new religious movement. One effect of that choice is to allow Wolfe to bracket his story within a trajectory that he can manage, allowing him to "predict" the responses that he (as a historical author writing after the fact in a tactic similar to the one I will trace for Reed in *Ten Days*) already knows will occur. For example, Wolfe cites Joachim Wach, a sociologist of religion, as predicting that "in all these religious circles," the group becomes tighter and develops its own symbols, words, and styles; rituals of music and art; and ecstatic experience (115–16). Some ninety pages later, then, Wolfe can introduce Kesey's concept of the "acid tests" and fulfill (complete with typographical pyrotechnics) his own (and Wach's) "prediction": "as it has been written: . . . *he develops a strong urge to extend the message to all people . . . he develops a ritus, often involving music, dance, liturgy, sacrifice, to achieve an objectified and stereotyped expression of the original spontaneous experience*" (205).

Taken as a whole, Wolfe's strategy is meant to reveal the level to which the Pranksters are deluding themselves, the path that will take them toward an ever tightening, ever irrelevant circle wherein rites "'grow out of the *new experience* and seem weird and incomprehensible to those who have never had it'" (Wolfe, quoting Wach, 115–16). Wolfe wants to assure us that, as outsiders, the events would strike us as simple, "coincidental, meaningless," and to assure us, with Wach, that we have all been here before. But as a whole the passage emits an almost lethal steam, a quality that Wolfe (much less Kesey) can't quite tame: the possibility of a deep and menacing synchronicity.

The Hell's Angels' visit to Kesey's La Honda compound heightens that menace even further. Wolfe introduces the Angels by reputation ("Ahor, the ancient horror, the middle-class boy fear of Hell's Angels, *Hell's Angels*, in the dirty flesh . . . that dark deep down thing" (152, ellipsis added) and then by sound, their Harley choppers descending from Hell's heaven like a runaway train:

> It was like a locomotive about ten miles away. It was the Hell's Angels in "running formation" coming over the mountain on Harley-Davidson 74s. The Angels were up there somewhere weaving down the curves on Route 84, gearing down—thragggggggggh—and winding up, and the locomotive sound got louder and louder until you couldn't hear yourself talk any more or Bob Dylan rheumy and—*thraaaaaaaaggggghhh*—here they come around the last curve, the Hell's Angels, with the bikes, the beards, the long hair, the sleeveless denim jackets with the death's head insignia and all the rest, looking their most royal rotten, and then one by one they came barreling in over the wooden bridge up to the front of the house, skidding to a stop in explosions of dust, and it was like a movie or something—each one of the outlaws bouncing and gunning across the bridge with his arms spread out in a tough curve to the handlebars and then skidding to a stop, one after another after another. (152–53)

The powerful "othering" attraction of the scene implicates most readers in a sticky web of complicity. We can not turn away; yet the scene's inescapable menace draws us. At first the Hell's Angels' visit reassures us in an admittedly unorthodox way; they don't really ever bash heads, most find LSD a mellowing trip, Mountain Girl soon has them in *her* movie. But Wolfe is there to remind us that this movie has another reel: "At big routs like this the Angels often had a second feature going entitled *Who Gets Fucked?*" (157). Tonight the target is "one nice soft honey hormone squash" of a "blonde" from "out of town." Though Wolfe assures the reader that the woman is a willing participant, he holds his readers' faces to a scene they can't quite watch and from which they can't quite turn, as the woman's ex-husband is brought in and "the girl rises up in a blear and asks him to kiss her, which he does, glistening secretions, then he lurches and mounts her and slides it in, and the Angels cheer Haw Haw—" (157).

The scene continues the developing theme in *Acid Test* of the manner in which responsibility may be sacrificed at the altar of sensation and how Kesey's "movie" is upstaged by a lurid second feature. Yet Wolfe is not ready to draw the curtain just yet, for the chapter ends with a moment when Kesey verbally disarms a hostile Sonny Barger, chief of the Angels' Oakland chapter, in a manner that other Pranksters determine to be further proof of Kesey's mystical power. In a 1983 interview with Ron Reagan Jr. for *Geo*, Wolfe said the gang-bang scene was the only one to which Kesey has ever objected, and that was because Wolfe was too "nice." Wolfe's comments reveal both the manner by which nonfiction can implicate real-life writers and readers and his recognition that the scene as originally written did not convey the sense of "tragedy" for which he was aiming in exploring the downward spiral of the Prankster experience:

> When I wrote *The Electric Kool-Aid Acid Test*, Ken Kesey was asked what he thought of it. He said, "It was okay. It was accurate, except for where he tried to be nice." Then he put his finger on the one place in the book where I had pulled my punch a little bit. This was a scene with a gang bang within the Hell's Angels. I couldn't bring myself to name the member involved or her former husband. It's a horrible scene. Kesey said that by not naming the individuals I had turned this tragic moment into a scene of low comedy. He was right. I just couldn't bring myself to do it, and it had nothing to do with libel. For some reason, I couldn't walk over that line. But strictly in terms of the standards I set for myself in writing now, I should have. (195–96)

In *On the Bus* Hunter S. Thompson, who, unlike Wolfe, actually witnessed the scene, reveals that the ex-husband was "Neal," a fact that he says he had never disclosed before. Even twenty-five years later Thompson wonders why he didn't leave the shack where the gang bang occurred but says as a reporter whose material was the Hell's Angels, he felt compelled to be a witness (134–135).

The interrelationship of sensation, witness, and control is further developed as the Pranksters begin to stage the "acid tests" that Wolfe believes are their attempts to institutionalize original religious ecstasy. The Pranksters build a panopticon-like tower to house the lights, tapes, loops, strobes, and projectors by which they (unseen) can master for their followers the movements and ecstasy of the re-created experience. The tower also assumes Babel-like dimensions in that it reaches upward in an effort (hence Wolfe's choice of the verb "mans" for Kesey's moment of control) to replace the power of the godhead: "Kesey looks out upon the stroboscopic whirlpool—the dancers! flung and flinging! *in ectasis* gyrating! levitating! men in slices! in ping-pong balls! in the creamy bare essence and it reaches a SYNCH he never saw before. Heads from all over the acid world out here and all whirling into the pudding. Now let a man see what CONTROL is. Kesey mans the strobe and a twist of the mercury lever UP and they all speed up" (217).

The Pranksters disintegrate physically as well as spiritually as Kesey and then others are forced either by legal hassles or by internal feuding to join the diaspora. By now, Wolfe notes with evident satisfaction, the politics of sensation has replaced the politics of engagement, even in Berkeley: "Some kid who could always be counted on to demonstrate for the farm workers . . . [or] work for CORE in Mississippi turns up one day—and immediately everyone knows he has become a head" (318, ellipsis added). The old activist ways are gone. For his part, Kesey is in Mexico, mired in his "rat" fantasies, while other Pranksters try to continue the acid test re-creations in their master's absence. One of those scenes sets in even bolder relief the choice between sensation and responsibility that has dominated the latter half of the book. At the Watts test a nameless girl freaks out on acid and begins to scream "Who Cares?" Rather than intervene, Ken Babbs—who has taken over as leader for Kesey—sticks a microphone into her face and broadcasts her tortured question over the tape loops and through the strobospheric, time-warped, lag-lifted brew for the benefit of the revelers: "Romney looks at Babbs and Who Cares—well, Babbs cares, with one part of him, but with another his devotion is to the Test, to the Archives, a freakout for the Archives, freaked out on tape in the Archives, Who Cares in the Prankster Archives, and the cry wails over the hall, into every brain" (251).

The book ends with the Acid Graduation and with a final gig at The

Barn near Santa Cruz. Wolfe can now fulfill his (and Wach's) prophesy: the religious circle, pulling tighter and tighter until even the true believers begin to drift off, spurning Cassady's interactive raps that had opened the book (if only a few days before in chronological time) with such menacing promise. "They just stare at [Cassady], freaking nuns, full of peace and tolerance and pity" (362). And Kesey, what of Kesey?—the Kesey who has served as Wolfe's alter ego in a fantasy of escape, who has provided a conduit to prank those pesky politicos strung out on activism, who has proven to the Richmond-born author that it is no longer hip to be black, who has bent the linear forms that rule the news rooms and publishing houses and exploded them into so many freaking Day-Glo bits—what of Kesey? He sits at the center of the ever-diminishing circle as Wolfe drifts away from him, out of the book, far away toward increasingly circumscribed reporting and writing, his escape recaptured:

> "WE BLEW IT"
> ". . . Ten millon times or more! . . ."
> "WE BLEW IT"
> " . . . it was perfect, so what do you do? . . ."
> "WE BLEW IT!"
> " . . . perfect! . . ."
> "WE BLEW IT" (368)

Read from the outside in, Wolfe's historical presence hovers over *The Electric Kool-Aid Acid Test,* adding a political and cultural interpretation to the book's effort to capture the history of psychedelic pioneers in the United States. The narrative presence that Wolfe reveals, underscored by his quotes outside the book and by the trajectory of his presence as a journalist within the dominant print media culture of the 1960s, breaks down the barrier between Wolfe the man and Wolfe the narrative presence in *Acid Test.* As many commentators have noted, Wolfe is everywhere in the book: his hectoring narrators always stem more from his own subjective consciousness than from what he insisted was a resolutely objective but relentlessly formal experimentation. If *Acid Test* is read over the edge as a nonfiction text rather than as a fictional text in which such issues as narrative omniscience and access are taken as a given, then Wolfe's work in the book and its rising and falling action will reveal the man and his work in the text.

John Reed and the Writing of Revolution

John Reed's historical presence offers a fascinating contrast to Wolfe when the two authors are subjected to an outside in reading of their work. Reed's first book-length nonfiction narrative, *Insurgent Mexico*, evidences a political sensibility not far removed from the contradictions that Wolfe displays. In his account of the Mexican Revolution Reed had not yet processed the fact of his marketing the experience of Mexico's insurgents to a magazine bank-rolled by Vanderbilt and Guggenheim heir Henry Payne Whitney (Rosenstone 209) and to an American reading public ready for the sensation of exotic rebels. Thus an outside in reading of Reed's history against his narrative presence reveals that Reed lied about his access to material, transferred actual characters into fiction, and made up fictional roles for characters to fill the gaps in his nonfiction.

In part because Reed had so deftly hidden and recaptured most of the social and political challenges which *Insurgent Mexico* had posed to its North American readers, his literary reputation was never higher than when the book was published. But Reed's increasing radicalism—particularly his opposition to World War I at a time when it became illegal to counsel against the draft or to oppose U.S. involvement in the Great War—pushed him toward a position where he was more willing to implicate himself in his writing as both a historic individual and a narrative character.

Reed faced in his writings after 1916 the specter of reporting subjects no longer willing to pose in docile subjection while a Western journalist markets their misery to his editors and readers back home. *Ten Days That Shook the World*, Reed's book-length narrative of the Russian Revolution, therefore, reenacts many of the key scenes and dilemmas that Reed faced in *Insurgent Mexico*. In *Ten Days*, however, Reed makes his presence in the narrative more clear and implicates himself and his reporting much more deeply in the events he covers. In part because of this, many of *Ten Days*'s readers resented the way the narrative tried to force them to identify with characters they could not accept in their extratextual lives as well as the manner by which Reed's narrative strategy made the events of revolution appear to be historically determined and inevitable. An analysis of Reed's writing from the outside in documents the stakes of this transaction for Reed, for his readers, and for his ever shrinking literary markets. In fact, by the end of his life Reed was writing openly as an author and reporter deeply alienated from the cultural, political, and legal power of his homeland. He suppressed

in fiction that which he could not admit in nonfiction. A careful reading of
the record will demonstrate not only the value of reading nonfiction from
the outside in but also something of the worth of retaining categories of
discourse that can distinguish (although not insist on a strictly fixed division)
between narratives traditionally labeled fiction and nonfiction.

The first long section of *Insurgent Mexico* construes Reed as a
youthful journalist slowly working his way into the graces not only of the
revolutionary outlaw/general Pancho Villa but, even more importantly, of the
Tropa soldiers with whom Reed shared a camp. Reed learns to drink
the fiery *sotol* of the Mexicans, eats the *carne crudo* ("we ripped meat from
the carcass and ate it raw"), argues the meaning of liberty and self-interest,
dances until dawn, and watches the *compañeros* fight the bulls (40–41, 45).
If Reed explicitly critiques his own interest in the sort of war-reporting "material" that is purchased at the death of his friends (98), he is not ready to
acknowledge an even deeper issue than the romanticization of "simple" for-
eigners and the purchase of material through bloodshed. Reed had construed a character for himself inside his nonfiction eager to accept the
peasants and their struggle, but he was not ready to reveal to his readers at
what price his reportorial access was purchased.

Although Reed took several chronological liberties within *Insurgent
Mexico* and presented English versions of Spanish dialogue that were no
doubt beyond his translation and transcription powers, careful readers like
Granville Hicks, Robert A. Rosenstone, Eric Homberger, and David C.
Duke are willing to grant him the license to rearrange and even enhance his
narrative version of truth. Rosenstone is perhaps the most articulate of
Reed's readers in summing up this permission:

> Suspended in John Reed's writings are incidents that float
> delicately between the realms of fact and fiction, with the
> narrator a character living in a world of romance, enacting
> a truth more emotional than literal. Details and dialogue
> altered for the benefit of dramatic structure, the result is
> an account of events that transcends the world of report-
> age. . . . A fusion of self with historical event occurred be-
> cause his writing reflected a search for meaning and self-
> definition. (150)

Although I have no desire to somehow disqualify Reed as a literary journalist
(as some critics might) because he might play loosely with the facts, neither

will I ignore the social and artistic implications that arise from his decisions. The essence of reading for the implicated author in nonfiction, as I have argued, compels the critic to examine the ways in which the narrative voice in the text cuts across the historical voice of the author as well as the traces of conflict that remain. *Insurgent Mexico* provides at least one example of such a conflict that is worth examining in detail.

In the book Reed lies about the manner by which he first gained access to Villa's Tropa. His daily log, contained among his papers at the Harvard Library, proves that without an American war profiteer and gun runner named Mac, whom he persuaded to take him into Mexico, Reed might never have been able to meet Villa's army train (Rosenstone 168). Both in the journal and in a short story Reed based on the figure, Mac is depicted as the prototypical ugly American: crude, misogynistic, chauvinistic. Yet other than in the daily log, which he never published, Reed hides the truth of his access to Pancho Villa behind a narrative he marketed as fiction: a tale entitled "Mac-American" published in the April 1914 edition of *The Masses*.

In that story, Reed writes of Mac as an "American in the raw" (43) whom the first-person narrator meets in a bar on New Year's Eve, 1913. Among other details, the story has the character of Mac say that all Mexican women are "whores," that Mexican men are "dirty skunks and greasers" (44), and that "the greatest sport in the world is hunting niggers" (47). In ironic contrast to these remarks are Mac's thoughts on American womanhood: "If any man dared to dirty the fair name of the American Woman to me, I think I'd kill him. . . . She is a Pure Ideal, and we've got to keep her so. I'd like to hear anybody talk rotten about a woman in my hearing" (45). Mac, who has worked as a law enforcement officer in the United States, recalls a time he was working as a southern deputy sheriff. One night he was writing a letter to his beloved sister (presumably one of the American Women whom he wishes to protect) when he was summoned to the bloodhound hunt of a black man through cotton fields, woods, across fences and rivers. He asks his audience in the story: "'Say, did you ever hear a *bloodhound when he's after a human*? It's like a bugle! . . . Of course,' he said, 'when we got up to him, the dogs had just about torn that coon to pieces'" (48–49, Reed's emphasis).

At the story's climax Reed's narrator quotes Mac: "'I wouldn't like to live here in Mexico,' Mac volunteered. 'The people haven't got any Heart. I like people to be friendly, like Americans'" (49). Although the first-person narrator is never developed as a full character in the story, his sensibility is certainly not that of Reed, for the narrator finds Mac to be "a breath from home" (43) and tells the reader he and his companions listen to Mac with "the solemn righteousness of a convention of Galahads" (43).[4]

Reed thus presents as a presumably fictional character in a deeply ironic "tale" his actual conduit to Villa's army in Magistral. Reed creates this subterfuge, most likely, because Mac, though actually a useful guide for a reporter desperate to see wartime action, does not square with the narrator's "self" nor with the political stance that Reed intends his nonfiction to present. Thus it is easier for Reed to hide his relationship with Mac behind the cloak of a fictional persona rather than to own up to it in a historical account. By contrast, Reed fashions *Insurgent Mexico* as a true account of the Mexican Revolution and presents himself as an actual (and thus historically implicated) character within that account. But if he acknowledges that his conduit to his "material" is a figure of American imperialism in microcosm, how is he to distinguish himself from the U.S. governmental interests whose presence in Mexico he means to criticize? Hiding his own sensibility behind the fictional narrator of "Mac-American" also offers Reed the advantage of effacing himself historically in that fictional story.

As in his other tales (most notably in his story "A Taste of Justice," in which he names his first-person narrator "George" and has him confess that, although he picks up streetwalkers, he never does so in front of his midtown club [133]), Reed creates a distance between himself and his fictional narrator and thus avoids the implications of a more strictly historical presence. Instead of giving Mac a place in his nonfiction, Reed chooses for the nonfictional text of *Insurgent Mexico* an actual Mexican character named Antonio Montoya, whom he met briefly in Jimenez. Montoya is presented in *Insurgent Mexico* as "a pock-marked officer with a big revolver" who surprises Reed in his room and threatens to kill the "gringo." Reed buys off Montoya by giving him his two-dollar wristwatch and observes as with "parted lips and absorbed attention [Montoya] watched it delightedly, as a child watches the operation of some new mechanical toy. 'A *compadre*,' he cried emotionally." Montoya then agrees to take Reed ("my *amigo*") to Magistral to meet Pancho Villa (163).

In addition to suppressing the "ugly American" character of Mac behind a fictional Mexican "stand-in" in a nonfictional text, *Insurgent Mexico* presents, apparently without irony, the tableau of an American buying the friendship of a childlike Mexican with cheap mechanical gifts. It is, therefore, the story of imperialism in microcosm and a startling contrast to the genuine scenes of friendship with rebel soldiers that Reed establishes elsewhere in the book. Normally well suppressed in the text, this aspect of Reed's character is much closer to the sort of nakedly ambitious journalist who surfaces in a June 10, 1914, letter to *Metropolitan* editor Carl Hovey. With characteristic braggadocio and startling candor, Reed tells Hovey he has "bought Villa a saddle and a rifle with a gold name plate upon it and a Maxim silencer. He is hugely delighted and will do almost anything for me now. The story is going to be not only exciting to the limit, but the greatest human document you have ever seen. It is a beat on the whole world" (qtd. in Rosenstone 163). The picture of Villa eating out of Reed's hand for the price of a saddle, rifle, and silencer is, of course, also silenced from the pages of *Insurgent Mexico*, its place taken by scenes of Villa's seemingly genuine liking for the North American (190) and his playful teasing of the "Señor Reporter" who comes south to cover the Mexican struggle (217).

Reed's biographers, even so astute a historian as Rosenstone, seem to want to apologize for his alterations of the truth in *Insurgent Mexico*, perhaps because they, like most readers, are so taken by the book's overall depth of insight. Although Rosenstone recognizes that a "brutish American . . . is hardly a suitable companion for the narrator as revolutionary sympathizer" (168), he explains the suppression of Mac for Montoya as "more dramatic." Choosing not to make an issue of the price for which Montoya's friendship was purchased, Rosenstone also sees Montoya as evidence of Reed's "ability to be embraced even by people who hated gringos" (168). David C. Duke and James C. Wilson are more forgiving. Wilson argues that Reed introduced Montoya to the pages of *Insurgent Mexico* to "personify both the revolution and the Mexican people . . . the spirit of Mexico" (69) while Duke goes even further and argues that Reed simply employs "a little literary license" (88) to add narrative excitement. Apparently without seeing Reed's own deep involvement in the same sort of project, Duke argues that Reed's "Mac-American" story "makes it clear that Mac is no different from the many other Americans he had met in Mexico. With their ugly nationalism and predatory instincts, their only goal was the pursuit of the dollar. For these 'friendly Americans' Mexico was a country to be exploited" (79–80).

While that is certainly a fair statement of the theme of "Mac-American," Duke neglects to see that Reed, too, had traveled to Mexico to pursue both fame and fortune and, in his own way, had treated the revolution as an event to be exploited for his growing journalistic capital. These impulses would not make Reed a singular reporter; indeed, profiting from the misfortunes of others is an occupational hazard of journalism. Fleeing from the Colorados and rejoicing in his "material," only to find it was undermined by the death of his friends—Reed is willing to implicate himself historically by enfolding these events in his nonfiction; buying off Montoya and Villa and burying Mac in fiction, he is not.

Recognizing an author's complicity and/or responsibility and noticing the ways that it is acknowledged or evaded are among the key insights that can be gained by reading nonfiction both inside and outside the text. It serves no purpose to deny that Reed hid his complicity behind a fictional persona, nor should a careful reader somehow banish *Insurgent Mexico* from the pristine nonfiction genre because she has caught its author in a lie. Exercises in checking facts against textual artifacts are never as "tedious" or "dreary" as critics who would collapse the distinctions between nonfiction and fiction would suppose. Although *Insurgent Mexico*, the "Mac-American" story, Reed's letter to Hovey—indeed, even Reed's memory of the events— are all texts, they are texts that can yield insights. Far better to read a text like *Insurgent Mexico* as an opportunity to "analyze the research and writing of a work as social acts" and to examine how "the reporting process implicates writer, subjects, and readers in relationships beyond a text" (Pauly 112).

For, finally, Reed—with some significant exceptions—makes it easy for his North American readers to swallow their complicity in Mexico's struggles even as he avoids some of his own deeper complicity. By concentrating on Villa's human side, his fierce individualism, his Robin Hood method of operations, and the ability of North Americans to take advantage of the "natural friendliness" of their neighbors to the south, Reed ensured himself a book that could be popular with most North American readers, despite the significant break it represented from the worst jingoism of the pre-World War I era.

After the success of *Insurgent Mexico* Reed was one of the highest-paid domestic and foreign correspondents in the country (Rosenstone 282) and had his pick of the major newspaper and magazine markets. But within little more than two years stunning changes ensued both in the political climate of the United States and in Reed's career. In that span Reed was to face federal charges under espionage and sedition acts for conspiracy to obstruct the military draft, see more than three hundred of his friends in the I.W.W. jailed on some 10,000 federal charges, and stand by as virtually all of his normal outlets for publication either refused to print his work or were forced out of business by postal regulators or federal indictments.

An exchange of letters between Reed and his longtime mentor Lin-

coln Steffens during June 1918 (cited by Rosenstone from the Steffens papers at Columbia University Library) offers insight into the critical decisions
Reed faced in his personal and professional future. He had just returned to
the United States after witnessing the Bolshevik uprising in Saint Petersburg
(Petrograd) and Moscow. On his return to Manhattan on April 28 (after being detained in Oslo for two months without a visa) he was interrogated and
strip searched. His trunks of notes, Russian handbills, newspapers, and
speeches were seized by the U.S. Department of State.

   Burning to write what he believed to be the greatest story of his life,
he asked for advice from Steffens, who for years was his role model as a
progressive journalist, muckraker, and the closest political associate to Reed's
late father. As the man who had arranged Reed's assignment to the Mexican
Revolution, Steffens was an important link to his success. Reed tells his mentor in the first letter that no newspaper will touch his syndicated series of
the events in Russia: "Collier's took a story, put it in type, and sent it back.
Oswald Villard told me he would be suppressed if he published John Reed!
I have a contract with Macmillan to publish a book, but the State Department took away all my papers when I came home, and up to date has absolutely refused to return any of them. . . . I am therefore unable to write a
word of the greatest story of my life, and one of the greatest in the world"
(qtd. in Rosenstone 319).

   Steffens's reply counsels patience. Publishing the story of the events
in Russia, even if truthful, might be undemocratic while the United States is
at war: "Jack, you do wrong to buck this thing. . . . It is wrong to try to tell
the truth now. We must wait. You must wait. I know it's hard, but you can't
carry conviction. You can't plant ideas. Only feelings exist, and the feelings
are bewildered. I think it is undemocratic to try to do much now. Write, but
don't publish" (qtd. in Rosenstone 320). Reed's response to his mentor is
brusque: "I am not of your opinion that it is undemocratic to buck this thing.
If there were not the ghost of a chance, if everybody were utterly for it, even
then I don't see why it shouldn't be bucked. All movements have to have
somebody to start them and, if necessary, to go under for them" (qtd. in
Rosenstone 320).

   What happened in those few years to force Reed to consider extin-
guishing his future as a publishing journalist on the altar of political and social change? Is it true, as Reed's only recent North American critic argues,
that Reed had become "an apologist of the regime and a political activist,
thereby ending his career as a literary journalist" (Humphrey 159)?

Reed was correct in predicting the suppression of messages such as these. *Seven Arts* ceased publication in December, when a major patron withdrew subsidy directly because of Reed's "This Unpopular War." Seventy-five publications, including several for which Reed wrote, were banned by the postmaster general under the Espionage Act, although the ban on *The Nation* was lifted after its editor refused to print any more articles by Reed. *The Masses*, which Reed coedited and which was his most reliable source of publication, was banned from the mails in August, then denied regular publication mail status for September because it had not mailed copies in August. Its five editors, Reed included, were indicted for conspiracy to obstruct the draft, primarily for an article Reed had written that had questioned the sanity of enlistees (Rosenstone 321–24). One cannot imagine any of these responses had Reed stuck to a fictional form. It is in this context that Reed, recovering from the removal of a kidney, wrote his brief autobiography, "Almost Thirty," whose title not only refers to his age but also to the common journalistic technique of signaling the end. "The War has been a terrible shatterer of faith in economic and political idealism," he confesses. "And yet I cannot give up the idea that out of democracy will be born the new world—richer, braver, freer, more beautiful" (142).

Reed was to devote the latter half of his short writing life to defining in his journalism those revolutionary impulses. He was to find for himself that "new world" in Bolshevik Russia. He was so taken by its creation that he penned his own prose nonfiction creation epic, *Ten Days That Shook the World*. The book was written during the last eight weeks of 1918, after Reed's papers were returned to him from seven long months in the custody of the U.S. Department of State. Reed rented the top floor of the Greenwich Village Inn and, with pamphlets, newspapers, notes, and memories crowded about him, wrote chapter after chapter whose titles reawaken the real-life drama of some monumental I.W.W. pageant: "The Coming Storm," "On the Eve," "The Fall of the Provisional Government," "Plunging Ahead," "The Committee for Salvation," "The Revolutionary Front," "Counter-Revolution," "Victory."

Although *Ten Days* is by far the most well known of Reed's writings, no commentator has yet discussed the source of its sweeping hold on many of its readers—those who support Reed's politics, those who despise them, and those who still aren't sure. In *Ten Days* Reed produces a narrative effect, virtually exclusive to nonfiction, that deeply implicates his readers. The "present action" of the narrative holds the reader inside the text in genuine suspense as it sweeps readers toward a conclusion (the triumph of Bolshevism) that both they and Reed outside the text already know will occur. Moreover, it is a conclusion that many of those very same readers, at least in North America, despise. The resulting fusion of narrative immediacy, historical context, and political and social implication at its best moments can achieve a disquieting and almost startling power.

For example, on the night of November 5 Reed is hurrying from his interview with Trotsky in the small bare room of the Smolny headquarters of the Bolsheviks toward the Marinsky Palace for the Council of the Russian Republic. For almost thirty pages he has carefully tightened the circle of revolution and counter-revolution, first interviewing Kerensky, then Trotsky—pitting the two in inevitable conflict—now traveling to the palace, now to Smolny, which "bright with lights, hummed like a gigantic hive" (87). Outside the Marinsky Palace "an armoured automobile went slowly up and down, siren screaming. On every corner, in every open space, thick groups were clustered; arguing soldiers and students. Night came swiftly down, the wide-spaced street-lights flickered on, the tides of people flowed endlessly. . . . It is always like that in Petrograd just before trouble. . . ." (75–76, Reed's ellipses).

The passage implicates the reader in several ways, partly because it is immediate and dramatic. The present tense verb of the last sentence ("it is always like that in Petrograd just before trouble") drags the reader into the immediacy of the scene as the sky darkens and lights flicker on. The dramatic effect pulls the reader inside the text, making that reader, willingly or unwillingly, suspend her knowledge of how soon or in what manner the "gathering storm" will break. The particular manner by which *Ten Days* deepens the stakes is by presenting these powerful narrative effects within the scope of an actual contemporary (and in many ways still on-going) political and social struggle. For example, Reed interviews Kerensky (probably on October 31) in *Ten Days*, noting that it is "the last time he received journalists," a comment that throws the reader outside the narrative and into history. Yet at the same time Reed quotes Kerensky: "The world thinks that the Russian Revolution is at an end. Do not be mistaken. The Russian Revolution is just beginning" (59). Reed provides the ironic aside: "Words *more prophetic, perhaps, than he knew*" (60, emphasis added).

In the time of action Kerensky means to say that the March revolution, the one he led and the one to which he was deeply committed, has not yet run its course and that the Bolshevik threat, which Kerensky never considered a true revolution, would be denied. In 1920 as well as now, of course, the great majority of readers of *Ten Days* know otherwise by the time they read the narrative and therefore see that the *Bolshevik* version of the Russian Revolution is "just beginning." Reed, as he sat in his rented room above the Greenwich Village Inn two years after the Bolsheviks took power, was just as aware of that fact. His use of the word "perhaps" is therefore rhetorical, meant to pull his readers back into the moment when he sat in Kerensky's study, the moment of action, as well as to milk the suspense (and the inevitability) of his narrative.

A brief contrast of that scene to a version Reed wrote soon after his interview with Kerensky for *Liberator* (the successor to *The Masses* after the latter was suppressed) might make these points more clear. In that article, written November 5, 1917, and published in April 1918 (Homberger and Biggart 64), Reed was not sure of the unintended irony of Kerensky's remarks and thus included no such quote. The article, unlike the book version of the interview, throws the reader much more often outside the time of action, breaking the narrative moment with asides such as Reed's first memories of Kerensky and his sardonic observation that Associated Press correspondents (one of whom was his companion at the interview) are prejudiced "against common peasants, soldiers, and workingmen who insisted upon calling one *tovarisch*—comrade" (66).

Reed seems to be quite aware of the narrative effect he is producing in *Ten Days;* even his chapter titles (as cited earlier) milk the suspense of present action at the same time the book's title trumpets its past-tense inevitability. Reed's ideology is revealed by this effect; he does believe that historical forces are aligned to produce a new heaven and a new earth and that the future is as inevitable as the present tense of the narrative is dramatic. Moreover, he will shift the reader out of present-tense suspense whenever it suits his purpose, so as to signal to us that history will not bear out certain present moments. For example, at the end of November 10 the book tells the reader that "counter-revolution *had* begun" (180, emphasis added), a verb that signals the past tense of counterrevolution even in its genesis.

Reed's introduction to *Ten Days*, written on New Year's Day, 1919, makes his belief in the power of history clear (and his rhetoric still has the power to unsettle many of its Western and Russian readers in this post-Soviet age):

> It is still fashionable, after a whole year of the Soviet Government, to speak of the Bolshevik insurrection as an "ad-

venture." Adventure it was, and one of the most marvelous mankind ever embarked upon, sweeping into history at the head of the toiling masses, and staking everything on their vast and simple desires. . . . No matter what one thinks of Bolshevism, it is undeniable that the Russian Revolution is one of the great events of human history, and the rise of the Bolsheviki a phenomenon of world-wide importance. (13)

Examples of present events trembling in the force of history are everywhere in the book: the night of November 7, when Reed states, "Now there was all great Russia to win—and then, the world!" (an observation that he knows will deeply trouble those readers who have reason to fear international revolution), is set against his readers' engagement in the present of the action: "night was yet hazy and chill. There was only a faint unearthly pallor stealing over the silent streets, dimming the watch-fires, the shadow of a terrible dawn grey-rising over Russia. . . ." (116, Reed's ellipsis).

Later that day Reed brings Lenin into the Second All-Russian Congress of Soviets in terms that stop only just short of hagiography. The passage, an example of Reed's gift for the brief word sketch as well as his lack of objectivity, stays in the present, even to clocking time as it passes, but shifts from the certainty of the past to the inevitability of the future as it suits Reed's needs:

It was just 8:40 when a thundering wave of cheers announced the entrance of the presidium, with Lenin—great Lenin—among them. A short, stocky figure, with a big head set down on his shoulders, bald and bulging. Little eyes, a snubbish nose, wide generous mouth, and heavy chin; clean-shaven now but already beginning to bristle with the well-known beard of his past and future. Dressed in shabby clothes, his trousers much too long for him. Unimpressive, to be the idol of a mob, loved and revered as perhaps few leaders in history have been. (128)

Reed almost revels in the scene that he is about to present, signaling his (and the readers') engagement with the adverb "now": "Now Lenin, gripping the edge of the reading stand, letting his little winking eyes travel over the crowd as he stood there waiting, apparently oblivious to the long-rolling ovation, which lasted several minutes. When it finished, he said simply, 'We shall now proceed to construct the Socialist order!' Again that overwhelming human roar" (129). Reed remembers to tell the reader that it was "exactly 10:35" when the proclamation to belligerent nations (which effectively ended Russia's involvement in World War I) was passed, then picks up the present, but inevitable, action with the adverb "suddenly":

> Suddenly, by common impulse, we found ourselves on our feet, mumbling together into the smoothing lifting unison of the *Internationale.* A grizzled old soldier was sobbing like a child. Alexandra Kollontain rapidly winked the tears back. The immense sound rolled through the hall, burst windows and doors and soared into the quiet sky. "The war is ended! The war is ended!" said a young workman near by, his face shining. And when it was over, as we stood there in a kind of awkward hush, someone in the back of the room shouted, "Comrades! Let us remember those who have died for liberty!" So we began to sing the Funeral March, that slow, melancholy, and yet triumphant chant, so Russian and so moving. (133)

The passage culminates with a line that brings full circle the Kerensky-Trotsky contrast that had informed the book's early chapters, a passage whose power to implicate at least some readers still results in its suppression from Communist Party–sponsored anthologies (Reed, *Education of John Reed* 206–7): "Then up rose Trotsky, calm and venomous, conscious of power, greeted with a roar."

If *Insurgent Mexico* exploited an Exodus motif, it is fair to say that *Ten Days*'s marching orders come from the Book of Genesis, although it is a decidedly secular version and, indeed, ultimately plays out against the grain of Biblical creation. In Reed's narrative the earth heaves and cracks and separates, light is created, the firmament is divided from the waters, the fragile planets are born. In the "Background" chapter a "ground-swell of revolt heaved and cracked the crust which had been slowly hardening on the surface of revolutionary fires" (51); the Bolshevik workers at the Ibukhovsky Zavod munitions plant are bathed in "sun, flooding reddish light through the skeleton windows upon the mass of simple faces upturned to us" (52); the revolutionary Smolny is "bright with lights, hum[ming] like a gigantic hive" (87); the workers in Red Square are thunderous as surf, "proletarian tide" (230). After the Bolshevik takeover, "Old Russia was no more; human society

flowed molten in primal heat, and from the tossing sea of flame was emerging the class struggle, stark and pitiless—and the slowly cooling crust of a
new planet" (147).

That new planet is a decidedly unorthodox creation, as Reed points
out in the section that ends the ten days proper of the narrative. Indeed, in
an unpublished sketch entitled "Foreign Affairs," which Reed wrote after
interviewing Trotsky at Smolny and which served as a prototype for the
Trotsky interview in *Ten Days*, Reed leads with the line "Two months ago,
at No. 6 Dvortsovya Ploschiad, I saw the new world born" (Homberger and
Biggart 147). In the sketch he presents Trotsky in decidedly Mephistophe-
lian terms: "His whole face narrows down to a pointed chin, accentuated by
a sharp black beard; and when he stands at the tribune of the Petrograd
Soviet hissing defiance at the Imperialists of the world, he gives the impression of a snake" (150).

Before sunrise on November 16 Reed sharpens the distinction between the old and new creations when he attends the funerals in Red Square
in the shadows of the street chapels that are now locked and dark, their
candles out for the first time since Napoleon occupied Moscow. The scene
begins in darkness, but Reed creates a light to replace that which has been
darkened: "The Holy Orthodox Church had withdrawn the light of its coun-
tenance from Moscow, the nest of irreverent vipers who had bombarded
the Kremlin. Dark and silent and cold were the churches; the priests had
disappeared. There were no popes to officiate at the Red Burial, there had
been no sacrament for the dead, nor were any prayers to be said over the
grave of the blasphemers" (228). The workers come to bury their dead as
men begin to shovel showers of dirt on coffin lids. The sun rises as the last
mourners pass the spot on Red Square where Reed himself will be buried
in only a few years' time: "I suddenly realized that the devout Russian people
no longer needed priests to pray them into heaven. On earth they were
building a kingdom more bright than any heaven had to offer, and for which
it was a glory to die. . . ." (230, Reed's ellipsis). Reed—who had declared a
year earlier in "Almost Thirty," "I haven't any God and don't want one; faith
is only another word for finding oneself" (143–44)—seems sure of his citi-
zenship in this new kingdom on earth, a significant change from his status in
Mexico, where he was always the outsider looking in, unable to shed the
privilege of race and nationality, no matter how deeply he had buried it in
his fictions.

Ten Days presents almost eerie repetitions of key identity moments that Reed faced in *Insurgent Mexico*. One of the most telling moments of repetition and adjustment is his journey with the Red Army to the front at Tsarskoye Selo on November 10 as the Bolsheviks attempted to respond to Kerensky's planned counterattack. As in his journey to the Mexican front with "Mac-American," Reed is less than candid with his readers but in an intriguingly different way. This time, instead of hiding his conduit out of shame for Mac's xenophobia, Reed hides his own identity to save the Bolshevik officers who are granting him access to the front without official authorization. Reed calls himself Trusishka (what an American might now call a "wimp" or a "nerd")[5] and reports that Trusishka "got in [the officers' car] and sat down and nothing could dislodge him" (172). Diffidently asserting that he sees no reason to doubt Trusishka's version of the trip, Reed weaves one of the few really comic tales in *Ten Days*, as the Peoples' Commissars for War and Marine first try unsuccessfully to borrow a military vehicle from the troops they now command, then must hail a battered taxicab flying the Italian flag. The Bolsheviks eventually must borrow a notebook and finally a pencil from the ever-accommodating Trusishka, so they can write a requisition for ammunition for the Red troops at the front. The significance of the scene is that Reed has such firm access to the material he wants that he is able to withhold evidence of his solidarity with the Russian insurgents, rather than to withhold evidence of his complicity with North American interests as he had in *Insurgent Mexico* by burying "Mac-American" in fiction.

Even more importantly, on a second trip to Tsarskoye Selo on November 13, Reed—without in any way acknowledging it—replays the scene he had drawn in Mexico on the way to the front with Urbina's troops. On both journeys, Reed is packed into a conveyance with a load of incendiary bombs. In both cases the bombs bump and jounce on the rutted roads as the good-natured Reed hangs on for dear life. The Russian journey even features the same sort of close questioning of Reed about United States embarrassments like Tammany or the Mooney case with which the Mexican rebels had challenged him in Mexico. Finally, on the road to Tsarskoye Selo, Reed is forced out of the Sixth Reserve Engineers truck and is interrogated by Red soldiers as a suspected spy. "The soldiers consulted in low tones for a moment," Reed reports, "and then led me to a wall, against which they placed me. It flashed upon me suddenly; they were going to shoot me" (213).

At the point of a gun in Mexico Reed had bought off his accuser Montoya with a two-dollar watch, then shared a private joke with his North American audience as the child-like Montoya marveled at the movement of the watch's hands and pledged his undying fealty to Reed. Here in Soviet Russia Reed—who had earlier donated his pad and his pencil to the cause under the pseudonym of Trusishka—finally finds a local committeeman who can read his pass from Smolny: "The bearer of this pass, John Reed, is a representative of American Social-Democracy, an internationalist. . . . Comrades, this is an American comrade. I am chairman of the committee and I welcome you to the regiment. . . . A sudden general buzz grew into a roar of greeting, and they pressed forward to shake my hand" (214–15, second ellipsis Reed's). As do so many in *Ten Days*, the scene closes the gap between Reed and his material but opens the gap between the author and a majority of his North American readers. Reed makes no pretense of objectivity in the scene; the Bolsheviks are his comrades and his story of their revolution will be impassioned and partisan.

Finally, in a scene not included in *Ten Days* but published in Reed's article "A Visit to the Russian Army" in the April–May issue of *The Liberator*, while Reed was waiting for the U.S. Department of State to return his Russia papers, Reed closes the book on the issue of bribing foreign subjects with cheap gifts. Although he had bought off Montoya with a cheap watch and Villa with a saddle, engraved rifle, and silencer, such gifts are identified as bribes in Reed's "A Visit to the Russian Army." In the scene Reed and his colleague Albert Rhys Williams of the New York *Evening Post* are traveling from Venden after having witnessed the funeral of three Lettish sharpshooters and revolutionaries:

> As we sat on the platform waiting for the Petrograd train it occurred to Williams that we might as well give away our superfluous cigarettes. Accordingly he sat down on a trunk and held out a big box making generous sounds. There must have been several hundred soldiers around. A few came hesitantly and helped themselves, but the rest held aloof, and soon Williams sat alone in the midst of an ever-widening circle. The soldiers were gathered in groups talking in low tones. Suddenly he saw coming toward him a committee of three privates, carrying rifles with fixed bayonets, and looking dangerous. "Who are you?" the leader asked. "Why are you giving away cigarettes? Are you a German spy, trying to bribe the Russian revolutionary army?" All over the platform the crowd followed, slowly packing

itself around Williams and the committee muttering an-
grily—ready to tear him to pieces. (56)

The article, stylistically an effective piece of artistic reportage, identifies Reed directly and immediately as the bearer of a note identifying him
as a member of the American Socialist Party "authorized to proceed to the
active army to gather information for the North American Press" (28).
Therefore, the access that Reed had hidden in *Insurgent Mexico* is laid bare
for his reader here. Reed remembered those Lettish men and women and,
as evidence of the way that his material was shaping his life even as he was
shaping his material, soon had reason to cast one such Lettish soldier in a
starring role. In *Ten Days* in the most pivotal scene of the most pivotal day—
November 7, at the Congress of the Soviets of Workers' and Soldiers' Deputies—Reed sets up the confrontation that symbolically passes the torch from
the Cadets (Constitutional Democrats) to the Bolsheviks. In his exhaustive
catalog of Russian factions in the "background" section of the book Reed
identifies the Cadets as the Russian equivalent of the (U.S.) Progressive
Party, Reed's boyhood heroes and the party of his father's and Lincoln Steffens's reform politics. As the argument at the Congress ebbs and wanes, and
as rumors spread that counterattack is on its way to Petrograd, a lean-faced
Lettish soldier stands amid the clamor and cuts the Russian reformers to
the heart:

> "No more resolutions! No more talk! We want deeds—the
> Power must be in our hands!" . . . The hall rocked with
> cheering. In the first moments of the session, stunned by
> the rapidity of events, startled by the sound of cannon, the
> delegates had hesitated. For an hour hammer-blow after
> hammer-blow had fallen from that tribute, welding them
> together but beating them down. Did they stand then
> alone? Was Russia rising against them? Was it true that the
> Army was marching on Petrograd? Then this clear-eyed
> young soldier had spoken, and in a flash they knew it for
> the truth. . . . *This* was the voice of the soldiers—the stir-
> ring millions of uniformed workers and peasants were men
> like them, and their thoughts and feelings were the same.
> (103, Reed's ellipses and emphasis)

Reed here symbolically disassociates himself from the reform politics of his father and fatherland. In the writing of *Ten Days* he resolutely will break Steffens's advice not to "buck this thing." "It is wrong to try to tell the truth now . . ." Steffens had counseled. "[Y]ou can't carry conviction. You can't plant ideas. . . . I think it is undemocratic to try to do too much now. Write, but don't publish" (qtd. in Rosenstone 319–20).

Ten Days That Shook the World is Reed's answer to Steffens, even as Reed summons Trotsky to answer the Russian reformers at the Second Congress of the Soviets of Workers' and Soldiers' Deputies. Trotsky, standing up with a pale, cruel face, letting out his rich voice in cool contempt, "'All these so-called Socialist compromisers, these frightened Mensheviki, Social-ist Revolutionaries, *Bund*—let them go! They are just so much refuse which will be swept away into the garbage-heap of history!'" (104). In his second-floor study above the Greenwich Village Inn, his contract with Macmillan canceled because of political pressure and his material only just returned after seven months at the Department of State, John Reed during the last two months of 1918 implicated himself about as deeply as any writer can. He had written the birth pangs of the nation that would become his own country's greatest enemy, and he had presented it as truth, as nonfiction, as living history with the power to attract and repel its readers both inside and outside its pages. "[A]n artillery shell, a peal of thunder, or ocean surf does not possess the power of the book that is lying on that desk," he said of *Ten Days* in 1919 (qtd. in Duke 54).

The price Reed paid for that power was that for most of the four decades after his death, his nonfiction was barely accessible—neither in the West nor in Stalin's Soviet Union. Trotsky had been banished to his own refuse heap, Lenin was dead, and Reed had committed the unpardonable sin of ignoring Stalin. The Soviet writer Anatoli Rybakov summarizes the case for the Stalinist prosecution: "The main task was to build a mighty so-cialist state. For that mighty power was needed. Stalin was at the head of that power, which meant that he stood at its source with Lenin. Together with Lenin he had led the October Revolution. John Reed had presented the history of October differently. That wasn't the John Reed we needed" (qtd. in Homberger 1).

Meanwhile, Reed's crime against the United States, if it was a crime, was that he believed in Petrograd that a new world was being born. And in his fervor to be the chronicler of that creation story he obliterated any opportunity he had to come back inside his nation's fold.

Reed's risk—complicated by subsequent events in Stalinist and Soviet Russia—was a risk that Wolfe was unwilling to take when faced with social upheaval in the 1960s. But as the histories of the two writers are read against their nonfiction texts, new worlds of interpretation are opened for the careful reader who remembers the power that nonfiction has to construe its authors both as narrative presences and actual presences. The revelation of inconsistencies in their work is no reason to abandon their claim to truth, but it is an invitation to read that claim for its artistic, social, and political implications.

For that task we will need readers who are prepared for the special challenge posed by nonfiction—that is, readers who recognize they are characters in the very texts they are reading. One of the most theoretically significant attributes of writing that claims to be true is that it will spill out into the readers' world, seeking to make sense or nonsense of the readers' own experiences. It is that recognition, I will argue, that brings nonfiction its greatest power and problems. The notion—even if highly compromised—that we are reading about events that really happened or characters that really lived will draw us into complicity with the narrative and its work. Many of these impulses, as I will show, are voyeuristic; often they are manipulated by the profit-making news industry. In the next chapter I will trace the way that readers are implicated both by standard journalism and by nonfictional narratives that have traditionally been studied as literature. Along the way I will not try to construct some ideal reading of nonfiction but will try to account for the way that nonfiction texts construe me as a reader and complicate my experience.

4.

READING INSIDE OUT:

Rupture and Control in the Construction of Reader

IF READING FOR AN IMPLICATED AUTHOR will require examining the narrator of the text against the grain of what I know of its actual author, then reading nonfiction for the manner by which it implicates me will require reading the "self" that is positioned by the text against the grain of what I know of myself outside the text. The "history" that I meet in the mirrored screen of the text is at once mediated and thus "other," yet the synthetic force of its fictionlike presentation can trigger powerful mimetic appeals: a narrative field that pulls the reader into the life of the text. Wayne Booth's response to Norman Mailer's *The Executioner's Song* shows that he experiences both inside and outside the text the book's depiction of Utah, its people, and Gilmore's family. Booth thus is a character, if unnamed, in the very text he is reading in a way he would not be were it fiction. He tastes the sting of this power firsthand when, because he is a product of Utah's Mormon culture, *his* culture is the one at stake in the novel. The "Utah" that Booth meets in the setting of *The Executioner's Song* cannot be neutral; Booth has been and can again be a character in that setting. And, as we have seen in the previous chapters, Mailer's own role as well is anything but neutral or aesthetically "implied." Mailer is, after all, at once a character interpreting Booth's socio-religious heritage, a historical figure, and an author ("implied" or otherwise) whom Booth has read and interpreted in texts over the years.

The multilevel vision thus created haunts an implicated reader like Booth or anyone with experience of the events and places described in the text. Although that power comes into play any time a fictional text builds a recognizable setting with which the reader identifies, most such texts do not bring with them a sense of what Booth calls "the harm that the book will do to many of those who are caricatured in it, including Gilmore's wife, children, and relatives" (210n). The deeper the reader's actual stakes are in that text, the more it will produce what Bill Nichols calls in his study of nonfiction film the "click of recognition" (161), the mirrored effect that forces a simultaneous outside/inside reading. In this sense the most deeply implicated reader will be the subject of the text itself, as any journalist knows who has ever misquoted a subject or who has construed a news source in a manner that the source considered unflattering. Against this recognition of the text's power to construe flesh-and-blood people and material events is the play of its mimetic appeal (so that there are "those who, like me," as Booth admits of Mailer's book, "somehow 'could not put the book down'" [208]) as well as—in a manner that seems particularly forceful in nonfiction—the evocation of memory (Booth's idea of "Utah," its people and culture, and its significance for his personal history).

The reverberations set in motion by the clash of synthetic and mimetic narrative strands—as well as by the personal and socially constructed memory that the reader brings to the event—are what set the reading of nonfiction apart from at least many readings of fiction and explain much of its affective power. For example, the reader captured by the sweep of revolutionary drama might build a strong textual identification with a Bolshevik revolutionary like Trotsky in Reed's *Ten Days That Shook the World* (which, as was demonstrated in the previous chapter, clearly is told from a narrative position that attempts to bind the reader to the revolutionary cause) and might, therefore, be thrilled when Trotsky rises in the Second Congress of the Soviets of Workers' and Soldiers' Deputies with a "rich voice in cool contempt" and consigns his enemies as "just so much refuse which will be swept away into the garbage-heap of history!" (104). But in the more than seventy years since Reed's nonfiction narrative was published it has been virtually impossible—in the United States, the Soviet Union, or post–Soviet Russia—for many readers to encounter that scene as if Trotsky and his revolutionary desires were merely someone's fictional construct. Most readers of the text are instead implicated in a clash of varying inside/outside responses: some of which are frankly disturbing to its capitalist or Stalinist or post-Soviet readers. Other less directly political implications echo the intertextuality of everyday life: was that really Trotsky? Or Reed? Or Warren Beatty playing Reed in *Reds*? Visual images, especially if they are representations, form our ideas of the way the world might be. We see less and less with our own eyes, and the uneasy feeling among many contemporary readers is that it has become increasingly difficult to distinguish the narrative of one's own memory from what is "mediated" or "constructed."

As I stated in the introduction to this study, I am certainly not claiming that such transactions never take place in fiction. Fictional accounts are not written or read in a social vacuum and frequently make use of recognizable social or political conflicts or, indeed, even "actual" names or characters. Occasionally, too, the status of fictional characters is challenged directly from across the divide, as when Harold Loeb challenged Ernest Hemingway's representation of Robert Cohn in *The Sun Also Rises,* or when the James J. Hill family sued Time, Inc., for revealing that they formed the basis of the crime novel *The Desperate Hours* (since the novel allegedly misrepresented their experience when the family was taken hostage by escaped convicts; Overbeck 157). But in most cases, as I believe the previous chapters have demonstrated, the "first cause" of the fictional text is assumed to be the author, and her power to construct that fictional world is not so seriously contested as is that of a nonfiction author.

As I stated in chapter one, Peter Rabinowitz's notion of the reader's role in the construction of genre can help us understand these sorts of constructions and help us resist essentializing them. He says that "genre is best understood . . . as a collection of texts that appear to invite similar interpretive strategies. And different readers, of course, are apt to apply different rules," although all strategies "always bring with them some kind of political edge" (137). Readers with no knowledge of the Hill family would most likely read *The Desperate Hours* according to its stated claim to be fiction and would invest no particular referential link between the novel's renamed protagonists and their alleged material counterparts, the Hill family. The family itself, however, did make that link and was able to convince a court to read the text as if it were (wrongfully presented) *nonfiction* and that Time Inc. had thus libeled them, despite the novel's claim to be fiction.

Naomi Jacobs's fascinating study *The Character of Truth: Historical Figures in Contemporary Fiction* traces the legal precedents of such considerations, contrasting Carol Burnett's successful libel suit against the *National Enquirer* to instances such as Robert Coover's characterization of Richard Nixon in *The Public Burning,* which was published without incident after a two-year delay during which lawyers studied its potential defamation (169).

> The one real difference between the *Enquirer*'s fact-fiction mix and that of fantasy fiction manipulating the images of famous people is that the *Enquirer* claims to be factually true, whereas the writers of 'faction' will generally say that they are referring not to the real person but to the person's

mythic self or persona, which is not at all congruent with the real self. Now, even a mildly sophisticated reader knows that the *Enquirer* is not factual, just as any sophisticated reader knows that symbolic or allegorical use of the name and image of a famous person does not constitute a literal reference to that person. *But to an unsophisticated audience, the effect of such knowing falsehoods is identical whether the publication purports to be factual or fictional.* (161, emphasis added)

The reader and her sense of implication by a text thus becomes a central player in both the recognition and effects of nonfictional narrative. A reader with no outside knowledge of actual events depicted by a narrative that claims to be true will experience the text as operating on actual material bodies if that reader believes—as I demonstrated in my analysis of Jane Kramer's *The Last Cowboy*—that the text intersects people in history. That belief carries certain ramifications, which Rabinowitz notes are both generic and political. But if the reader does not know (or does not care) that tragedies portrayed in such texts affect or have affected actual people, then the text will be read primarily as fiction, regardless of its author's intent. Similarly, a reader with no knowledge of the Mexican Revolution, or even the Russian Revolution or Kennedy assassination, will not be implicated in the same way as a reader who recognizes actual characters and cares about how the memories of such events are preserved and adjusted.

Such texts that purport to reenact for the reader an experience the reader understands is at least potentially available elsewhere will tend to *force* those readers onto the plane of multireferentiality and social contest. M. M. Bakhtin has written in *The Dialogic Imagination* of the disorientation that can result when one's experience, even one's words, has been recontextualized by an "other" discourse:

Any sly and ill-disposed polemicist knows very well which dialogizing backdrop he should bring to bear on the accurately quoted words of his opponent, in order to distort their sense. By manipulating the effects of context it is very easy to emphasize the brute materiality of another's words, and to stimulate dialogic reactions associated with such "brute materiality." . . . Another's discourse, when introduced into a speech context, enters the speech that frames it not in a mechanical bond but in a chemical union. (340)

It is that sort of "chemical union" that can create Booth's contradictory claims that Mailer's text in *Executioner's Song* takes "the easy way of simply reporting a world that you are to accept as actual without having to work much at it" (208) and that this so-called lazy text yet has the verve to "harm . . . many of those caricatured in it." The aim here is not to side either with Booth or with Mailer on the value of the text itself (I am not particularly taken with *Executioner's Song*) but to explain (with Bakhtin) the uneasy relationship that blooms when an author assumes narrative control over an actual experience shared, even obliquely, by the reader. "To see oneself (differently from in a mirror): on the scale of History" (12) is how Roland Barthes explains the nonfiction discourse of photography in *Camera Lucida* and the sensation of experiencing oneself in a reenacted text:

> For the photograph's immobility is somehow the result of a perverse confusion between two concepts: the Real and the Live: by attesting that the object has been real, the photograph [or nonfiction text] surreptitiously induces belief that it is alive, because of that delusion which makes us attribute to Reality an absolutely superior, somehow eternal value; but by shifting this reality to the past ("this-has-been"), the photograph suggests that it is already dead. (79)

Like the photograph, nonfiction narrative rubs differing planes of actuality together in the narrative present or mixes the real with the referential in a way that recalls the impulses of surrealism or metafiction. That disquieting, almost chemical, union, in fact, accounts more significantly for the affective quality of reading nonfiction than does some sort of empirical "truth" test of the text itself. The text creates an implicated reader, a reader who has lived within the world the text purports to reveal (and is thus at least a potential character), who is now reading about that world (and is also an audience), and who may have experienced that world through competing representations (and is therefore an even more complicated or intertextual audience).

The implicated-reader model accounts for the affective power of a text like Don DeLillo's *Libra*, which—while it is marketed as fiction—clearly forces many readers to interact with the text of Lee Harvey Oswald's involvement in the Kennedy assassination as both audience and character. Those readers who have considered conspiracy theories for Kennedy's death, even if only to question why so many theories persist, will be implicated. Some readers have "met" Lee Harvey Oswald in the televised images of his death at the hands of Jack Ruby and now are mimetically engaged in Oswald's thoughts, which DeLillo presents with full narrative force from the factual record of Oswald's diaries, a device that distinguishes *Libra* from standard realistic fiction. Some readers have seen the Zapruder film's depiction of Kennedy's death and now are engaged by *Libra's* reenactment of those moments immediately preceding and after the limousine rounded the corner near the Texas School Book Depository. The readers' extratextual world, in which we try to reconcile those conflicting images and arrive at some master narrative of the event, interplays with DeLillo's created world, in which Nicholas Branch, the government official who has been asked to review the case, tries to reconcile those conflicting images and arrive at some truth of Kennedy's death. Both Branch and many of the book's readers are forced to recognize that no ground is solid here—that we have experienced Kennedy and Oswald primarily through mediated images and that the labyrinth of espionage and intrigue cannot be, or at least has not been, solved in either "fiction" or reality.

It is from this potentially fruitful tension that I believe those critics who would collapse all distinctions between fiction and nonfiction—or at least texts that intersect material bodies and events and those that do not—would release the reader too easily. The inside/outside interplay depends on the tension between an implicated (outside) and reading (inside) audience. Similarly, to grant actuality to nonfiction while releasing the reader from an ongoing struggle to reconcile her experience to a created text would seem to diminish the power and effects of the nonfiction form. As Barthes says in *The Pleasure of the Text:* "The reader can keep saying: I *know these are only words, but all the same* . . . (I am moved as though these words were uttering a reality). Of all readings, that of tragedy is the most perverse: I take pleasure in hearing myself tell a story *whose end I know.* I know and I don't know. I act toward myself as though I did not know" (47, Barthes's emphases).

The task of assessing the chemical reaction of the implicated reader will not be to posit some "ideal" or "implied" reader by which to measure scientifically these responses, but to gather something of the range of responses that are possible when actual readers read a nonfiction text from the outside in or the inside out. For example, the analysis of narrative expression has long since taught us that a reader's sympathy might be engaged by reading the thoughts of others and by building a close textual identification with their hopes, dreams, and fears. But when those others are nonfiction characters whom (outside the text) the reader might also experience as exotic, alien, or even menacing, complex and potentially incendiary reactions are produced. The "friend" created by narrative effects inside the text can become the "enemy" of outside memory. The historian Hayden White in his extended critique of historiography, *The Content of the Form,* outlines the "uncanny" union of narrative mastery and untamed actuality:

> As distinct from the present the past is alien, exotic, or strange; as continuous with it, this past is familiar, recognizable, and potentially fully knowable. The historical past is, in a word, "uncanny," both known and unknown, present and absent, familiar and alien, at one and the same time. Thus construed, the historical past has all the attributes that we might ascribe to the psychological sphere of "the imaginary," the level of infantile fantasies and narcissistic projections that feeds off dreams of uninhibited mastery and control of objects of desire. (89)

The appeal of the nonfiction narrative for many readers thus becomes its ability to create a fantasy of rupture accompanied by one of mastery and control, the ability to gain some power over the shock, the scandal, the formlessness or ambiguity of the past. Ironically, then, nonfiction can produce both a disquieting effect *and* a promise of formal control that releases that anxiety.

Nonfictional Narrative and the Impulse of Voyeurism

The power of these narrative sensations of rupture and control has long been of interest to the journalism industry, which, after all, originates many of the nonfiction narratives that are produced each day for mass consumption. The industry even adopts terms that betray the economic underpinning of such considerations: events are considered to have more or less "value" for their power to implicate readers; these competing values are assessed and assigned credits or debits in the daily "budget" of the news product. The industry responds in a more direct but similar way to the same effects that draw readers to more nominally "literary" nonfiction—effects that are produced when readers encounter "real-life" others in narrative. Journalism has codified those sensations into six enduring standards of news value: conflict, unusualness, impact, prominence, proximity, and timeliness—close variations of which are taught in every basic journalism class in America and codified near the front of every standard news-writing and -editing textbook. These standards are what makes news "fit to print," and they enjoy a special status in the profit-making news industry that exceeds even that of the "inverted pyramid" or the "who-what-when-where-why" lead. The first four standards succinctly define the power of the "real-life other," the markers of the past that White calls "alien, exotic, or strange," while the last two standards promise to bring that textual power to the consumer/reader with its juices still hot. These standards help to explain why in the vast majority of American newsrooms—where representations of reality are marketed each day along with advertisements for clothing, cars, and entertainment—a house fire is news while a house raising might not be, why reporters regularly visit police stations but rarely classrooms, why the media cover political campaigns far more closely than the inner workings of policy, why Donald Trump is hotter news than David Dinkins, why Jeffrey Dahmer or O. J. Simpson gets more press than Bishop Tutu. In a manner similar to that outlined by Hayden White, standard forms of nonfiction narrative—newspaper and magazine accounts, network television, and the like—play off the sensation of "othering" experience against its recapture and release at the level of "infantile fantasies and narcissistic projection" (89). The mastery of both news values and the fairly rigid forms that channel such values is in fact the principle requirement that the profession demands of the beginning journalist.

A close reading of conventional journalism news-writing texts, therefore, can offer insights into the way that desire and recapture work to implicate nonfiction readers, at least within contemporary standards of news value and news-writing form. Gerald Stone's *Newswriting*, an introductory college text marketed by HarperCollins Publishers and adopted by many journalism schools, offers an example of the way the industry begins to build a standard of news value for its neophytes. It defines its six enduring news values as consequence, prominence, proximity, timeliness, action, and novelty.[1] Corollary values are attributed to sex and humor. The very first words of Stone's discussion sound the continuing theme of reader implication:

> News values that affect the largest number of people have
> the most consequence. The news value of consequence
> should be considered at every level, both for good news
> and bad. . . . And the consequence principle is applied eas-
> ily to money: a $1 million bank heist generates much more
> reader interest than a $10,000 robbery. Remember conse-
> quence is the rule of "greater" effects. The greater the
> numbers—the more people, places or things affected—
> the greater the consequence. Greater consequence means
> more reader interest. (3–4)

Consequence is closely aligned with "human interest," which, Stone reminds
his readers, "involve[s] the reader by arousing feelings such as joy, hatred,
sorrow, understanding or sympathy" (8).

The textbook, like all standard journalism news-writing texts, defines the news value of "prominence" along economic and class lines, devot-
ing special emphasis to spectacular professions like movie or rock stars or to
titled professionals or managers. "[T]he title of doctor and kidney specialist
suggests a higher news value than if the person were a paramedic," Stone
reminds his students. The rock star is more newsworthy than the stage hand.
And "people in the spotlight—whether government officials, educators,
business people, labor leaders or movie stars—rate higher in general reader
appeal than less conspicuous people" (4). Similarly, conflict is measured according to its ability to be conspicuous, not necessarily by the number of
people who are hurt by it. Therefore an unusual, highly visible conflict would
be more important than a chronic problem that affects even more people in
a less dramatic way. "[D]isruption of the status quo is news" under the rubric
of "action," Stone tells beginning journalists: "The more disruptive an action,
the more likely it will grab attention. But the 'action' news value is also at
play when a definitive action preserves the status quo" (7).

The news value of "novelty" corresponds to a market demand for
diversified news product as well as for the reporting of "freak" events that
excite an otherwise routine news consumption pattern. "Reporters chronicle
novel ways of committing crimes," Stone observes. "Hospitals provide a mul-
titude of both miracles and inexplicable tragedies" (8). In all cases the emphasis is on events that break normal patterns, that offer their readers a "real-
life" experience that is exotic or strange, though safely mediated. Stone suggests examples. "Robberies occur in most medium-sized cities every day, but

seldom does a thief mistakenly break into a police precinct. A local hotel owner defies superstition and numbers the 13th floor. From that time forth, every misfortune that occurs at the hotel happens on the 13th floor, including fires, police raids, and leaky plumbing. A woman has a baby in a local cab, and although that's happened before, this is the third time she's had a baby in a taxi" (8). Proximity and timeliness are discussed as corollary values to the initial four; both are important enough to be mentioned high up in a news story so that the product can be marketed as fresh and relevant. But even proximity, Stone says, does not outweigh the spectacular effects of the prominent or unusual. An event like the firing of a local government official may be upstaged by the "news that a famous Hollywood actress has died," the textbook suggests, recalling that every U.S. newspaper and television station devoted "conspicuous and extensive coverage to the death of John Wayne." According to Stone, "this famous actor's death must have lowered the news budget priority of a lot of more-local stories at many papers and stations" (9).

Although most news-writing texts are not candid enough to grant sex its own news-value category, the HarperCollins text shows no such squeamishness. Reminding beginning journalists that "sex is one of the basic human needs," Stone counsels them to remember its power in determining news value, whether it be "titillating, shocking or shameful" or a combination of the three (9): "This news value has been recognized as a separate category, although it frequently accompanies other discrete news values, but it also can be identified as a major aspect of human interest. The embezzling of bank funds might be just another theft except that the vice president falsified the books to keep a lover. Police raids resulting in a drug bust are common until linked with a wife-swapping club" (9).

The value of this sort of close reading for my study of the nonfiction narrative and its implication of readers is that standard journalism—like its longer or more adventurous nonfiction counterparts—also works an inside/outside, attraction/repulsion edge. Because it is a more immediate and simpler form, and because novices must be efficiently taught the rules of the system, its underlying ideology is more readily spelled out, even if it is rarely shared with "common" readers. Its lessons show that readers are attracted to the spectacular and to the scandalous; the reenactment of history as narrative allows the reader to replicate the "othering" experience without necessarily surrendering to it.

Richard M. Barsam's critical history of nonfiction film demonstrates how a similar "reenactment" quality pervaded early movies. Audiences were attracted by "real-life" films that depicted war, by images of the "Wild West" or Native American life, or by travel films of exotic locations (particularly, we can assume, if the "natives" might be expected to wear less clothing than Westerners). One of the earliest manifestations was George C. Hale's "Pleasure Railway," debuting at the 1904 St. Louis World's Fair, which "gave audiences the illusion of actual travel: good sightlines to a life-size image on a large screen and vibrations with sound effects adding to the overall effect" (30). Ushers dressed like conductors to welcome patrons to the "Pleasure Railway"; each week featured a new destination. Like today's "virtual reality" computer projections, the lure of Hale's "Pleasure Railway" was not so much that it could produce a more convincing picture than the naked eye (the films were in fact available only in black and white), but that it allowed its viewers to experience simultaneously *both* real and fantastic effects, the power (gained for the price of admission) to "transgress" safely, to travel to places they had not yet been with the assurance that they might safely return.

When audiences tired of the travel films, Barsam notes, producers upped dramatic values by "restaging and outright deception" (30). One of the more popular film series was George Milies's *actualité reconstituée*, reenactments of war and disasters contrived to reproduce the effect of reality. "[M]any of the faked films were carefully produced to seem authentic," Barsam notes. "Thomas Edison, who shot all his Boer War series in the Orange Mountains of New Jersey, was particularly adept in this respect" (32). One can readily see how such depictions mirror the concepts of theme parks and thrill rides, where a consumer is allowed to experience a controlled but fantastic "real-life" effect. If, as in the island park depicted as Jurassic Park, the regenerated dinosaurs sometimes exceed their bounds, at least the audience for the film *Jurassic Park* is granted the assurance (purchased along with its admission) that it might safely leave the theater once the film has ended.

Mainstream journalism is equally effective at safely recovering its evocation of "othering" desire through news-writing conventions. Spelled out in great detail over the hundreds of pages that follow the discussion of threshold news values in textbooks such as HarperCollins's *Newswriting*, these conventions include "objectivity," the "inverted pyramid" news hierarchy, the cultivation of official sources, and the reliance on legally privileged (and often governmental) sources for quotes and documentation that establish an epistemologically firm footing and a "top-down" view within the news text. Similarly, reading more adventurous nonfiction texts for the specific ways in which they implicate their readers will entail a consideration of how the readers are positioned against the text.

We might want to assess as carefully as possible the sources of "othering" desire as well as the manner by which those desires are channeled by the underlying forms of the texts. Generalizations, of course, are shaky, particularly in nonfiction. Not all readers will read a text in the same way, particularly if that text explicitly recalls the reader's extratextual experience. A Russian citizen, for example, might read *Ten Days That Shook the World* much differently than a reader who has never been to Russia, but the content and form of the text nonetheless can reveal its constructedness, its ideology, to the careful observer by the manner in which it positions its readers.

An initial example might be drawn from two nonfiction film texts that culminate with the death of one or more human beings from the weapons of war. The first nonfiction film text is *The Battle of Chile,* a documentary described by Bill Nichols in his thoroughgoing study of nonfiction film, *Representing Reality.* In the making of the documentary, Nichols tells us, a camera operator was shot and killed; the footage from the operator's camera became part of the finished film: "The endangered camera may even record the final moments of a fatally jeopardized camera person. One of the most compelling examples of this gaze, if we can still call it a gaze rather than a look or line of sight, occurs in *The Battle of Chile.* We see the killer and witness the moment at which the bullets are fired, their impact inscribed in every jolt and jostle of falling man and camera before the machine stops running and the image turns to black" (84). The second nonfictional film text is documentary footage of a precision bomb "kill," footage supplied by the U.S. government and widely aired on television and cable during the 1991 Desert Storm war in Iraq. It is described by Richard V. Vincent in his study of Cable News Network published in *Triumph of the Image:*

> The black-and-white grainy footage always showed pin-point accuracy of this high technology as the target entered the cross hairs of the camera and moments later the screen went blank. The released footage was always of a perfect hit. Rarely could human activity be seen on the ground prior to the explosion. It was all so sterile. Yet people un-

doubtedly were inside some of the buildings that were obliterated. The destructive power of these bombs and missiles was appalling—people unfortunate enough to be caught at the center were not identified, their arms, legs, and flesh scattered in small pieces. (188)

Set side by side, the two slices of nonfiction film offer intriguing similarities and differences. Both are constructed yet carry the power of actuality. Both help to demonstrate that no matter how artificial the nonfiction representation might be, there is no point to collapsing all distinctions between fictional and nonfictional representation. Film, of course, differs somewhat from written text because of its ability to construe the replica of a material body. But there is something to knowing that the victim is actual, not an actor or a fictional construct, in either film or written text. Real people die. No actor got up and walked away from either of the fatal attacks chronicled by the camera footage. As Nichols says, "Danger, in documentary, is real. Contingency abounds . . . risks will have real consequences" (84).

Yet the viewer is positioned much differently in each of the documentaries. The bombing of the Iraqi installations is viewed from the top down. The viewer rides the projectile into the building; the explosion is proof that the viewer has successfully penetrated the defenses of the enemy. But in the Chilean footage the viewer is positioned at the receiving end of the projectile. The view is bottom up, and the explosion is proof of the viewer's failure to mount a successful defense against the enemy. The blank screens that end each segment, even though identical in form, thus convey vastly different meanings because of the manner by which they position and implicate their viewers. One becomes the celebration of victory from which all evidence of death is effaced; the other is mute proof of death's certainty. Both depictions carry the force of an actual war representation that meets the test of nonfiction's power mutually to attract and repulse our interest. Yet, in the Chilean footage the blank screen tastes of death, while in the Iraqi footage it tastes of American power and victory. Paul Virilio explains how the Iraqi war thus became a battle to control the mechanics of vision, "images and sounds, rather than objects and things" in which the struggle became that for a centralized point of view, the skirmish to control narrative as well as property. "The will to see all, to know all, at every moment, everywhere, the will to universalized 'illumination': a scientific permutation on the eye of

God which would forever rule out the surprise, the accident, the irruption of the unforeseen" (70).

Reader Positioning within the Nonfiction Canon

Careful assessment of reader positioning can also be applied to more canonical nonfiction texts like Charles Dickens's "A Visit to Newgate Prison," Henry Mayhew's *London Labour and the London Poor,* or William Hazlitt's "The Fight." Each of these three writers offers his readers a top-down voyeuristic discourse that will remove the "wall" that separates readers from the objects of repulsion/desire while at the same time avoiding the danger of interaction in the "top-down" narrative position we have just identified. As such, the authors produce what Mary Louise Pratt in "Scratches on the Face of the Country," her analysis of colonial travel narratives, calls "informational" discourse: "textually produc[ing] the Other without an explicit anchoring either in an observing self or in a particular encounter in which contact with the Other takes place" (140) or what Peter Stallybrass and Allon White call "balcony" discourse, a downward view that allows for the gaze while restricting the contaminating touch (136).

 In his visit to Newgate Prison Dickens positions his reader as a man in the street, minding his business,[2] oblivious to the squalor and death just inside the prison wall. Dickens takes that reader by the hand, transgresses the wall, and invites his reader to confront a scrupulously depersonalized Other from an intimate but slightly elevated distance:

> There is one object, too, which rivets the attention and fascinates the gaze, and from which we may turn horror-stricken in vain, for the recollection of it will haunt us, waking and sleeping, for a long time afterwards. Immediately below the reading desk, on the floor of the chapel, and forming the most conspicuous object in the little area, is *the condemned pew;* a huge, black pen, in which the wretched people, who are singled out for death, are placed on the Sunday preceding their execution, in sight of all their fellow-prisoners. (209, Dickens's emphasis)

Dickens asks his readers to imagine "the hopeless clinging to life to the last" and the "wild despair" with which the felons meet their death, but he never wades into the "huge black pen" to ask the "wretched people" themselves, much less forces his reader inside. His narrative, therefore, has the power of actuality—we are, after all, inside the notorious prison witnessing the last moments of people who will actually die—but maintains both a reportorial and a formal distance.

Mayhew's *London Labour and the London Poor,* a "Cyclopaedia of the Condition and Earnings of Those that *Will* Work, Those that *Cannot* Work, and Those that *Will Not Work,*" also virtually precludes interaction between the observer and subject and removes the reader to a safe narrative distance while at the same time the reader is explicitly—indeed sometimes gleefully—held close to the repulsive subject. Mayhew's "cyclopaedia" of subjects includes street peddlers, criminals, prostitutes, deviants, entertainers, garbage collectors, sewer sweeps, and—in the case of the redoubtable Jack Black—rat exterminators. Mayhew meets Jack Black (whom he bills as the "Queen of England's ratcatcher," thereby invoking the news values of unusualness, impact, and prominence at one sweep) on the streets of London where Black is peddling rat poison.

Black has a cage of rats with which to demonstrate his virtually erotic powers: "I saw him dip his hand into this cage of rats and take out as many as he could hold, a feat which generally causes an 'oh!' of wonder to escape from the crowd, especially when they observed that his hands were unbitten. Women more particularly shuddered when they beheld him place some half-dozen of the dusty-looking brutes within his shirt next to his skin" (11). The reader here again is a voyeur in the crowd, though he no doubt is construed among the crowd's male members, who, after all, are treated to the spectacle of female reaction as well as to Black's prowess. Black, as it turns out, is not above demonstrating his prowess by thrusting the heads of live rats into his mouth and, moreover, proves a master of dramatic discourse (though Mayhew's presumed lack of a recording apparatus would place Black's exact "voice" in some doubt, as the previous chapter would demonstrate).

Perhaps the most chilling of Black's narratives involves the extermination of rats that have invaded the house of lord of Hay, Hempstead. The specter of rats in the houses of royalty, presented as a nonfiction narrative, must have produced a sensation for Mayhew's middle-class audience as well as reminding them of the terrors of the underground sewers and the thin line that separates the high from the low, the exalted from the underworld. In his lord of Hay narrative, Mayhew, through Black, inscribes the rats, "a dreadful spiteful feller—a snake-headed rat" (17), with virtually serpentine force as they attack their Edenic victims:

> [They] must have come up from the bottom of the house to the attics. The rats gnawed at the hands and feet of the little children. The lady heard them crying and got out of her bed and called to the servant to know what the child was making such a noise for, when they struck a light, and then they see the rats running away to the holes; their [the children's] little nightgownds was kivered with blood, as if their throats had been cut. I asked the lady to give me one of the night-gownds to keep as a cur'osity, for I considered it a *phee*nomenon. (17, Mayhew's emphasis)

Hazlitt's "The Fight" allows for slightly greater interactivity between the reporter and his subject, but Hazlitt, like Dickens and Mayhew before him, seems primarily content to be the professional voyeur, enticing his readers with promises of real-life blood and potential death at the illegal bare-knuckles venue. "Reader, have you ever seen a fight?" he asks. "If not, you have a pleasure to come, at least if it is a fight like that between the Gas-man and Bill Neate" (637). For readers of "The Fight," pleasure mixes with desire and death, which begins when Tom Hickman (the "Gas-man") unveils a right hand and promises "this will send many of them to their long homes" (638). Ironically, it is Hickman who approaches the death whose prospect Hazlitt has used to entice his readers. When the moment of death comes, the reader is implicated by explicitly demonic imagery, borrowed from Milton and Dante, to inscribe the scene's "otherness." Hit full in the face by Neate's tremendous lunge, the Gas-man

> hung suspended for a second or two, and then fell back, throwing his hands in the air, and with his face lifted up to the sky. I never saw anything more terrific than his aspect just before he fell. All traces of life, of natural expression, were gone from him. His face was like a human skull, a death's-head, spouting blood. His eyes were filled with blood, the nose streamed with blood, the mouth gaped blood. He was not like an actual man, but like a preter-natural, spectral appearance, or like one of the figures in Dante's *Inferno*. (641–42)

In each of these three examples the reader is allowed to witness the deeply "othering" sensation of "real-life" death. Though the reader is permitted to view closely the results of violence, the positioning remains as resolutely top-down as in the grainy footage of the U.S. bombs that penetrated the Iraqi defenses. It is, after all, the denizens of the condemned pew who are executed, the lord of Hay's children who are bloodied by rats, the Gas-man who dies; the reader is permitted to watch but is never personally threatened. But that very safety heightens the tension that voyeurism produces in the observing of actual death.

Each writer is careful to remind his readers that the deaths are "real," not staged. It is this distinction that removes the thousands of staged deaths that one routinely can observe any week on network television from the scrupulously suppressed "snuff" film in which a real victim dies. No doubt our historical implication in the Dickens, Mayhew, and Hazlitt texts is blunted somewhat by having no specific outside knowledge of the victims, as we might in late-twentieth-century America if the Gas-man were Mike Tyson, or if the lord of Hay were Senator Robert Dole, or if the condemned pew held Ted Bundy or Jeffrey Dahmer. But even across the years, it seems to me, many readers will recognize they have participated in the artful reenactment of an event that ended in the death of a person, not merely a character. As Nichols reminds us, "History kills"; there is a materiality to the body and to death that is not entirely discursive, even if its meaning and social value is (109).

Against the Dickens, Mayhew, and Hazlitt accounts I will briefly consider two other literary texts that are presented by their authors as nonfiction and that position the reader at the receiving end of the narrative's force. Thomas De Quincey's *Confessions of an English Opium-Eater* suggests a link with a twentieth-century narrative like Michael Herr's *Dispatches* in that each implicates the reader by asking her to consider her complicity with guilty experience. Their and their readers' positioning recalls the category that Pratt describes as experiential discourse in her analysis of colonial travel narratives. The journal of the experiential nonfiction discourse, Pratt says, "narrates the journey as a kind of epic-style series of trials and challenges—often erotic ones" (150).

De Quincey draws his reader into the text experientially through a double-edged confessional mode, both evoking opium's magical charms and demonizing it for its attack on the autonomous self. The reader encounters a distinctively epic voice for the narrative journey as De Quincey frequently invokes his nemesis openly for its power to soothe the savage soul. De Quincey directly tempts his reader with a long catalogue of opium's charms, for its "assuaging balm," for its potent rhetoric, for its gift of brief oblivion, for its power to deliver to "the guilty man, for one night givest back the hopes of his youth" (44). But as the narrative progresses, opium reveals itself as the explicitly demonized Other. In a discourse with interesting reverberations for Pratt's colonial literature readings De Quincey explicitly compares his opium hallucinations to "Oriental dreams" (70), the foreign, the Other that will not be colonized by the Western rationalized self. De Quincey evokes a self subsumed by the Other, a life with "lunatics and brute animals," "Oriental imagery and mythological tortures," "cancerous kisses," "confounded with all unutterable slimy things, amongst reeds and Nilotic mud" (69).

The "self" that is under attack in this scene is looking upward into the trajectory of a weapon that has an Oriental face, the weapon that can end its life. The reader—whatever her feelings about the actual or extratextual essence of Orientalism—is dragged along in De Quincey's project. To the extent that the reader has developed any textual association with De Quincey's tortured revelations, she will be challenged by his enemy, even if she would not share that challenge outside the text. De Quincey's Oriental dreams, he tells us, are of Southern Asia, "the seat of awful images and associations," the "ancient, monumental, cruel and elaborate religions of Indostan. . . . Man is a weed in these regions" (69).

Herr's *Dispatches* offers a way to culminate this part of the chapter's discussion of the manner by which nonfiction implicates its readers. In a way that resembles De Quincey's work, the book also is about the accounts that one must pay for guilty experience. And like De Quincey Herr merges the drug experience and the Asian experience as mutual challenges to Western rationalism and conquest. But in addition *Dispatches* offers both informational and experiential challenges to its readers as it promises to give us the story of the Vietnam War that the official histories will not dare to communicate. That very premise, of course, powerfully implicates the book's late-twentieth-century American readers, for whom the war lives on both in memory and in its continuing power to alter current events. In *Dispatches* Herr draws in his readers by bringing the Western ego-ideal into direct confrontation both with what De Quincey had earlier termed the "awful images" of Southeast Asia and with itself. The former challenge Herr constructs for his readers in the typically top-down manner that Pratt has identified as informational colonial discourse. But the latter challenge—the Western ego-ideal in direct confrontation with itself—Herr is able to meet in a powerfully intersubjective way as he brings his readers into the trenches along with the Marine Corps grunts as each braces himself against the rounds of "incoming" fire. To address the initial strand first: for a book about Vietnam, *Dispatches* manages virtually to ignore the country and its people, most likely because Herr was dressed as a soldier and was reporting within a powerful military machine that effectively separated him from the land. When we do meet Vietnam and its people in Herr's text, we see them always from a distanced, slightly elevated perspective (often literally from a U.S. helicopter), positioning the reader in a manner not unlike that which I have earlier identified in Dickens. For example, of the Vietnamese Montagnards Herr writes:

> Their nakedness, their painted bodies, their recalcitrance, their silent composure before strangers, their benign savagery and the sheer, awesome ugliness of them combined to make most Americans who were forced to associate with them a little uncomfortable over the long run. It would seem fitting, ordained, that they should live in the Highlands, among triple canopies, where sudden contrary mists offered sinister bafflement, where daily heat and the nighttime cold kept you perpetually, increasingly, on edge. (99–100)

By contrast Herr will bring his reader into a prolonged close-up view of the subject he knows far better: the Marine Corps grunts, the Green Berets, the Lurps, and the rest of the U.S. forces fighting the generals' war. The thrust of Herr's narrative is to bring (indeed, even force) the reader into closer and closer contact with these subjects and with their battle. The reader first encounters them as the Other personified, as in this prolonged view of a Lurp, which opens the book. "He wore a gold earring and a headband torn from a piece of camouflage parachute material, and since nobody was about to tell him to get his hair cut it fell below his shoulders, covering a thick purple scar. Even at division he never went anywhere without at least a .45 and a knife, and he thought I was a freak because I wouldn't carry a weapon" (4).

Both the Lurp and the battle itself are experiences that the reader must confront if she is to hear the story that Herr insists no one else seems to be able to tell about Vietnam. And so for the reader the book is a long double experience as Herr moves closer and closer to ground zero both in his original experience and in his drive to reexperience and rechannel its power through its retelling. Symbolically, Herr pulls the reader into the reexperience of the war when he moves underneath the voyeuristic position and climbs into the trenches with the grunts, closing the distance between the high and the low, between observer and observed in both social and epistemological terms. Herr seems to grab his readers, telling us that we cannot read about the war until we can experience the battle as "incoming" fire:

> dreaded and welcome, balls [a term that "genders" his reader inside the text and will implicate him or her outside] and bowels turning over together, your senses working like strobes, free-falling all the way down to the essences and then flying out again in a rush to focus, like the first strong twinge of tripping after an infusion of psilocybin, reaching in at the point of calm and springing all the joy and all the dread ever known, *ever* known by *everyone* who *ever* lived, unutterable in its speeding brilliance, touching all the edges and then passing, as though it had all been controlled from outside, by a god or by the moon. (144, Herr's emphasis)

To summarize the arguments of the chapter thus far, I have demonstrated that nonfiction narratives implicate their readers by seducing the reader into the text at the same time the reader may read the text through the screen of outside knowledge. That "double" inside/outside vision explains many of the sources of nonfiction's power—not the least of which is the reader's ability to transcend his own limitations through imagination, with the guarantee of a safe return. Mass market journalism, like the movies or like theme-park adventure rides, is particularly adept at marketing that sensation, selling the thrill of "othering" implication while recouping it through "safe," top-down structures and practices.

A reading of nonfiction narrative that is alive to its underlying ideology will try to assess the manner by which a text positions its reader. Because real-life readers differ according to their experiences and closeness or remoteness from the events described by the text, it will be impossible to nail down some sort of ideal reading. Yet we can begin to determine how a text positions our own readings. If, as I demonstrated in the previous chapter, reading for an implicated author will require reading the narrator of a text against the grain of what we know of its actual author, then reading nonfiction for the manner by which it implicates us will require reading the "self" that is construed and positioned by the text against the grain of what we know of ourselves outside the text.

As historian Hayden White reminds us in *The Content of the Form:* "The act of reading requires that the subject assume a particular position vis-à-vis the discourse, on the one side, and the system of beliefs, values, ideals, and so on, that comprise his cultural horizons, on the other. To acquiesce in the adequacy of a given way of representing 'reality' is already to acquiesce implicitly to a certain standard for determining the value, meaning, or worth of the 'reality' thus represented" (88). To recognize that a U.S. military videotape positions us on the nose of an invading "smart" bomb should force a historical as well as a textual reaction; similarly, seeing that a Michael Herr normally permits us to experience the Vietnamese people only from the psychic distance of a hovering U.S. helicopter will help us to assess the manner by which Herr constructs our reading of the war.

Nonetheless, a book as powerful as *Dispatches* will (and, I believe, should) inevitably produce strong reactions and identifications inside its text. The enduring charm of literature, after all, is its power to draw us into the people and events that are at its core. But when those events assume a historical and material dimension as well (even if, as Fredric Jameson argues, "history is inaccessible to us except in textual forms" [82]), we will read them for the ways that those texts create our own histories.

Joan Didion and the Reader in Radiation

A close reading of the way Joan Didion positions her readers in her nonfiction will demonstrate what can occur when a writer constructs her reader inside a radically destabilized universe. Building on the analyses developed so far in this chapter, I begin this section with a brief contrast of the way Wolfe and Didion position their readers and conclude my discussion of Didion's texts in a specific way that points toward chapter 5's outside in reading of the narratives of Tim O'Brien, an author who similarly destabilizes facts at the same time he insists that they matter.

> [I]t never occurred to me that I would not sooner or later—most probably sooner, certainly before I ever grew up or got married or went to college—endure the moment

> of its happening: first the blinding white light, which appeared in my imagination as a negative photographic image, then the waves of heat, the sound, and, finally, death, instant or prolonged, depending inflexibly on where one was caught in the scale of concentric circles we all imagined pulsing out from ground zero. (*After Henry* 122)

> I was supposed to have a script, and had mislaid it. I was supposed to hear cues, and no longer did. I was meant to know the plot, but all I knew was what I saw: flash pictures in variable sequence, images with no "meaning" beyond their temporary arrangement, not a movie, but a cutting-room experience. In what would probably be the middle of my life I wanted still to believe in the narrative and in the narrative's intelligibility, but to know that one could change the sense with every cut was to begin to perceive the experience as rather more electrical than ethical. (*White Album* 12–13)

For a writer who, since childhood, has walked the waking bad dream, alert for the "blinding white light" that will signal the world's end, the stroboscopic pulse is the flash of the negative, of cataclysmic ends, of undoing. And so Didion sits in a nearly empty restaurant on Miami's Biscayne Boulevard, buildings swimming free against the sky, causeways adrift, angles oblique, surfaces "reflective, opalescent" (*Miami* 31), and listens to a reporter and a prosecutor chat up fraud cases within ever larger, ever more fluid, fraud cases: money washed, diverted, channeled, submerged, bodies rising to the surface. As the voices rise and fall, the rains begin once more; sheets of warm rain wash across the windows. Over Biscayne Bay the white light flares all around her: "The lightning was no longer forking now but illuminating the entire sky," she recalls, "flashing a dead strobe white, turning the bay fluorescent and the islands black, as if in negative" (38).

Didion has been here before, ever in her waking dreams, crouched under her desk at school, covering her eyes and brain stem, waiting, waiting, waiting for "the blinding white light," the "negative photographic image," the "waves of heat, the sound, and, finally death," a "seductive reversal of the usual associations around 'light' and 'white' and 'radiance,'" the "logical conclusion" (*After Henry* 122–23). The subtext of Didion's nonfiction—a subtext that she has nourished like a cool blue flame over twenty-five years even as it threatens to erupt in a blinding flash—is its desire to snare her readers by the illogic of "logical conclusions," that white vision of apocalypse by which Didion herself has been implicated. She will admit the stakes of that transaction, as she did in her essay "Why I Write," will admit that her intentions are "aggressive," even "hostile," an "imposition of the writer's sensibility on the reader's most private space" (5). And, therefore, Didion would pull us inside a shifting, liquid world where the flashes burn brilliant and reversed, inside a stroboscopic vision from which we cannot escape.

Didion's own position as writer and her positioning of the reader within that vision offers both a transition from and a suggestive contrast to Tom Wolfe, who also made consistent use of the strobosphere image, particularly in *The Electric Kool-Aid Acid Test*. But there, despite Wolfe's seductive narrative mannerisms (sweeping lights, flaming loudspeakers, strobes exploding, black lights, and Day-Glo paints), the writer's presence remains outside and above the maelstrom, looking down through Ken Kesey's mind to Kesey's human hand firmly on the controls in the swirling, stroboscopic dome:

> "Kesey looks out upon the stroboscopic whirlpool—the dancers! flung and flinging! *in ecstasis* gyrating! levitating! men in slices! in ping-pong balls! in the creamy bare essence and it reaches a SYNCH he never saw before. Heads from all over the acid world out here and all whirling into the pudding. Now let a man see what CONTROL is. Kesey mans the strobe and a twist of the mercury lever UP and they all speed up" (217).

Even when he gives voice to a subject on the floor, caught up in the intensity of the white flash, Wolfe's narrative presence remains safely past tense, reassuring us that Clair Brush, the point-of-view character here, has been recaptured, even as she mouths the memories of escape. The strobe, Brush recalls for Wolfe, "disturbed that part of me that was trying to hang onto reality . . . playing with time-sense was something I'd never done . . . and I found it irresistible but frightening" (246).

By contrast Didion positions her reader so the white strobe is all around. We have moved out of Herr's helicopter hovering safely overhead and are now on the floor of the jungle, disoriented and involved. Didion's "flash pictures in variable sequence" (*White Album* 13) are the flash of the apocalypse; no hand is on the control, and the flash is always most menacing when it is least expected. Fire, rain, wind, race riot, assassination, mass murder—all are the manifestations of the flash by which Didion will implicate her readers. Behind us lies the constant threat of the blue pool in the nuclear reactor. The pool for Didion is unfathomable, seductive, and forever poses a challenge to the dynamo of infinity and human progress that Henry Adams in his *Education* had discovered on his journey to the 1900 Paris Great Exposition. Then, Adams had contemplated the great gallery of machines as a moral force. Didion recalls in her article "Pacific Distances," collected in her most recent book of nonfiction, *After Henry,* that Adams studied science as he had studied Mont-Saint-Michel and Chartres, and she plots that Chartres image to her own post-nuclear devices. When she first visits the TRIGA Mark III nuclear reactor in the basement of Berkeley's Etcheverry Hall, she muses:

> It had been thirty-four years since Robert Oppenheimer saw the white light at Alamogordo. The "nuclear issue," as we called it, suggesting that the course of the world since the Industrial Revolution was provisional, open to revision, up for a vote, had been under discussion all those years, and yet something about the fact of the reactor still resisted interpretation: the intense blue in the pool water, the Cerenkov radiation around the fuel rods, the blue past all blue, the blue like light itself, the blue that is actually a shock wave in the water and is the exact blue of the glass at Chartres. (124)

If the logical conclusion of that "blue past all blue" is the white light of sudden death, then it is by illogic that Didion will contest its presence. Hence, she tells us that actuality, even if it can be glimpsed, is a story for a madwoman to tell, and she parades her qualifications in no less than her own psychiatric report that she reprints in her article "The White Album." Emotionally alienated, regressive libidinal, conflicted, devious, preoccupied with the distorted and bizarre: this is the diagnosis by which Didion implicates herself, as both a historical and a narrative presence, about as personally as any writer can. "It is as though she feels deeply that all human effort is foredoomed to failure," her psychiatric work-up concludes (*White Album*

14–15). What other "illogical" response is possible to the "logical" conclusion of the white blast, Didion seems to wonder, then concludes, "By way of comment I offer only that an attack of vertigo and nausea does not now seem to me an inappropriate response to the summer of 1968" (19).

Many of Didion's best readers seem to underestimate the radical decentering of reader position that is produced by an inside out reading, preferring to discuss Didion's method as a rhetorical strategy toward elusive truth rather than as an image of the danger (and even insanity) of presenting uncontested "truth" in a postnuclear world. Second, these critics underemphasize the effects of what happens when such a strategy is applied to nonfiction—a form that makes the readers *characters* in Didion's swirling and liquid style as well as consumers of her narrative strategy. Didion's most often-quoted description of her own work, offered to an audience at the University of California during her 1975 return to her alma mater and reprinted as the essay "Why I Write," raises the possibility that the writer and reader must be positioned on the edge of insanity to qualify as witnesses in the postmodern world. The description concerns the sketches of cats drawn by a patient in varying stages of psychosis:

> This cat had a shimmer around it. You could see the molecular structure breaking down at the very edges of the cat: the cat became the background and the background the cat, everything interacting, exchanging ions. People on hallucinogens describe the same perception of objects. . . . Look hard enough, and you can't miss the shimmer. You can't think too much about these pictures that shimmer. You just lie low and let them develop. You stay quiet. You don't talk to many people and you keep your nervous system from shorting out and you try to locate the cat in the shimmer, the grammar in the picture. (7)

Didion seems to suggest that the postnuclear world creates in human beings the quality of the schizophrenic condition. The shimmer, therefore, is the flash and menace of the radioactive universe, a destabilized universe, interacting and exchanging ions.

Many of Didion's best readers seem to underestimate the image, preferring to discuss it as a rhetorical strategy toward elusive truth rather than as an image that poses for implicated readers the danger (and even insanity) of presenting the uncontested "truth" in a postnuclear world. For example, Chris Anderson in *Style as Argument* discusses Didion's "shimmer" as a virtual synonym for formal resonance or ambiguity, evidence of "her capacity to project apocalypse in rhetorically effective and engaging ways" (152). He sees no crisis of underlying fact for Didion. She, like Orwell, "believes in the inextricable relationship between words and ideas . . . ," Anderson concludes, "that words can corrupt ideas, that the truth or falsity of ideas is directly reflected in the truth or falsity of the language used to express them" (165). Similarly, Barbara Lounsberry in *The Art of Fact* suggests that Didion can find the "truth" behind experience and present it to her readers. Hence, even though Didion "*locates 'truth' obliquely, in the slippage or breakage, between the lines and over the border*" (108, emphasis added), Lounsberry argues that "her effort to discipline her illusions likewise becomes a model for reader behavior" (136). Finally, Mark Muggli in his essay "The Poetics of Joan Didion's Journalism" argues that Didion enacts an "emblematic" significance to her work that finally imposes a meaningful order to a work such as *Salvador.*

Each of these readings is most helpful in establishing certain of Didion's formal strategies, but none is adequate to describe the way she positions her reader in her narratives. In contrast to Wolfe Didion issues a deep challenge to the "sanity" of a factual hierarchy whose logical conclusion is a tangible threat of annihilation and most often refuses to offer the reader a safe passage back to the world of predictability. (Granted, the article in which Didion discusses most overtly her obsession with the nuclear holocaust was not collected until 1992 in the *After Henry* collection, since the publication of the critical studies I have cited.) The shimmer of the blue pool and the shimmer of schizophrenic vision are not merely Didion's self-selected artistic methods; she presents them as the only way possible to write about the insanity of an air-raid drill that would tell a child to protect her brain stem function by crossing her fragile arms against the fury of a fifty-megaton bomb. And so Didion recalls "listening all one Sunday afternoon to a special radio report called 'The Quick and the Dead,' three or four hours during which the people who had built and witnessed the bomb talked about the bombs and 'by extension' their own eerie and apparently unprecedented power, their abrupt elevation to that place from whence they had come to judge the quick and the dead" (*After Henry* 122).

Where unprecedented power over the future of the universe is presented as scientific discourse by calm and rational discussants, Didion stakes out a resolutely posthumanist course beyond that suggested by any of her published critics: "You are getting a woman who somewhere along the line misplaced whatever slight faith she ever had in the social contract," she tells us, "in the meliorative principle, in the whole grand pattern of human endeavor" (*White Album* 133). Normal definitions of sanity and insanity, Didion suggests, are reversed in the shadow of the bomb, as journalist Ron Rosenbaum noticed when he traveled to ICBM launch sites somewhere near South Dakota for *Harper's* magazine in search of the government-certified "sanest men in America," whose fingers are on the trigger. "No one would think that a man able to participate in the launch of up to thirty separate nuclear warheads and help extinguish human civilization with a twist of his key would be a bull goose loony. . . . The implication here is that sanity in a launch means *not* thinking about this reality, sanity means the kind of studied insanity or fugue state that ignores one's true relation to the world" (288).

Didion, on the contrary, will serve as a doomed witness to that doomed world, plunging to its depth, writing inside its turmoil, even if it costs the privileged position of authorial sanity. In one of her earliest published essays, "On Morality," which though it is not strictly a journalistic narrative reveals much about how Didion writes such narratives, she seems to define and symbolically prefigure her role as postnuclear reporter. She recalls the tale of Nevada sheriff's deputies diving for ten days into a dark, apparently bottomless pool in an effort to recover a "drowned boy" while the boy's eighteen-year-old pregnant widow stands silent vigil and stares into the black water. The divers have found "no bottom to the caves, no bodies and no trace of them, only the black 90 degree water going down and down and down, and a single translucent fish, not classified. The story tonight is that one of the divers has been hauled up incoherent, out of his head, shouting—until they got him out of there so that the widow could not hear—about water that got hotter instead of cooler as he went down, about light flickering through the water, about magma, about underground nuclear testing" (*Slouching* 160).

Didion will be that witness, even if she must dive again and again into the hot radioactive light and even if robs her of her coherency upon return. For it is the only way she can report "the monstrous perversion to which any human idea can come" (*Slouching* 161). Her readers will be those silent watchers, waiting for the word, pregnant with possibilities. The transaction is a harsh one, as her "moral" lesson suggests, sometimes so harsh that the witness and the one who waits for the word must be forcibly separated.

Didion recognizes in this, one of her earliest published pieces, that the trans-action's stakes are both intensely moral as well as intensely implicating: "Of course you will say that I do not have the right, even if I had the power, to inflict that unreasonable conscience upon you; nor do I want you to inflict your conscience, however reasonable, however enlightened, upon me" (*Slouching* 161).

As if to respond to the domestication of the New Journalism project that Wolfe had underway by the publication of his theoretical essay "The New Journalism" (1973), Didion further explores the demands and limits of reporting history in the title essay of *The White Album* (1979). Initially Did-ion seems to be making the case that Anderson, Lounsberry, and Muggli would have us accept, that the creation of story ("We tell ourselves stories in order to live" [11]) is the highest human act imaginable in a chaotic age: "We look for the sermon in the suicide, for the social or moral lesson in the mur-der of five. We interpret what we see, select the most workable of the multi-ple choices. We live entirely, especially if we are writers, by the imposition of a narrative line upon disparate images, by the "ideas" with which we have learned to freeze the shifting phantasmagoria which is our actual experi-ence" (11).

No sooner has Didion created this notion of story, however, than she deconstructs it with an "or" clause and opts out of the promise of intelli-gible story: *"Or at least we do for awhile"* (11, emphasis added). Then we lose the script, she says; all we can see is "flash pictures in variable sequence" (13), and in the most extreme cases we learn that the stories we tell ourselves in order to live often are merely delusions of sensation, new narrative cir-cuitry, scar tissue to cover the raw nerve: "During the years when I found it necessary to revise the circuitry of my mind I discovered that I was no longer interested in whether the woman on the ledge outside the window on the sixteenth floor jumped or did not jump, or in why. I was interested only in the picture of her in my mind: her hair incandescent in the floodlights, her bare toes curled inward on the stone ledge" (44). Even then Didion will not stop at the altar of pure aesthetic sensation, rightly dismissing it as the essay continues as "sentimental . . . equally meaningful, and equally senseless" (44).

What is most important for my study of implicated writers and read-ers is that Didion's nonfiction insists on the social context of a teller and a hearer together by the pool; indeed that is part of the reason why, it seems, she has chosen to present so many of her stark narratives as nonfiction: a form that, as this study argues, almost inevitably links its readers and writers in a social and historical—as well as in an artistic—transaction. From the ashes of an "equally meaningful, equally senseless" narrative condition she will rebuild the possibility of reporting informed by, if not quite adequate to, the imminence of apocalypse as well as the intertextuality that complicates our interactions.

Didion wants to suggest that her nonfiction will do more than market reality in timely fashion. For her, all writing, especially the nonfiction writing of human beings in "disorder," is a potentially moral, if often desperate, act. In "On Morality," an essay in *Slouching Towards Bethlehem*, Didion says morality became concrete in the story of a talc miner who had stayed on the highway through the night to guard the body of an accident victim while the miner's wife drove 185 miles across the desert and three mountain ranges for help. Had he not stayed the coyotes would have torn the corpse's body and eaten its flesh. Didion concludes, "One of the promises we make to one another is that we will try to retrieve our casualties, try not to abandon our dead to the coyotes. If we have been taught to keep our promises—if, in the simplest terms, our upbringing is good enough—we stay with the body, or have bad dreams" (158).

Given that concrete example of moral behavior, how difficult it must have been in 1982 for Didion to turn her back on a young Salvadoran civilian near the Boulevard de los Heroes as soldiers herded him into a van, "their guns at the boy's back" (36). Didion is the reporter who has come to El Salvador to bear witness to the *desapariciones,* to document the atrocities committed by the regime supported by her American readers' government. But when the lad is kidnapped before her eyes, she can tell those readers only that "I walked straight ahead, not wanting to see anything at all" (36).

From that start, as the 1980s progress, Didion burrows toward a more deeply implicated reporting capable of recognizing political and cultural *desapariciones* of the late twentieth century. She may be no more sure of an overarching truth than before, no more certain that either she or her readers will escape the blinding white flash of the apocalypse, no more certain that it is possible to pull apart the strands of competing narratives to get at something hard and fast. But in the 1980s Didion moves beyond her confession in *Salvador* that she will turn her back on deeply implicating material. It is as if she has concluded—along with Jane Tompkins in the quote that I cited near the beginning of this study and in a way that I will apply even more specifically to Tim O'Brien in the next chapter—that recognizing that facts always are embedded in narrative does not excuse a writer or reader from trying to sort out those facts. For as Tompkins reminds us:

> [If] you are convinced . . . that there really are no facts ex-
> cept as they are embedded in some particular way of seeing
> the world, then the argument that a set of facts derives
> from some particular worldview is no longer an argument
> against that set of facts. If all facts share this characteristic,
> to say that any one fact is perspectival doesn't change its
> factual nature in the slightest. It merely reiterates it. . . .
> [Y]ou can't argue that someone else's facts are not facts *be-
> cause they are only the product of a perspective,* since this
> will be true of the facts that you perceive as well. (76, em-
> phasis added)

And so, while the latter Didion never changes her obsessions with holocaust and hyperreality, she seems to equip herself for a serious nonfiction capable of burrowing into the postmodern world of intrigue and shadowy plots amid the stroboscopic flashes of white light. Throughout this evolution Didion continues to open her reporting to her readers, allowing them to see the quality of her evidence, the constructedness of her narrative, and to compare its validity to that of competing narratives. Somehow, through it all, she becomes an artist who might be worthy of being called a reporter, as well as a reporter who might be worthy of being called an artist.

Didion is honest enough to confess those moments (as in the San Salvador kidnapping) when her nerves or her natural reserve cause her the bad dreams of immoral inaction, and she wants to produce the same feeling in readers confronted by characters who live both in the world and on the page. At the end of her "Slouching towards Bethlehem" tale about Haight Ashbury's wasted dream, Didion sees a three-year-old child who had burned his arm playing with fire chewing on a live electric cord while the mother's "macrobiotic friends" are busy "trying to retrieve some very good Moroccan hash which had dropped down through a floorboard damaged in the fire" (128). Didion ends the long article about the Haight-Ashbury culture with that vignette, the chillingly ironic note about a culture that promises to love in principle but is selfish in practice, a culture that would rather see a child abused than lose good drugs.

More than ten years after she filed the story Didion shows she has not forgotten that boy and his burned arm; the odor of burned flesh implicates her (and any reader who can recognize the distinction between the odor of "actual" and "fictional" flesh) across time as no fictional situation could. Like many reporters, she recognizes that she might have reached out to save the boy, but had she done so she would have lost not only her detachment but perhaps the vignette that perfectly captured her theme. She still doesn't rest easily with that decision and confesses to Susan Stamberg in an interview reprinted as "Cautionary Tales": "I was terribly worried, because my child was almost that age. His mother was yelling at him in a kind of desultory way. There had been a floorboard damaged in the fire, and some hash had dropped down through it, and everybody else was trying to dash around and get this hash back. I wanted to take the child out, but I had no business doing that" (25). Didion can recognize the fictionlike power of the evocative narrative detail as well as how the writing of actual characters and events forces both writer and reader into moral choices that leap off the printed page into history. This is without doubt her greatest dilemma as well as her greatest achievement.

Her book-length nonfiction narratives, *Salvador* and *Miami,* force their readers into a similar dilemma, particularly those readers who are citizens of the United States and who are exploring the details of policies carried out in their names. In *Salvador* the mimetic pull of the narrative—the tension of a plot in which its reporter/protagonist is placed in a milieu where weapons are brandished and eye contact is avoided—plays against the recognition by many readers that a reporter who fears eye contact will leave San Salvador without being the witness she should have been.

The reader caught up in the book's narrative present follows Didion as she tries to discover information about the deaths and disappearances in El Salvador. She tries to make sense of death statistics whose numbers never add up and which seem to change every day; she looks through photo albums containing the photographs of dead bodies. She learns that vultures "go first for the soft tissue, for the eyes, the exposed genitalia, the open mouth" (21). She even visits a well-known body dump one morning to see the bodies for herself; when she gets there she finds a man giving a woman a driving lesson in the sort of truck that has been linked to the deaths and disappearances. The truck inches back and forth while three small children play in the wet grass. The reporter, meanwhile, walks down the steep mountainside—which itself is the subject of a tourist bureau boast as El Salvador's most beautiful natural attraction—and finds "what is left of the bodies, pecked and maggoty masses of flesh, bone, hair" (21).

The sense of generalized danger that has complicated Didion's reporting soon is directed more specifically at the reporter herself. She goes for a walk, opens her handbag to check an address, and hears "the clicking of metal on metal all up and down the street" (22). One night, while she and her husband are dining alone on the porch of a restaurant, she sees two men, one carrying a rifle, crouched between the pumps at a gas station next door. She fights an urge to blow out the candle on her table, "in a single instant demoralized, undone, humiliated by fear" (26). At first Didion tells us that she maintains her work habits in spite of this sense of now-personal as well as generalized danger. She interviews the country's president, the U.S. ambassador, reads histories and embassy reports. She is able to draw metaphorical connections, such as the fact that only the U.S. embassy with its inflexible foundation is damaged badly by an earthquake that rocks the ground under her feet; other buildings shift with the shifting earth and are not damaged (53). But she no longer seems ready to face the facts that a reporter is expected to report. She has already, on one occasion, closed her notebook and turned her back on the obvious kidnapping; language (65), even *verdad* itself, is "a degenerated phrase" (66), has come to mean "the truth according to Roberto D'Aubuisson" (67), the government official widely believed to be behind the majority of the killings.

Finally, Didion wrangles an exclusive interview with Victor Barriere, grandson of the demented Salvadoran former dictator General Maximiliano Hernandez Martinez and the namesake of the country's most notorious death squad. She interviews the grandson, learns that he reads Nietzsche and Schopenhauer, that he lives with his "Mommy" and keeps an eighteen-year-old peasant boy (whom he is teaching to be a primitive painter) as a companion, that he equates the martyred Archbishop Romero with Adolph Hitler. Faced with an unparalleled opportunity to engage her reporting, Didion declines to ask the grandson any questions, even though he seems eager to talk. She confesses: "It occurred to me that this was the first time in my life that I had been in the presence of obvious 'material' and felt no professional exhilaration at all, only personal dread. One of the most active death squads now operating in El Salvador calls itself the Maximiliano Hernandez Martinez Brigade, but I had not asked the grandson about that" (56). She travels, instead, to the cathedral where Archbishop Romero has been shot and finds it a "vast brutalist space" with an unlit altar that "seemed to offer a single ineluctable message: at this time and in this place the light of the world could be construed as out, off, extinguished" (79). In her last act as a reporter Didion asks an embassy staffer about an obvious distortion in U.S. Ambassador Deane Hinton's speech, but the staffer assures her that it will not matter; the only important thing is that the ambassador's speech will be front-page news in both the *Washington Post* and the *Los Angeles Times* (98).

During one of Didion's last days in El Salvador the sense of generalized dread that implicates and defeats her as a reporter becomes even more specific. A car in which she is riding is surrounded by young men on motorcycles, one of whom caresses a machine gun propped between his thighs. No one says anything; the young men smile but will not make way for her car. While her driver maneuvers the car out of the tight spot, she can only study her hands and conclude that it was "a pointless confrontation with aimless authority" and that "any situation can turn into terror" (104–5).

The growing tension keeps Didion awake during her last night in the country as she listens to a band blare "Malaguena" until dawn; on the way to the airport she is sure she is being kidnapped. Once there: "I sat without moving and averted my eyes from the soldiers patrolling the empty departure lounges. When the nine A.M. TACA flight to Miami was announced I boarded without looking back, and sat rigid until the plane left the ground. I did not fasten my seat belt. I did not lean back" (106). On the plane she meets a student missionary who has brought the Good News of Jesus to the people of Belize, another Central American nation. From an immediate perspective his mission of witness has been successful while the reporter's witness has not. The young man has renewed his commitment to bring Jesus Christ as personal savior (*salvador*) to the world. Didion has been undone. Once back in the United States she can report only that "the State Department announced that the Reagan administration believed that it had 'turned the corner' in its campaign for political stability in Central America" (107–8). Although Didion is deep into irony here, the government's is the last word of the book; she must depend on an ironic effect for the evidence of United States government complicity in the events of El Salvador that her reporting cannot uncover.

To understand the manner by which *Salvador* has implicated many of its North American readers, it might be worthwhile to try to imagine the narrative as if a reader knew nothing of El Salvador in the 1980s nor of the United States' policies toward Central American dictatorships that El Salvador reflects. For that reader Didion has emerged alive from a situation when there was a real chance that she would not. She has plunged at the story's beginning "directly into a state where no ground was solid" (13) and come

out alive. On the other hand, a reader purely inside the text, with no knowledge of external events, would seem to be aware that her safety comes at
some cost, that she seems less free to communicate the truth as she sees it
than she hoped to be able to do at the beginning of the book. Even more
important, that reader would be drawn to a rather unambiguous conclusion:
the United States, a nation which the reporter, as a citizen, has a right to
believe will protect her, has in fact done nothing to assure her of its protection. In the world inside the narrative, the reporter's nation clearly is aligned
with evil. It is protecting the terrorists of El Salvador while it has largely
abandoned her.

     That sort of reading, of course, becomes much more complicated
for the vast majority of *Salvador*'s audience. These are readers who might
know something of the history of El Salvador (whether they were supporters
of U.S. policies during the 1980s or not), readers whose taxes may have paid
for the elaborate appointments at the United States embassy where Didion
is told that her nation is making strong progress in its efforts to "save" El
Salvador. That sort of reader—as this book has argued throughout—would
be "implicated" by the events of the text, in that those events would assume
an "actual" dimension for that reader outside the book as well as a "narrative"
dimension inside the book. Ever more disconcertingly Didion undermines
at every turn any attempt at an uncomplicated historical *or* narrative reading
of the text. "[N]o ground is solid, no depth of field reliable, no perception so
definite that it might not dissolve into its reverse. The only logic is that of
acquiescence" (13). Didion will repeat that essential message from the first
page to the last. The visitor to El Salvador is told unambiguously that to
survive he will need to function exactly opposite the manner in which a reporter should: by concentrating only on present details, by averting eyes
from danger, "to the exclusion of past or future concerns, as in a prolonged
amnesiac fugue" (14).

     Thematically, Didion is on familiar turf here, that which pervades
her work from beginning to end. The mass destruction represented by the
body dumps and disappearances is El Salvador's holocaust, while the pervasive intertextual propaganda of the Salvadoran and U.S. governments is its
hyperreality. Official statistics, official reports (perhaps even those in the
newspapers that an actual reader might value) are exposed as worthless, but
no worthwhile figures are put in their place. Government memos (most
likely paid for by a vast majority of the book's actual readers) use other discredited government memos to support their statistics; such memos are in

turn used to buttress (actually undermine) the factual basis of the text the implicated reader is reading. Even presumably actual places such as the Puerto del Diablo body dump are rendered not so much as evil but as "a place [which] presents itself as pathetic fallacy" (20). Signs and significance are unhinged: the simple act of checking an address is read as menace; a candle on a dinner table is insupportable danger. The face of Ronald Reagan (commander-in-chief to many of the book's actual readers at the time of its publication) saluting the Salvadoran commitment to freedom and political self-determination dissolves into the televised image of actor Ronald Reagan (complete with Spanish overdubbing) playing opposite Doris Day in *The Winning Team,* a movie that any member of the book's actual reading audience could—and maybe has—rent at a local video store or watched on a cable movie channel. Meanwhile, Roberto D'Aubuisson takes part, wittingly or unwittingly, in an actual performance of a cinema verité scene shot by a Danish film crew for a (fictional) movie about a foreign correspondent

> in which the actor playing the correspondent "interviewed" D'Aubuisson, on camera, in his office. This Danish crew treated the Camino Real not only as a normal location hotel (the star for example was the only person I ever saw swim in the Camino Real pool) but also as a story element, on one occasion shooting a scene in the bar, which lent daily life during their stay a peculiar extra color. They left San Salvador without making it entirely clear whether or not they had ever told D'Aubuisson it was just a movie. (62)

The effect of *Salvador* seems markedly different than it would be if, say, the reader were involved in a narrative with no "actual" dimension. The almost pointless government regulation, the uneasy sense of generalized menace without clear cause, the mixing of realistic detail and surreal effects like the D'Aubuisson filming or the Reagan-Doris Day movie make *Salvador's* plot read like a modern-day Kafka novel, to be sure, but it is a Kafka novel that the majority of its readers are living as well as reading. The props in this narrative—the chilled wine in crystal at the U.S. embassy, the fish on American eagle porcelain—are supplied in the names of the U.S. citizens who make up many of the book's actual readers when Didion is told (against all evidence) that U.S. interests are prevailing in Salvador.

Ultimately Didion leaves those readers hanging in *Salvador,* depending for ironic effect on her refusal to make final sense out of the hyper-real terrorist society she has encountered. The *Heart of Darkness* epigraph will instead be her testament. In it Marlow reflects on the power of Kurtz's language, the report that "vibrates with eloquence," that "soars," that makes the reader "tingle with enthusiasm" born of "burning noble words" and the "magic current of phrases" (qtd. in *Salvador* 9). It is that sort of message that at least some portion of *Salvador*'s readers might want, the eloquence that will assure us that some savage customs in El Salvador are being suppressed in our names or at least that the artist/reporter can make some sense of the experience.

By making a reader care about her narrator on the mimetic level Didion is following the conventions of latter-day New Journalism: realistic narrative that promotes reader identification. But by denying that part of many readers who want to be reassured by this technique she is striving to be adequate to the facts even as she undermines her text's ability to present facts:

> This was a shopping center that embodied the future for which El Salvador was presumably being saved, and I wrote it down dutifully, this being the kind of "color" I knew how to interpret, the kind of inductive irony, the detail that was supposed to illuminate the story. As I wrote it down I realized that I was no longer much interested in this kind of irony, that this was a story that would not be illuminated by such details, that this was a story that would not be illuminated at all, that this was perhaps even less a "story" than a true *noche obscura.* As I waited to cross back over the Boulevard de los Heroes to the Camino Real I noticed soldiers herding a young civilian into a van, their guns at the boy's back, and I walked straight ahead, not wanting to see anything at all. (36)

Didion, it seems, will refuse the Kurtz solution. She will refuse to produce the searingly beautiful, the elegantly ironic text about extermination. Hers, finally, is the voice of confession. She has played her readers' desire to engage in the text's suspenseful narrative against our desire to escape from its history. If the reader is not implicated directly and historically by this nonfiction text, he might complete it by being satisfied with its achingly ironic art-istry and turn to the next book on his reading list.

For the fully implicated reader, however, Didion's confession that she is not up to turning terror into unambiguous art comes at a cost. She has made that reader the witness to an *actual* kidnapping in this pivotal scene; an actual boy has disappeared, a gun at his back, and Didion will not, and will not let her reader, stay and bear witness. The similarities and contrasts to *Heart of Darkness* are instructive here. Surely *Heart of Darkness* also im-plicates its author and readers in the historical events of imperialism, a power that I do not wish to discount in any manner, but in *Salvador* the reader has witnessed the kidnapping of a flesh-and-blood character, one who almost surely will be tortured and killed. Didion has turned her (and our) back on that character rather than bearing witness to that disappearance no matter its cost—as she had urged in her "On Morality" essay many years before—against the coyotes who would rip the boy's flesh. The reader, of course, has the option to treat the disappearance as that of a fictional character, but to do so would be to negate its power and responsibility. Didion has made met-aphorical and artistic use of the kidnapping's terror, but has finally turned her back on it and, moreover, has made the reader an accomplice in her project. She implicates us even as she frustrates us. We have come to under-stand Kurtz's brutes in a new way, Didion suggests by this strategy, and a vast majority of *Salvador's* North American audience might be intimately acquainted with the brutes that act in its name.

In *Miami* (1987), published in book-length form some four years after *Salvador*, Didion seems to make more of an effort to bear witness to the actual violence she depicts in her narratives as well as its ramifications for her reporting and her nation. In *Miami*, Didion blends far more substantial documentation with her trademark hallucinatory style. Here she brings her tropical topics that much closer to the bulk of her North American reading audience. As the discussion earlier in this chapter documents, *Miami* is set in the liquid world of political intrigue, gun running, and drug trafficking. As in *Salvador*, challenging a dominant political ideology might have stern consequences: Didion documents bombings at Kennedy Airport, at the Ven-ezuelan Mission to the United Nations, and at the Cuban Missions to the United Nations in two separate Manhattan locations (101), as well as car ignition bombings (100), beatings (107), and plastique dynamite (103). Most are linked to the Cuban exile community in Miami, which Didion covers in detailed fashion.

The reader coming to Didion's *Miami* after reading her other book-length collections of nonfictional narrative immediately notices the depth of her reporting: the scores of interviews that bolster its research, the numbers of government documents, and the reams of official and semiofficial records. Didion presents some fifteen pages of scrupulously detailed notes after the main body of the narrative, each designed, chapter by chapter, to establish her narrative's factual status. And yet *Miami* also remains demonstrably within the Didion tradition: the eerie apocalypse of lightning's white flash; the ever shifting, ever slippery versions of official "truths"; and the layers of lies and half-truths that both support and undermine those claims.

I want first to focus on Didion's presence in the book, particularly suggesting the ways in which it differs from her presence in *Salvador* and ultimately to discuss what those differences tell us about Didion's nonfiction as the end of the century approaches. Like John Reed in his nonfiction narratives *Insurgent Mexico* and *Ten Days That Shook the World*, Didion almost seems destined to replay pivotal scenes from *Salvador* in an effort to establish the changes she has made in her commitment to reporting.

If Didion closed her notebook during the interview with Victor Barriere in El Salvador, no longer interested in "material" but only in her own "personal dread" (56), she will keep that notebook resolutely open in *Miami*. In a chapter that details the pervasive terrorism to which Cuban exile groups have subjected those few Miami-based Cubans who have dared to suggest *dialogo* with Castro, Didion unflinchingly lists the names of those who have died: Carlos Muniz Varela, Eulalio José Negrin, Luciano Nieves. Varela was murdered in San Juan by a group calling itself "Comando Cero" (114), Negrin by two men in ski masks who surprised him and his son in a Union City, New Jersey, parking lot (114), Nieves was shot and killed in the parking lot of Variety Children's Hospital in Miami (106). Despite this menace, Didion will interview Bernardo Benes, the architect of the proposed *dialogo* with Castro and "its principal surviving victim" (111). He tells Didion that he is construed by the exile community as "the Captain Dreyfus of Miami" (112), that he has lost all his car dealerships and his positions on bank boards because he dared to suggest that Miami-based Cubans might do better to talk to those Cubans back home rather than to prepare endlessly to invade the island.

As the interview progresses, the stakes of the narrative deepen as its participants begin to comprehend the implications of Benes and his wife talking to a reporter on the record about political repression in Miami: "We were sitting at the kitchen counter, drinking the caffeine and sugar infusion that is Cuban coffee, and as Bernardo Benes began to talk about the *dialogo* and its aftermath he glanced repeatedly at his wife, a strikingly attractive woman who was clearing the breakfast dishes with the brisk, definite movements of someone who has only a limited enthusiasm for the discussion at hand" (112). It is the sort of increasingly tense and implicating scene that would be much more difficult to imagine were the text fiction and the characters imaginary. "[P]eople tend to forget that my presence runs counter to their best interests," Didion had said of her nonfiction as long ago as the introduction to *Slouching towards Bethlehem.* "And it always does. That is one last thing to remember: *writers are always selling somebody out*" (xvi). Benes and Didion continue to talk about the way the Spanish-language radio stations in Miami have routinely denounced him as a Communist, or at best an *idiota util,* or useful idiot, for Castro (113).

"This is Miami," Benes finally tells Didion. "Pure Miami. A million Cubans are blackmailed, totally controlled." It is, he says, the same condition that Castro has imposed on Cuba: "Total intolerance. And ours is worse. Because it is entirely voluntary" (113). He tells Didion how he could not go to a restaurant without people coming to his table and calling him names, how the friends of his children were forbidden to visit because their parents did not want them there "when the bomb went off" (114), how a Burdines clerk had refused to accept the credit card offered by Benes's daughter (115). As he talks he continues to glance at his wife, who stands now against the kitchen sink, her arms folded. Didion reports:

> From the windows of that house it was possible to look across the bay at the Miami skyline, at buildings through which Bernardo Benes had moved as someone entitled. Mrs. Benes spoke only once, to interrupt her husband with a protective burst of vehement Spanish. "No Cubans will read what she writes," Bernardo Benes said in English. "You will be surprised," his wife said in English. "Anything I say can be printed. That's the price of being married to me. I'm a tough cookie," Bernardo Benes said in English. "All right," his wife said, in English, and she walked away. "You just make your life insurance more." (115)

There is a recognition here that narrative that intersects with actual lives, narrative that goes against the grain of official "truth" in pursuit of facts and their implications, will affect its readers and subjects in powerful ways. Didion reports in detail such activities as the meetings of the Freedom Research Foundation, which procures funding for paramilitary groups, and reports briefings on the eve of the 1984 Salvadoran election that targeted "people like Tom Brokaw" as the enemy of Cuban expatriates (191–92).

Despite, or indeed perhaps because of, such carefully drawn and researched polemics, *Miami* does not have the critical reception that *Salvador* enjoys. Many of its readers are correct in noting that *Miami* presents a vast amount of sometimes only partially digested information, perhaps too much for some of its literary critics, who are more comfortable with Didion's trademark minimalist irony. Certainly the book lacks the elegant structure of *Salvador,* where the narrative begins and ends with the arrival and departure of the ultimately undone reporter and frames her increasing sense of personal danger and moral dread. *Miami,* by contrast, is sprawling. In the words of Peter Elbow in another context: "it does its cooking out on the table" (237). And it is not ashamed of its status as nonfiction, resolutely detailing its sources and access to the sensibilities and scenes she construes in her narrative. Both texts deliver on the apocalyptic themes that have marked Didion's prose since the beginning, but in *Miami* Didion seems to shed her embarrassment at fact-based prose and to recognize in a deeper way the power of facts to implicate her North American readers.

Reading Inside Out in the Age of AIDS

After detailing the ways in which readers can be positioned in nonfiction texts, and exploring the manner by which Didion has become increasingly willing to make her readers equal partners in a search for the truth about American complicity in international violence, I want to turn to my personal experience as a reader of nonfiction. As in my discussion of Didion, I will be contrasting texts in an effort to show what sort of narratives find ways to implicate their readers without resolving their anxiety with easy resolutions. But on this occasion I am most interested in the way that the written nonfictional text intersects with my own memory or "text." I thus will end this chapter with a close personal reading of a less well-known author, Jacqui Banaszynski, whose three-part series, "AIDS in the Heartland," published in the *St. Paul Pioneer Press,* won the 1988 Pulitzer Prize for feature writing. An analysis of "AIDS in the Heartland," similar to the analysis of Freud's

Dora presented in chapter 2, which considered the writer from the inside out, will permit me to show in a very specific way something of the value of reading a text against the grain of a specific reader's history.

Katie Dyer presents a reading model for me to follow:

> What is my job as critic here? To help you understand these words, the experience offered by the text. But what words other than these are available? Only my own. Words from my own life, personal words, words you might not want to hear. If my own subjectivity is my passageway to this text, how can I share that with you in a language that won't make you squirm? The complex dynamics between empathy, sympathy, and judgment, the way I am positioned/position myself in the world of this text compose my engagement with the malady of death and with the possibility/burden of life. I *empathize* with characters I feel close to. I am involved, implicated in their lives. It's as if parts of us were mixed up in each other. (8)

As it happens, Dyer is writing about fiction: Marguerite Duras's *The Malady of Death*. But the reading she suggests, it seems to me, rings all the more true for nonfiction, in which characters assume a material as well as a textual dimension and in which a death diminishes the population of the actual world, not only the literary world, by one more body. I am but one reader of "AIDS in the Heartland"; I do not insist that mine is the "ideal" reading of this nonfiction text. What I want to do instead is to model the sort of reading that is possible when a conscientious reader reads both inside and outside a nonfiction text, alive for the way that the reading entangles his aesthetic judgment and his own memory. This is that space that Dyer calls "this place where the force of the reader's life breathes being into the text and where, then, we must go back to the text, to be true to it and to see what it may have to teach us about the life that we have been" (6).

"AIDS in the Heartland" is Banaszynski's story of the sickness unto death of political activist Dick Hanson on his farm in rural Glenwood, Minnesota. Hanson lived there with his lover, Bert Henningson, a researcher for Minnesota's Department of Agriculture who also tested positive for the HIV virus. Despite the fact that the series of three stories was published in a mainstream commercial newspaper, the *St. Paul Pioneer Press,* Banaszynski writes frankly of Hanson and Henningson's relationship: how "Henningson had gathered Hanson into his arms and said, 'I'll never leave you, Dick,'" when the two tested positive for HIV (261); how Hanson's seventy-five-year-old mother, before her death, had served the lovers a breakfast of caramel rolls in bed to show that she accepted their relationship (266); how the two men had celebrated their first five years together with an exchange of rings before a gathering of friends (265).

Banaszynski has said it was important to her to write a series about gay AIDS patients rather than the usual "family newspaper" choices of hemophiliac or blood-transfusion victims. She knew the choice would be controversial, but with the full support of her editors she searched for more than a year until she found a gay couple who was willing to be openly identified for the article.[3] "I have found it absolutely essential to be perfectly honest. I think a lot of reporters go into things and try to dance around the issues, the tough stuff," Banaszynski now says. "I think it's much better if you go and say 'This is what I'm about. This is why I need to know these things.'" (Friedlander and Lee 258).

I turn the pages of Hanson and Henningson's lives and become enfolded in Hanson's approaching death. I wonder what has happened to Henningson in the six years since the story was published. Then he was HIV-positive but asymptomatic; has he too now died? I can see the Kaposi's sarcoma sores that disfigure Hanson's face and arms, the lesions that attack his eyes and mouth, for it was in 1985 and 1986 that I also wrote a series of articles in which I had the grim task of watching an AIDS patient grow progressively ill and die. The young man had called the *Charlottesville Daily Progress,* where I worked as a reporter, and asked if anyone wanted to write an article about the unwillingness of Charlottesville landlords to rent an apartment to a gay, sick man. I almost immediately agreed, in part because he also said he had been accepted as a subject in the first official medical trial of the drug AZT at the National Institutes of Health (NIH), and so his story, in that way if in no other, had the sort of news value that I could sell to my editors.

Like Banaszynski I recognized that naming names, particularly in a story such as this, was an act that would profoundly impact the young man who was the subject of my articles. Although he was trying to find a place in town, the young man then lived in rural Nelson County, a poor and transcendently conservative area about thirty miles south of Charlottesville. This was long before Earvin "Magic" Johnson's diagnosis, a time when Rock Hudson's illness was just a whispered rumor and when radio announcers were demanding that a studio be fumigated after the visit of an HIV-positive guest. Because the young man who approached me was unwilling to face the prospect of discovery in his community, I agreed to call him "John" in the articles. Even then, as an active journalist, I reflected on how seldom it is that fictional representation invests the naming of characters with such devastating political and social ramifications.

In retrospect, and after reading Banaszynski's articles, I believe I should have worked harder to convince "John" of the public value of his name. It is, after all, the name and the body that are the most powerful facts in stories such as these; the fact is that the body will die and that the name will bear witness that an actual person has been sacrificed to this plague. In no way do I blame "John" for not agreeing to come forward. In fact, like Freud in his case study, the maintenance of anonymity had certain advantages for me in that it allowed me to control the textual presentation more closely. But I can see the power that Banaszynski's stories have that my own did not. In addition to her superior reporting and writing, the name of the subject, Dick Hanson, and the carefully developed public character she builds for him assume a presence in her articles that simply will not let her readers assign the story to some "fictional" space where they don't have to deal with the personal implications of this character's future and that of his lover:

> The tiny snapshot is fuzzy and stained with ink. Two men in white T-shirts and corduroys stand at the edge of a barnyard, their muscled arms around each other's shoulders, a puzzled bull watching them from a field. The picture is overexposed, but the effect is pleasing, as if that summer day in 1982 was washed with a bit too much sun. A summer later, the same men—one bearded and one not, one tall and one short—pose on the farmhouse porch in a mock American Gothic. Their pitchforks are mean looking and caked with manure. But their attempted severity fails; dimples betray their humor. (260)

Banaszynski reports that the pictures in the photo album become sharply fewer after 1985. One shows "the taller man, picking petunias from his mother's grave. He is startlingly thin by now; as a friend said, 'like Ghandi after a long fast.' His sun-bleached hair has turned dark, his bronze skin pallid. His body seems slack, as if it's caving in on itself. The stark evidence of Dick Hanson's deterioration" (260).

Banaszynski, again in a way that contrasts with my stories, writes of the manner by which the men contracted the disease, disclosing Hanson's practice—until he met Henningson—of traveling to Minneapolis each weekend "for anonymous encounters at the gay bathhouse. 'I had to taste all the fruit in the orchard,' he said" (266). But she and her subjects never allow the disclosures to fold back into stereotypes. Hanson is unashamedly spiritual, so those traditional readers who will want to criticize his choices will also have to make sense of this comment: "I believe that God can grant miracles. He has in the past and does now and will in the future" (263). Near the end of the opening story in the series, Banaszynski even states matter-of-factly that Hanson the night before has heard his mother speaking to him from beyond the grave: "'It wasn't part of any dream,' he said. 'Just her voice, crystal clear, calling'" (269).

As it happens, I am not one of those readers who would have a strongly negative reaction to Hanson and Henningson's sexuality. But the manner by which Banaszynski writes the story makes it difficult even for those readers who do reflexively hate or fear gays to dismiss the lovers. The story opens and closes with the two together; their farm-bred vigor is as pervasive to the pieces as is Hanson's illness. In their sickness and health, Banaszynski writes clearly and persuasively of their thoughts and desires for the future. Any reader identification created at all by the articles (and it seems substantial to me) flows naturally toward them, seducing even those readers who would want to criticize them. Banaszynski has said that when the first article in the series was published the newspaper received responses that it was "glorifying homosexuality," but by the time the last segment was published, "readers were calling and writing to say the stories had changed the way they viewed AIDS and its victims" (Friedlander and Lee 257).

Like Banaszynski I found that many people wrote to me and asked what they could do to help "John" in his economic and medical struggle. Several landlords offered their apartments in response to my first story, but by then John was too ill to live alone; enough other benefactors contacted me that I was able to set up a fund where readers could donate money to meet John's ever mounting medical bills. Other than a smattering of letters to the editor, I didn't hear from those readers who thought the series was wrong, but John did. Despite the care we took, several Nelson County readers (again in ways that recall Freud's *Dora*) guessed that the story was about him; his sister and her children were ostracized, and the family was asked to stop attending their conservative Baptist church "for health reasons, you understand."

But what implicates me now most strongly about Banaszynski's stories is the simple fact that they force me to watch a man, an actual man, die in front of my eyes. Perhaps the stories assume this power partly because I sat in a University of Virginia Hospital room and watched John, now too ill to recognize me except in far-flung moments, vomit into his pillow; watched his sister carefully wash him for the tenth time that day; watched him sweat and shiver and rave. The last coherent thing he ever said to me was that he wished he had defied those doctors who had warned him that animal fur could worsen his pneumocystic pneumonia. His eyes opened wide against the drawn white blinds of the hospital room, and he looked squarely at me for the last time. "I just want a cat near me for the long nights ahead," he said. "You know what I mean?" I ended my stories with that image. John died.

In "AIDS in the Heartland" Hanson and Henningson sit in the hospital room and on television Jeff Reardon is losing a lead for the Minnesota Twins in the late innings of a baseball game. Hanson has been given a spinal tap to see if the virus has entered his brain; he and Henningson discuss funeral plans in matter-of-fact tones. As the two talk quietly, Banaszynski subtly shifts the focus to the survivor as Henningson ponders the possibility of having Hanson's ashes sprinkled in one tributary of the Mississippi River and his own in another: "He sits at the window next to Hanson's hospital bed, and holds his hand. Finally, he abandons the diversionary talk and cries. He is worried about losing the farm, about the political hassles involved in getting housing assistance, about getting a job after his contract with the state expires, about not having enough time left with Hanson. And he can't help but worry about the AIDS virus in his own body and his own health prospects" (270). Banaszynski ends her story with this image: the ashes of two gay men flowing down the Mississippi River to entwine in the warmer waters of the Gulf of Mexico. "You can't control what happens to people after they're dead," Henningson says. "But even if it doesn't happen, it's a lovely, consoling thought" (270).

Banaszynski later talked to the editors of a feature-writing textbook about the structure of her article, saying that she carefully chose her final image. "I like my endings to be as strong as my beginnings," she said. "I save some of my best quotes for the ending, for the kicker. . . . My goal is to bring the reader back so that the ending is as *satisfying* as the beginning was" (Friedlander and Lee 271, emphasis added). As a reader of nonfiction, one who deeply identifies with Banaszynski's profession and who salutes her ability to get a story as sensitive and important as this into a mainstream newspaper, I both praise and curse her for this "satisfaction." For Dick Hanson, after all, not some fictional character, is dead, and I can take little satisfaction in that ending. I recognize here, as in my own work, the insidious way in which the journalism market (in a way that resembles all nonfiction) will entice readers to dip into Hanson and Henningson's stories with morbid fascination; how a resolved, personal, quietly ironic ending to this love story might release those readers' anxieties.

I ended my own series with a perhaps harder-edged image. The young man's wish—even in his moment of death—to take a "cat" to bed with him, especially against his doctors' wishes, carried an inside message of final resistant desire in the face of death that only a few of my readers may have gleaned. Most would read it as the story of the healing power a cuddly kitten might bring to a dying man, and they would not be wrong either. But either way the stories that Banaszynski and I wrote position their readers at the bedside of a dying man, ready to leave the room when the death is fulfilled, when the ending of the series of stories fulfills their opening, finally outside the grief and consoled by the power of resolution.

To draw out (as well as culminate) my implicated reaction to Banaszynski's "AIDS in the Heartland" series, I must turn to Randy Shilts's remarkable article "Talking AIDS to Death," first published in *Esquire* and later reprinted in *The Best American Essays 1990.* As the author of *And the Band Played On,* the book-length narrative chronicle of the origins and spread of the AIDS plague, Shilts has become what he admits is "the world's first AIDS celebrity" (233). His article is about the difficulty of recognizing that one has mastered the discourse of a disease that refuses to be mastered. The piece details Shilts's experience on the talk-show circuit after publication of his book, honing his responses to the inevitable questions about AIDS with flash and brilliance. But at night, when the television lights dim, he dreams of "talking to my friend Kit Herman when I notice a barely perceptible spot on the left side of his face. Slowly, it grows up his cheekbone, down to his chin, and forward to his mouth. He talks on cheerfully, as if nothing is wrong, and I'm amazed that I'm able to smile and chat on, too, as if nothing is there. His eyes become sunken; his hair turns gray; his ear is turning purple now, swelling into a carcinomatous cauliflower, and still we talk on. He's dying in front of me. He'll be dead soon if nothing is done" (231).

Herman's dying body haunts the piece, brings both Shilts and his readers back again and again to the rot, to the death that defies the domestication of discourse. When Shilts returns to San Francisco's gay community "from network tapings and celebrity glad-handing," he sees his friends back home dying. "The lesions," he says, "spread from their cheeks to cover their faces, their hair falls out, they die slowly, horribly, and sometimes suddenly" (234). As he talks AIDS to death, "they die in my arms and in my dreams, and nothing at all has changed" (234). In his desperation Shilts plies his audiences with more and more gruesome statistics, scribbling notes in his margins to update the ever growing mortality figures. It works for a time, and then his audiences grow bored with the death count, and he must think of new ways to satisfy their demands for novelty.

But the enduring difference between Shilts's story and those that were written by Banaszynski and me is that he places the personal tragedies that are AIDS into a social and political context in a way that reminds me of Didion's *Miami*. He details how the stock NIH responses that AIDS drugs were forever "in the pipeline" were the direct result of the Reagan administration's willingness to fund only 11 of 127 positions requested by Dr. Anthony Fauchi, associate NIH director for AIDS. "The lives of 1.5 million HIV-infected Americans hung in the balance, and the only way you could get a straight answer out of an administration official," says Shilts, "was to put him under oath and make him face the charge of perjury. Where I went to journalism school, *that* was a story" (237).

But the reporters to whom Shilts suggests the story only want to know what actor will play Shilts in the television miniseries of *And the Band Played On*. So Shilts fashions ever more glib, ever more effective responses on the talk shows, and his friend Kit Herman dies in excruciatingly slow tortured stages. And then Shilts cracks on a radio call-in show in the San Fernando Valley and begins to scream in an insane rage, which, the article suggests, is his first sane response to the crisis. In his mind he hears the "dissembling" NIH researchers go home to their wives at night and "complain about the lack of personnel" and sees them shrug in frustration:

> They'd excuse their inaction by telling themselves that if they went public and lost their jobs, worse people would replace them. It was best to go along. But how would they feel if *their* friends, *their* daughters, were dying of the disease? Would they be silent—or would they shout? Maybe they'll forgive me for suspecting they believed that

ultimately a bunch of fags weren't worth losing a job over.
And when I got home, I was going to have to watch my
friends get shoved into powder-blue vans [on their way to
the morgue], and it wasn't going to change. (245, Shilts's
emphases)

In San Francisco gay men and lesbians have the economic and political power to ensure that a reporter who writes such an article still will have
a job at one of the city's two principal daily newspapers. Elsewhere it is more
difficult. In Charlottesville, a town where doctors number a higher propor-
tion of the population than in any city except Rochester, Minnesota, home
of Mayo Clinic, readers and editors will respond far more gracefully to a
story that depicts the AIDS patients as individuals whose heroic doctors are
struggling against all odds to save them. There is no time or money to assign
a reporter like Shilts to uncover the complicity that government policy shares
in a continuing health emergency.

I am insisting that the deaths of "John," of Dick Hanson, of Kit
Herman carry a special sting because they are characters in nonfiction and
as such are irreplaceable. Certainly fictional depictions, such as the widely
seen motion picture *Philadelphia,* also have the power to implicate many
viewers and to produce real changes in the way straight audiences perceive
gay men and others who are dying from the AIDS pandemic. Moreover,
Philadelphia's moment of death is shot from the point of view of the patient
as his lover, family, and friends look on in consternation, thus avoiding the
presentation of the inevitable death scene only from the top-down point of
view of the survivors. But I am also insisting that the vast majority of audiences are aware that Tom Hanks, the actor, will stand up and walk away from
the bed as soon as the cameras stop rolling. He retains the aura of actor, not
the sting of actual death.[4] In fact, many viewers—particularly younger
ones—were far more affected by the death of Pedro Zamora on MTV's *Real
World* than by Tom Hanks's "death" in *Philadelphia.* Despite the many obviously scripted moments of *The Real World,* its characters are actual and the
audience developed a relatively intense identification with them over the
months of the series, particularly with Zamora. The revelation that Zamora
had AIDS and his willingness to talk about his experience during the months
that the disease progressed gained tremendously effective implications, in
my judgment, and his eventual death carried a tangibility and focus that for
me and many other viewers surpassed that of the fictional character in
Philadelphia.

Similarly, as I close the book on "AIDS in the Heartland" I see how at last the stories that Banaszynski wrote—despite their many values—position their readers far differently than does Shilts. As a reader I am permitted to walk away from Dick Hanson's bedside, or at least it seems so from Banaszynski's articles. But neither Shilts, nor I as his reader, can walk away so easily. His piece, as they all do, ends at the bedside of a dying man, his friend Kit Herman. The two discuss their frustration at how the longer that Shilts works to uncover the scandal of AIDS policy, the more it seems to be ignored. Herman, who the day before has tried unsuccessfully to take his own life with an overdose of morphine, tells Shilts that the reporter has got to keep trying: "Kit closed his eyes briefly and faded into sleep while plastic tubes fed him a cornucopia of antibiotics. After five minutes, he stirred, looked up, and added, as if we had never stopped talking, 'But you don't really have a choice. You've got to keep doing it. What else are you going to do?'" (246).

Three years after his essay was printed in *Esquire,* and less than a decade after the publication of *And the Band Played On,* Shilts died of complications caused by the HIV virus. A bout of pneumocystic pneumonia in August 1992 signaled his contraction of fully developed AIDS. He had known he was HIV-positive since the day he had finished the manuscript of *And the Band Played On* in 1987 (Schmaltz G6), though he did not disclose that fact in his *Esquire* essay. But the evidence in that essay is everywhere, I now see. And it raises the stakes of his narrative and explains what I thought I had intuited from Shilts's text. "[Y]ou don't really have a choice," his dying friend told Shilts (246). As it turned out, Shilts didn't. And his readers don't either. "Yeah, I have a good life," he told the *New York Times's* Jeffrey Schmaltz. "I'd be a lot happier if I didn't have to worry about dying" (G6).

Sometimes the readers of nonfiction narratives would be a whole lot happier as well if we didn't have to worry about the sting of actual death in the narratives we read. But as the next chapter will show, a method of reading nonfiction narrative as an engaged reader from the outside in will defeat the possibility of such an easy reading. It turns out that facts matter when they intersect with the lives of actual writers and readers outside the written artifact even if those facts are difficult to ascertain and would cause some readers to abandon all distinctions between fact and fiction.

5.

READING OUTSIDE IN:

Over the Edge of Genre in the Case of Private O'Brien

READING OUTSIDE IN MEANS TO ASSESS outside knowledge (including one's own memory) against the knowledge constructed by a narrative that is nonfictional or depicts the lives of flesh-and-blood characters whose presences spill outside the text. Read in that fashion, contemporary American novelist and sometime journalist Tim O'Brien enacts across the body of his work the epistemological stakes of representation that lie at the forefront of a critical discussion of history and textuality. Perhaps best known as the author of *Going after Cacciato,* the winner of the 1979 National Book Award in fiction, O'Brien obsessively blurs the lines of fact and fiction in his half-dozen major texts about Vietnam—some of which he has portrayed as truth and others as invention. O'Brien has never written a line of nonfiction whose factual status he has not contested at some other moment of his writing. For example, he has presented himself as a historical character in his nonfiction memoirs of Vietnam (*If I Die in a Combat Zone*); enacted himself as an equally plausible character in his fictional memoirs of Vietnam (*The Things They Carried*); altered the names of living characters and events in his nonfiction; constructed the extratextual identity of his fictional characters so compellingly that he could dedicate a book to them; caused historical characters like Lieutenant William Laws Calley Jr. to confront fictional characters in the dialogue of his recent novel, *In the Lake of the Woods;* blended scrupulously researched footnotes to that novel with others that just as surely are invented; and re-created key scenes of reunion trips to Vietnam ostensibly experienced before he made those trips in history.

Yet with all that blurring—whose summative effect would seem to pose O'Brien as the poster boy for theorists who collapse meaningful distinctions between fact and fiction—no major writer so clearly insists on his own accounting and on his readers' accounting for the status of outside events through and against text. For O'Brien, the outside/inside question of truth matters. His varying texts will afford me a sustained opportunity to build on everything that I have tried to establish in this study—that is, how the text of events intersects the written text, how different written texts intersect with each other, and how the inescapable presence of human subjects makes facts matter in nonfictional stories.

In his texts O'Brien prowls and reprowls the horror of Vietnam's "Pinkville" Quang Ngai province: from that day on March 16, 1968, when Calley's Charlie Company killed anywhere from 343 to 504 Vietnamese women, teenagers, infants, and old men at My Lai until slightly more than a year later when O'Brien's Alpha Company trudged over the same "Pinkville" turf and O'Brien saw his buddy, Chip Merricks, blown into a hedge of bamboo (*Lake* 301, "Vietnam" 53). O'Brien is haunted by Vietnam because actual people have died, most overwhelmingly the Vietnamese and, significantly, members of the platoon with which O'Brien marched. His writing—whether presented as fiction or nonfiction—never lets him or his readers retreat from the combat zone of factual implication into the safe zone where text consumes all and outside facts do not matter.

My reading of O'Brien's writings places me squarely at odds with such critics as Steven Kaplan, who contends that O'Brien's genre-bending style exemplifies Wolfgang Iser's theory that what happens inside texts "is relieved of the consequences inherent in the real world referred to" (48). Of O'Brien's *The Things They Carried* Kaplan argues, "The facts about what actually happened, or whether anything happened at all, are not important. They cannot be important because they themselves are too uncertain, too lost in a world in which certainty had vanished somewhere between the 'crazy and almost crazy'" (49). My contention, by contrast, is that although certainty may have vanished in O'Brien's universe, the facts most certainly *are important* to him, even as they are important to the reader posited by the epigraph to this book, the one who wonders, "Is it true?" and cares deeply about the answer. O'Brien forces his American readers, particularly those of age during the Vietnam War, to experience their implication in history in more than academic terms and to bring that history inside the text created by the nonfiction account.

In so doing O'Brien engages the troubling interrelation of history and textuality in holocaust narrative: a flashpoint issue for theorists who have abandoned a positivist view of history. Historiographer Hayden White sums up the stakes of the argument in *The Content of the Form* by voicing the doubts of his detractors in a series of rhetorical questions:

> Do you imply that any account of [the Holocaust] is as valid as any other account so long as it meets certain formal requirements of discursive practices and that one has no responsibility to the victims to tell the truth about the indignities and cruelties they suffered? Are there not certain historical events that tolerate none of that mere cleverness that allows criminals or their admirers to feign accounts of their crimes that effectively relieve them of their guilt or responsibility or even, in the worst instances, allows them to maintain that the crimes they committed never happened? (76)[1]

White ultimately argues for an engagement with Holocaust history that almost exactly mirrors O'Brien's continuing project. Resisting a positivist view of the past does not mean that one avoids its implications, White contends, insisting instead that historians adopt "a conception of the historical record as being not a window through which the past 'as it really was' can be apprehended but rather as a wall that must be broken through if the 'terror of history' is to be directly confronted" (82).

O'Brien batters his head against that very wall in his writings about Vietnam's Quang Ngai province. Vietnam is our holocaust, he suggests; we caused it, and we must reckon with that guilt. In a range of texts written over nearly twenty years O'Brien has never claimed anything other than that he was a moral coward for not resisting the Vietnam War when he was drafted, and he forces his reader toward that same sort of honest revelation. In "The Vietnam in Me," a remarkably tortured confessional of his February 1994 trip back to Vietnam, O'Brien complains that his discussion of My Lai in American high schools and colleges these days mostly brings on "dull stares, a sort of puzzlement, disbelief" (52) as our nation reinvents its history in the texts by which it evades responsibility. "Now, more than 25 years later, evil has been pushed off to the margins of memory," O'Brien says in the *Times* piece, "Evil has no place, it seems, in our national mythology. We erase it. We use ellipses. We salute ourselves and take pride in America the White

Knight, America the Lone Ranger, America's sleek laser-guided weaponry beating up on Saddam and his legion of devils" (52).

I have chosen O'Brien as the culminating demonstration of this study because his writing demands the sort of outside/inside engagement of history and text for which I have argued throughout. The status of truth is always problematic for O'Brien. He takes advantage of the conventions of fiction, memoir, and journalism even as he deconstructs them. He defeats the possibility that truth can ever be certain at the same time he defeats the possibility that truth can be marked off from the texts' claims. To demonstrate these contentions, I will look closely at the four O'Brien texts centered in Vietnam's "Pinkville" district: *If I Die in a Combat Zone* (1973), *The Things They Carried* (1990), *In the Lake of the Woods* (1994), and "The Vietnam in Me" (1994).[2] O'Brien presents the four texts respectively as non-fictional memoir; as a series of interrelated stories that, while fictional in several details, also makes use of many of the same facts as did the earlier memoir; as a fictional novel, albeit one that makes use of several actual characters, the documentary apparatus of footnotes, and a metafictional narrator who strongly resembles in many historical details the actual O'Brien; and as nonfictional reportage in the "all the news that's fit to print" newspaper whose traditional claims of fact-checking give O'Brien a strong, if thoroughly contested, aura of truth status.

What makes the quartet of texts intriguing (and the point from which I will begin my discussion with a reading of the texts from the outside in) is that O'Brien covers and adjusts many of the same events within the various textual conventions that he adopts and challenges. Once I have demonstrated that pattern of intertextuality, I will show how O'Brien constructs himself in all four texts as a character and author deeply implicated in the horror of Vietnam and positions his readers—both inside and outside the written text—in a complicated interplay with his own history and authority. Finally, in White's terms, I will demonstrate—through the outside in reading of My Lai and its aftermath—how O'Brien batters through the wall of history and text to make the terror of Vietnam matter to his readers.

The essentials of O'Brien's Vietnam narratives are remarkably similar, though they are not so developed in the shorter "The Vietnam in Me" as in *If I Die in a Combat Zone* and *The Things They Carried* and are complicated by the separation of narrator from main character in *In the Lake of the Woods*. A college-educated native of Minnesota is drafted amid a conscience-tortured summer and fall of 1968 in which he seriously considers draft resistance or Army desertion; the soldier loses his nerve to resist and is placed in a platoon of Army grunts chiefly stationed in Quang Ngai province; the soldier fires on a Vietnamese silhouette he sees walking along a trail near the My Lai villages in "Pinkville"; the soldier's best friend steps on a mine and is blown into a tree or hedge; the soldier later walks into an ambush in a drainage field (or "shitfield") near the village of My Khe 3 that results in the deaths and maiming of several other friends; the soldier enters a Quang Ngai province village with a vengeful platoon and witnesses atrocities; the soldier's platoon stumbles onto a beach on the South China Sea to the east of the My Lai villages that is more beautiful than anything he has ever seen although its waters are mined and deadly; the soldier ultimately is rotated to back-line duty near Landing Zone Gator; the soldier's tour ends and he is flown back to the United States in a single day, changing from his Army issue to civilian clothes in a rest room at the rear of the aircraft on his final flight connection into Minneapolis St. Paul.

  If I Die in a Combat Zone positions its narrator as an earnest young veteran eager to tell what he has learned of war and bravery as well as of the awful confusion, death, and waste he has seen in Vietnam. O'Brien writes in his own name, although he tells us in an author's note that the "names and physical characteristics of persons depicted in this book have been changed" (7). In the book O'Brien reveals that he went to war because he was trapped in "an intellectual and physical standoff, and I did not have the energy to see it to its end" (31). While stationed at Fort Lewis, Washington, O'Brien secures a weekend pass to Seattle and packs an AWOL bag, ready to desert the army for Vancouver. A long night in his hotel room ends with his vomiting bile and deciding not to desert because "I was a coward. I was sick" (73). He summarizes the moral stakes of his decision in unequivocal confession: "I was persuaded then, and I remain persuaded now, that the war was wrong. And since it was wrong and since people were dying as a result of it, it was evil" (26).

  O'Brien presents *The Things They Carried* as "a work of fiction." Except for "a few details regarding the author's own life," he claims, "all the incidents, names, and characters are imaginary" (copyright page). Yet the book's narrator shares much in common with the earlier war memoir's narrator, including the long tortured night of the soul which ends in the vomiting capitulation to military service. Here the narrator (called "Tim," or "Timmy," or "O'Brien" at several locations in the book) spends a week during the summer of 1968 on the Rainy River that separates Minnesota from Canada, contemplating flight to avoid the draft. An old man befriends the narrator and offers him the means to escape on a boat, but the narrator ultimately decides to serve. Like O'Brien in his memoir, the "O'Brien" who is the narrator of *The Things They Carried* recognizes that his decision to fight in Vietnam was nothing short of an act of cowardice: "What it came down to, stupidly, was a sense of shame. Hot stupid shame" (54); "Embarrassment, that's all it was. And right then I submitted. I would go to war—I would kill and maybe die—because I was embarrassed not to. That was the sad thing" (62); and "I was a coward. I went to war" (63).

In "The Vietnam in Me" O'Brien writes in his own name in a *New York Times Magazine* text that accompanies pictures of the author during his 1994 trip back to the My Lai area where he had served. His confession of his Vietnam War participation, viewed backward over more than twenty-five years and anchored by the depiction of his physical presence in the text's accompanying photographs, is again unequivocal: "I thought about Canada. I thought about jail. But in the end I could not bear the prospect of rejection: by my family, my country, my friends, my hometown. I would risk conscience and rectitude before risking the loss of love. I have written some of this before, but I must write it again. I was a coward. I went to Vietnam" (52). Even in *In the Lake of the Woods*, where O'Brien complicates his presence by appearing as an unnamed "narrator" in several of the novel's footnote sections, the echoes are unmistakable. That narrator reveals (as O'Brien has in his nonfictional and fictional memoirs) that he served in the "Pinkville" district almost a year after Calley's company and patrolled the same Quang Ngai villages. The tone again is confessional. "Twenty-five years ago, as a terrified young PFC, I too could taste the sunlight," the narrator says. "I could smell the sin. I could feel the butchery sizzling like grease just under my eyeballs" (203n).

To understand how the varying narratives position their author and readers I shall take a close look at the texts' construction of the soldier's firing on the enemy and of the death that same day of the narrator's friend and fellow soldier, characterized variously as Chip, Curt Lemon, or Chip Merricks. In *If I Die in a Combat Zone*, O'Brien tells his readers that he saw "the living enemy" only once in Vietnam: three silhouettes tiptoeing out of a hamlet near My Lai while O'Brien's unit had staged a predawn ambush of one of the villages: "They were twenty yards away, crouching over, their shoulders hunched over. It was the first and only time I would ever see the living enemy, the man intent on killing me. . . . We stood straight up, in a row, as if it were a contest. I confronted the profile of a human being through my sight. It did not occur to me that a man would die when I pulled the trigger of that rifle. I neither hated the man nor wanted him dead, but I feared him. Johansen fired. I fired. The figures disappeared in a flash of my muzzle" (101–2). When the unit checks the casualties at dawn, they find one dead man with a bullet hole in his head and are uncertain which one of the three has killed him or if another body or bodies has been dragged away. For his part, "I could not look," O'Brien reports, though he hopes the dead man is not named "Li," a North Vietnamese lieutenant whom O'Brien had met on a college trip to Prague in 1967 and with whom O'Brien had discussed the war late into the night (97–99).

The "O'Brien" character in *The Things They Carried* raises the stakes of the episode considerably; this time he is unable to stop looking at the man killed by gunfire. O'Brien first reveals the killing in a chapter called "Spin," in which he constructs his narrative presence as a forty-three-year-old author (his actual age at the time of the book's writing, though the narrator, unlike the actual O'Brien, has a daughter) still obsessed by war stories (38). Later, in a chapter he entitles "The Man I Killed," O'Brien supplies the physical detail of the body that he had refused to witness in *Combat Zone*: "there was a butterfly on his chin, his neck was open to the spinal cord and the blood there was thick and shiny and it was this wound that had killed him. He lay face-up in the center of the trail, a slim, dead, almost dainty young man" (139).

O'Brien's narrator imagines the life that ended on the trail as a life that virtually doubles his own: the same birth year, a university background, a soldier who "in the presence of his father and uncles, pretended to look forward to doing his patriotic duty," but who at night prays for peace (142). In the story, as his friend Kiowa urges him to shake the guilt and move on, O'Brien's narrator is unable either to talk to Kiowa or to look away from the dead man's face.

> The blood at the neck had gone to a deep purplish black. Clean fingernails, clean hair—he had been a soldier for only a single day. After his years at the university, the man I killed returned with his new wife to the village of My Khe, where he enlisted as a common rifleman with the 48th Vietcong Battalion. He knew he would die quickly. He knew he would see a flash of light. He knew he would

fall dead and wake up in the stories of his village and
people. . . . He was a slim, dead, almost dainty young man
of about twenty, his face neither expressive nor inexpres-
sive. One eye was shut. The other was a star-shaped hole.
"Talk," Kiowa said. (144)

In "Ambush," the following chapter of *The Things They Carried,*
the narrator "O'Brien" discusses the war with his daughter, who asks him
why he continues to write war stories and if he killed anyone in Vietnam. He
tells the daughter he has not killed anyone, but the reader is expected to
understand here that the narrator is not telling the truth, even if O'Brien,
the author (who does not have a daughter), is uncertain whether he actually
killed anyone on the trail that day in Vietnam. In "Ambush," the narrator
"O'Brien" recalls the killing and imagines a different ending:

Even now I haven't finished sorting it out. Sometimes I
forgive myself, other times I don't. In the ordinary hours
of life I try not to dwell on it, but now and then, when I'm
reading a newspaper or just sitting alone in a room, I'll look
up and see the young man coming out of the morning
fog. I'll watch him walk toward me, his shoulders slightly
stooped, his head cocked to the side, and he'll pass within
a few yards of me and suddenly smile at some secret
thought and then continue up the trail to where it bends
back into the fog. (149–50)

Reading inside the texts, most readers will experience something
far different in *If I Die in a Combat Zone* than in *The Things They Carried.*
In the first book O'Brien presents a scene in which the standards of truthfulness seem relatively secure even if all the facts aren't known. Both O'Brien
and his reader are allowed to turn away from the body on the trail, and
O'Brien depends for irony on the reader's linking the name "Li" with the
North Vietnamese soldier O'Brien had befriended in Prague. In the second
book truth seems far less secure, though ironically more important. O'Brien's
method forces the reader into what Frus calls a "reflexive" reading and one
that I would call "implicated": a struggle to understand the difference between what happened and what did not, even as O'Brien complicates (and
virtually collapses) that difference. O'Brien takes much more pains in the

second text to build reader identification with the Vietnamese soldier, using his power of imagination to construct a life for the soldier that mirrors the life of the American. The reader—even inside the text—recognizes that the narrator tells a lie to his daughter about his culpability in the death, which derails both our identification with that narrator and his reliability as a narrator.

Finally, O'Brien's narrator complicates the truth status even further by having his narrator assert in a later chapter, titled "Good Form," that "It's time to be blunt." The narrator admits that, "I'm forty-three years old, true, and I'm a writer now, and a long time ago I walked through Quang Ngai Province as a foot soldier." He says he watched a man die on the trail but did not kill him, then moments later says, "But listen. Even *that* story is made up." O'Brien's narrator distinguishes between "story-truth" and "happening-truth" and concludes this to be "happening-truth": "I was once a soldier. There were many bodies, real bodies with real faces, but I was young then and I was afraid to look. And now, twenty years later, I'm left with faceless responsibility and faceless grief" (202). The narrative thus doubles back toward the "truth" that O'Brien had revealed in *If I Die in a Combat Zone:* someone died on the trail, and O'Brien does not know if he caused that death.

The Things They Carried, through its multileveled, even palimpsest presentation, succeeds in questioning not only whether truth can be fixed but also whether O'Brien can be trusted to tell the truth even if he could know it. In that way the book reenacts the epistemological challenge that is the history of U.S. involvement in Vietnam. What does the reader do with an author who declares in the middle of a "story" that he is about to tell the "happening truth," by which he appears to mean facts that transcend text, even as the text consumes their telling? Of course the O'Brien who wrote *The Things They Carried* could always wink at his reader and say, "I told you on the title and copyright pages that this is 'a work of fiction' and that 'except for a few details regarding the author's own life, all the incidents, names and characters are imaginary.'" The reader encountering O'Brien's work across the varying texts, however, would do well to refuse that easy solution, even if it might satisfy a scholar who depends for truth status solely on the author's intent or a scholar who ascribes no meaning to events that underlie text.

O'Brien insists on the importance of those events in the case of his friend Alvin "Chip" Merricks, an African-American specialist fourth class from Orlando, Florida, whom Vietnam War casualty lists document as having been killed on May 9, 1969, while O'Brien's unit was in Quang Ngai province.[3] In *If I Die in a Combat Zone* O'Brien calls the soldier "Chip" and reveals that he and a squad leader named Tom were "blown to pieces" as they swept one of the My Lai villages (101). O'Brien later discusses the deaths in more detail in a chapter called "Step Lightly."

> More destructive than the Bouncing Betty are the booby-trapped mortar and artillery rounds. They hang from trees. They nestle in shrubbery. They lie under the sand. They wait beneath the mud floors of huts. They haunted us. Chip, my black buddy from Orlando, strayed into a hedge-row and triggered a rigged 105 artillery round. He died in such a way that, for once, you could never know his color. He was wrapped in a plastic body bag, we popped smoke, and a helicopter took him away, my friend. (125)

In "The Vietnam in Me," the other Vietnam narrative that O'Brien presents as nonfiction, he amplifies his memory of Chip. O'Brien reveals that he and Chip wrote letters to each other's sisters and that they were called "Black and White" by their platoon mates because of their inseparability in combat, even if they had to go their separate ways "by color, both of us ashamed" at the rear (51). O'Brien writes in the *New York Times* account, published in 1994, that "Chip was blown high into a hedge of bamboo. Many pieces. I loved the guy, he loved me. I'm alive. He's dead. An old story, I guess" (51).

If the nonfiction accounts of Chip's death present the factual book-ends, O'Brien's fictional accounts unpack the emotional toll of Chip's death even as they complicate the factuality. For example, the details of Chip's death show up in a footnote to the fictional *In the Lake of the Woods*, published the same year as "The Vietnam in Me," and establish an important link between the facts of O'Brien's life (backed up by independent Vietnam casualty records) and the identity of the unnamed narrator who repeatedly inserts his own voice into the novel's documentation. Near the end of the novel (which I will discuss in more detail in the last third of this chapter) O'Brien's unnamed narrator footnotes a comment about the novel's protagonist with a list of war memories that directly recalls key scenes from O'Brien's nonfiction. "For me, after a quarter century," the narrator writes, "nothing much remains of that ugly war. A handful of splotchy images. My company commander bending over a dead soldier, wiping the man's face with a towel. A lieutenant with a bundled corpse over his shoulder like a great sack of bird feed. My own hands. A buddy's bewildered eyes. A kid named Chip Merricks soaring into a tree. A patch of rice paddy bubbling with machine-gun fire. Everything else is a smudge of hedgerows and trails and land mines and snipers and death" (301n).

Several facts of these accounts resonate for an outside in reading of O'Brien's work: the revelation from "The Vietnam in Me" that O'Brien and Chip wrote letters to each other's sisters and the description in the *In the Lake of the Woods* footnote of Chip Merricks's "soaring into a tree." In both cases, the details recall key scenes of perhaps the most harrowing and widely anthologized chapter from the ostensibly fictional *The Things They Carried* collection: "How to Tell a True War Story." The chapter details the death of one "Curt Lemon," an American soldier who died when a "booby-trapped 105 round blew him into a tree" (89). As was the shooting of the Vietnamese soldier on the trail, the scene is foreshadowed in the "Spin" chapter, in which the "Tim O'Brien" narrator sits at his typewriter and stares through his words into memory: "Curt Lemon steps from the shade into bright sunlight, his face brown and shining, and then he soars into a tree" (36).

"How to Tell a True War Story" organizes itself in an ever tightening spiral whose horrifying core is that moment when the narrator and a soldier named Dave Jensen must climb the tree to throw down the pieces of what remains of Curt Lemon. "I remember the white bone of an arm. I remember pieces of skin and something wet and yellow that must've been the intestines," the narrator says. ". . . But what wakes me up twenty years later is Dave Jensen singing 'Lemon Tree' as we threw down the parts" (89). The dead soldier's name[4] seems calculated to resonate the lyrics of the popular song: "Lemon tree very pretty / and the lemon flower is sweet / but the fruit of the poor lemon / is impossible to eat," but the details of face and dismemberment seem to recall Chip Merricks's death for the author.

Other links between "How to Tell a True War Story" and both earlier and later narratives include the reference to writing letters to sisters, which O'Brien carefully inserts in his subsequent 1994 *New York Times* piece. In "How to Tell a True War Story," Curt Lemon's sister never writes back to the American G.I. who provides her an emotional recounting of Lemon's death. And the story's most harrowing scene—the torture of a "baby VC water buffalo" by that vengeful G.I.—echoes the moment in *If I*

Die in a Combat Zone, where, in response to the never-ending tension of the mines and mortars that had killed Chip and other fellow soldiers, the soldiers opened fire on several boys and a cow who had strayed into a free-fire zone. What follows reminds O'Brien of target practice in boot camp at Fort Lewis: "The boys escaped, but one cow stood its ground. Bullets struck its flanks, exploding globs of flesh, boring into its belly. The cow stood parallel to the soldiers, a wonderful profile. It looked away, in a single direction, and it did not move. I did not shoot, but I did endure, without protest, except to ask the man in front of me why he was shooting and smiling" (139).

In the "How to Tell a True War Story" version the scapegoat beast becomes a "baby VC water buffalo" shot by Curt Lemon's companion Rat Kiley after Lemon's death.

> Rat took careful aim and shot off an ear. He shot it in the hindquarters and in the little hump at its back. He shot it twice in the flanks. It wasn't to kill; it was to hurt. He put the rifle muzzle up against the mouth and shot the mouth away. . . . He shot off the tail. He shot away chunks of meat below the ribs. All around us there was the smell of smoke and filth and deep greenery, and the evening was humid and very hot. Rat went to automatic. He shot randomly, almost casually, quick little spurts in the belly and butt. Then he reloaded, squatted down, and shot it in the left front knee. Again the animal fell hard and tried to get up, but this time it couldn't quite make it. It wobbled and went down sideways. Rat shot it in the nose. He bent forward and whispered something, as if talking to a pet, then he shot it in the throat. (85–86)

"How to Tell a True War Story," and indeed the entire *The Things They Carried* cycle, appears to be calculated to make its readers care desperately about truth and responsibility even as it is calculated to frustrate any effort to pin down some sort of exact truth about what happened. "If the answer matters, you've got your answer" (89), O'Brien's narrator says of its truth claim. But he undermines certainty at every turn: "It's all exactly true. It happened, to *me,* nearly twenty years ago" (77), he says at one moment, then later, "in a true war story nothing is ever absolutely true" (88), and still later, "No Lemon . . . beginning to end . . . it's all made up" (91). It is this sort of multileveled claim, each level of which can flip or cancel out another claim, that causes a critic like Steven Kaplan to conclude that O'Brien "liberates himself from the lonesome responsibility of remembering and trying to understand events" and creates a community of readers who understand that "events have no fixed and final meaning" (51).

My sense, however, is that O'Brien, both in this text and in later Vietnam narratives, wants to do anything but "liberate" himself or his readers from the responsibility and anxiety for our culpability in deaths like those of Chip Merricks or the Vietnamese soldier on the trail. For in "How to Tell a True War Story" O'Brien saves his most withering vitriol for an unnamed listener who "likes" the artistry of his story about Curt Lemon's death, especially the water buffalo scene, which made her weep a bit, and who suggests that O'Brien "put it all behind me. Find new stories to tell" (90).[5] By building clear links between Curt Lemon's fictional death and the nonfictional death of Chip Merricks in his earlier and subsequent Vietnam narratives, O'Brien refuses to mark off Merricks's death—even in its evocation as the death of Curt Lemon—as another closed chapter in another fictional narrative. What he is after is implication, not "liberation" from that responsibility. Inside the texts, O'Brien positions his readers in the uncomfortable stance of knowing that one bears responsibility for the evil one sees, even if one is never quite certain that the "truth" can be determined and thus disarmed of its tension.

Tracing the narrative presence that O'Brien constructs for himself in the texts is one good way to unmask O'Brien's sense of personal implication as we begin to shift our strategy toward an outside in reading of O'Brien's work (that is, one that considers the text in light of what we know of its author and characters in history). O'Brien shoulders increased responsibility and willingness to implicate himself as his work progresses. He moves from a relatively straight depiction of himself in *If I Die in a Combat Zone* as a young veteran confused about what happened in the Vietnam War to a depiction that consistently undercuts its own authority. In *The Things They Carried* O'Brien makes his readers wonder how much he can be trusted, what is true or not true, and whether he can hold a confidence. Finally, in "The Vietnam in Me" and *In the Lake of the Woods*, both published in 1994, O'Brien appears to want to implicate himself much more deeply as a historical character: names and key dates become more specific, and O'Brien provides more distinction between facts and imaginative text, although he never offers himself or his readers an easy way to mark off truth and thus dismiss anxiety.

In *If I Die in a Combat Zone,* O'Brien presents himself as an observer capable of presenting a truthful, if never quite certain, record of his experience in Vietnam. As Maria S. Bonn has shown, O'Brien seems to subscribe to the Platonic ideal that the citizen can demonstrate the "terribleness" of war "by creating a straight historical text rather than a fictional one" (6). But if that is so, then O'Brien also finds the certainty of that assertion slipping away from him as the book progresses. Early in the book O'Brien had trusted in his friendship with Erik Hanson at boot camp in Fort Lewis for the honest discussions that might help him resist the dehumanization of the war machine. "[T]alking about basic training in careful, honest words was by itself an insult to army education," he suggests. "Simply to think and talk and try to understand was evidence that we were not cattle or machines" (43). Now, war ended, "all I am left with are simple, profound scraps of truth," he says. "Men died. Fear hurts and humiliates. It is hard to be brave" (31).

That movement toward uncertainty is exemplified by the "Step Lightly" chapter, wherein O'Brien sets out to catalogue all of the varieties of enemy land mines in an effort to build some predictability in the midst of what a fellow soldier calls the "absurdity" of walking on mined land, "the certainty that you're walking in the mine fields, walking past the things day after day; the uncertainty of your every movement" (127). But as O'Brien strives to place each of the devices in its proper file and describe their effects in precise unemotional language, the hidden bombs do their damage, including taking the life of his friend Chip. The occasion leads to a device that O'Brien will develop and complicate much further in subsequent books: the method of questioning his writing while he writes, of recognition that the very act of "making sense" of senseless war is in its own way part of the problem:

> In the three days I spent writing this, mines and men came together three more times. Seven more legs, one more arm. The immediacy of the last explosion—three legs, ten minutes ago—made me ready to burn the midsection of this report, the flippant itemization of these killer devices. . . . But only to say another truth will I let the half-truths stand. The catalog of mines will be retained, because that is how we talked about them, with a funny laugh, flippantly, with a chuckle. It is funny. It is absurd. (129)

Second-guessing his own perspective is complicated to an almost infinite degree by *The Things They Carried*. Not only is its truth status equivocal, as I have demonstrated previously, but O'Brien willfully undercuts his own authority at almost every turn even as he implicates himself historically. The book's most developed stories—"The Things They Carried," "How to Tell a True War Story," "The Man I Killed," "Speaking of Courage" and "In the Field"—are each qualified by a later chapter in which O'Brien comments on their creation from the perspective of a writer with an astonishing number of similarities to the actual author. Writing about the book, *New York Times* reviewer D. J. R. Bruckner contends that this "writer" and the actual author are originally from Minnesota and forty-three but that "everything else, even most of the convincing personal details about his life and family, is made up" (16). But, as I have already shown by the links to O'Brien's firing on the soldier on the trail and his loss of Chip Merricks, the link between the actual O'Brien and his narrative presence is far stronger.

One example is the story "Speaking of Courage" and its aftermath story, "Notes." Here, O'Brien writes about the return of fellow soldier Norman Bowker to an Iowa town where no one much cares about his experiences in Vietnam. Updating Hemingway's "Soldier's Home" to the Vietnam era, "Speaking of Courage" depicts Bowker driving idly around the town's central lake, composing a mental conversation with his father (who doesn't really care enough to talk to his son and is home watching baseball on television) about a failure of moral courage that abandoned his buddy Kiowa to sink to his death in a "shit field" near the My Lai villages:

> And then he would have talked about the medal he did not
> win and why he did not win it.
> "I almost won the Silver Star," he would have said.
> "How's that?"
> "Just a story."
> "So tell me," his father would have said. (161)

As Bowker continues around the lake he circles closer and closer to the kernel of his hypothetical conversation with his father—a structure that echoes the spiraling search for truth of "How to Tell a True War Story." What comes out as Bowker circles is that his friend "Kiowa slipped away that night beneath the dark swampy field" while Bowker backs off and watches him and the Silver Star disappear. "'The truth,' Norman Bowker would've said [on the eleventh revolution of the lake], 'is I let the guy go'" (172). On his twelfth revolution, "the sky went crazy with color," and Bowker wades into the lake without undressing, watching the town's Fourth of July fireworks: "For a small town, he decided, a pretty good show" (172–73).

"Speaking of Courage" is an achingly successful story, full of regret and bitter irony, but O'Brien presses it into more unsettling service than if one were to read it solely within its boundaries. In the "Notes" chapter that immediately follows the narrator "O'Brien" discusses the story's genesis in terms that intersect startlingly with what we know of O'Brien's own life and build a complicated metafictional—indeed meta-nonfictional—web. The story, the narrator tells us, was written after Bowker read *If I Die in a Combat Zone*, recognized himself as one of O'Brien's characters "even though almost all of the names were changed" (178), and challenged the narrator "O'Brien" to write a story about a veteran who "wants to talk about it, but he can't" (179). The narrator explains that he wrote the story as a chapter of *Going after Cacciato*, changed Bowker's name to that novel's protagonist, Paul Berlin, and lifted the setting from O'Brien's home town of Worthington, Minnesota. Although the narrator doesn't say it, the device of circling the town's lake almost certainly comes from O'Brien's own experience in the months before he was drafted, "driv[ing] a car around and around the town's lake, talking about the war . . . trying to make it a dialogue and not a debate" (*Combat Zone* 25).

The narrator "O'Brien" recalls in "Notes" that he abandoned the chapter of *Going after Cacciato*, published it as "Speaking of Courage" in a small magazine and then in an anthology, and sent the story to Bowker for comment. "'It's not terrible,' he wrote me, 'but you left out Vietnam. Where's Kiowa? Where's the shit?' Eight months later he hanged himself" (181). The narrator O'Brien then reveals that he has rewritten the story, placed Bowker's "real" name in it, and for the first time told the true story of Kiowa and the shit field. The "real name" status, of course, is decentered both by the story's publication in the ostensibly fictional *The Things They Carried* collection and by the book's dedication to Bowker, among other (presumably fictional) members of Alpha Company. "Norman is back in the story, where he belongs," the narrator "O'Brien" tells his readers, "and I don't think he would mind that his real name occurs" (182).

Even read inside the text the claims create the palimpsest effect that I have identified earlier in O'Brien's writing and that is related to such metafictional writing as Didion's *Democracy*, Paul Auster's *The New York*

Trilogy, or Italo Calvino's *If on a winter night a traveler,* wherein an "author" appears as a character and comments on the story's construction. What complicates O'Brien's technique, however, is that he has a body of nonfiction that (unlike Didion's work, for example) covers virtually the same events as his metafiction. Read from the outside in, O'Brien closes the distance between his historical presence and the "O'Brien" he has constructed as narrator of the story. For example, the actual O'Brien did publish an early version of "Speaking of Courage" in *The Massachusetts Review* in 1977. The story's protagonist was Paul Berlin, and the text, although many of its paragraphs are virtually verbatim to the later version, does avoid any reference to Kiowa or the shit field incident. There, the soldier who dies is named "Frenchie Tucker," and Berlin's failure of nerve is that he will not follow into a Vietcong tunnel the enemy who has shot Frenchie. Berlin thus must be dragged out of the tunnel "by his heels, losing the Silver Star" (250). Mirroring what the narrator discloses in "Notes," the early version of "Speaking of Courage" also was published in a short-story anthology, *Prize Stories: The O. Henry Awards.*

The distance between what we know of the actual Tim O'Brien and the "Tim O'Brien" who serves as the author character in *The Things They Carried* is clearly collapsed by this strategy and, as such, is much different from what Auster attempted in *The New York Trilogy.* In that novel the narrator at one point knocks on the door of a New York apartment only to have it answered by one "Paul Auster." But that "Auster" is never characterized across the boundary of fiction and fact in the manner that O'Brien accomplishes. Indeed, in discussing his trilogy Auster told interviewer Sinda Gregory that the device was an effort to confront his "author" self in the text rather than his actual self:

> I think it stemmed from a desire to implicate myself in the machinery of the book. *I don't mean my autobiographical self. I mean my author self,* that mysterious other who lives inside me and puts my name on the covers of books. What I was hoping to do, in effect, was to take my name off the cover and put it inside the story. I wanted to open the process, to break down walls, to expose the plumbing. There's a strange kind of trickery involved in the reading and writing of novels, after all. . . . It's as though no one has really written the words you're reading. I find that "no one" terri-

bly fascinating—for there's finally a profound truth to it. On the one hand it's an illusion; on the other hand, it has everything to do with how stories are written. For the author of a novel can never be sure where any of it comes from. The self that exists in the world—the self whose name appears on the covers of books—is finally not the same self who writes the books. (*Art of Hunger* 301, Auster's emphasis)

Auster's strategy with his characterized author appears to foreground the fictivity or constructedness of fiction, while O'Brien appears to want to force his readers to confront the factuality (or historical implication) that grows out of his Vietnam experience. While the actual Auster distances himself from his characterized presence in the novel ("Auster" turns out not to be the "author," who in fact is an anonymous narrator "who comes in on the last page and walks off with Quinn's red notebook" [*Art of Hunger* 301]); the actual O'Brien continuously shortens the distance between himself and his narrative alter ego as the reader learns more and more ways that O'Brien was culpable for the events his company faced in Vietnam's "Pinkville."

Read from this perspective, O'Brien rather clearly has constructed a web in which texts become interchangeable with the events that precede and follow them, as on other occasions O'Brien has reenacted the epistemological dilemma that defeats the generic certainty of either fiction or nonfiction. But what makes my approach to the narrative problems posed here unique is that I am less concerned with that generic certainty than with the alchemic reaction that arises when texts operate on flesh-and-blood characters, specifically, the way in which a text that makes use of actual events entangles its author and its characters as historical presences outside the text. For his part, O'Brien manages to implicate his narrator and ultimately himself in ways that metafictionists like Didion, Auster, or Calvino have not contemplated. And his use of actual characters who intertwine with fictional ones and force readers to negotiate the difference creates a somewhat different effect than even the most deeply implicating fictional war novels such as *A Farewell to Arms*.

For example, the "Speaking of Courage" chapter in *The Things They Carried* concludes: "Kiowa, after all, had been a close friend, and for years I've avoided thinking about his death and my own complicity in it. Even here it's not easy. In the interests of truth, however, I want to make it clear that Norman Bowker was in no way responsible for what happened to Kiowa. Norman did not experience a failure of nerve that night. He did not freeze up or lose the Silver Star for valor. That part of the story is my own" (182). What are we to make of this confession? Does O'Brien mean "my own" in the sense that it was *his* failure of nerve that doomed Kiowa or in the sense that the Kiowa plot twist is his own invention? The question is complicated further because we are reading the words of a narrator who shares many biographical details—but not all—with the author. Thus the confession potentially leaps off the pages to implicate O'Brien personally.

The strategy draws a range of responses from readers. A critic like Bruckner is unworried about O'Brien's potential implication in Kiowa's death because he believes in strict genre separation and takes at face value O'Brien's insistence on the copyright page that the book is fiction and the incidents and characters are imaginary (17). Bonn interprets the passage that "O'Brien explains that he, not Norman Bowker, was the friend unable to save Kiowa that night," although she believes that "truth" is further undercut by later qualifications in the text (13). Kaplan raises the possibility of both interpretations in a footnote, but because he collapses distinctions between fact and fiction he ultimately believes, in a move not unlike Bruckner's, though it comes from the other direction, that O'Brien takes refuge by demonstrating that "events have no fixed or final meaning" (51, 52n).

I have no definitive evidence to add here, no "proof" that O'Brien was or was not responsible for Kiowa's death in the realm of fiction or non-fiction. Vietnam casualty lists record no "Kiowa" dying in Vietnam in 1969, but what of that? It is most likely a nickname, and O'Brien has already told us the names in his book aren't actual. None of the named characters who dies in *The Things They Carried* is named on casualty lists, even though O'Brien dedicates the book to them. What counts for me is less generic certainty than the affective quality of O'Brien's approach, its ramifications for him as a storyteller and Vietnam veteran and for me and other American readers who were alive during the Vietnam years and who struggle with those memories.

O'Brien is forcing the reader to reckon with the author's credibility and ultimately with our own responsibility. What if the relatively factually secure O'Brien of the nonfictional *If I Die in a Combat Zone*—the O'Brien who witnessed atrocities but did not directly participate in them, who shot at a man but isn't certain he killed him—is the fiction? Would he be the first to lie about his implication in the war's horror? Would we be the first to be taken in by fiction masquerading as nonfiction or by nonfiction masquerading as fiction? Didn't that happen in Vietnam? In what other areas of our lives do we lie about our involvements and responsibilities? These are the dangerous questions posed by O'Brien's labyrinthine strategy in *The Things They Carried* if we refuse to take refuge in a safe zone where rigid genre rules obviate the need for careful negotiation or the equally safe zone where all is text and the facts don't matter. The strategy raises questions about truth and responsibility in a different way than does standard realistic fiction, which depends on mimetic identification rather than actual implication. "[Y]ou ask, 'Is it true?' and if the answer matters, you've got your answer" (*The Things They Carried* 69). Facts do seem to matter to O'Brien, but he won't make it easy for his reader: "Right here, now, as I invent myself, I'm thinking of all I want to tell you about why this book is written as it is" (203) the narrator "O'Brien" tells us, and we believe he speaks for the author as well.

If the metafictional qualities of *The Things They Carried* deliberately blur the boundaries of fact and fiction, O'Brien's two texts published in 1994—"The Vietnam in Me" and *In the Lake of the Woods*—appear to implicate him even more deeply as a historical character even as they require the reader to measure the texts against outside evidence. The two pieces come at the problem from different directions: "The Vietnam in Me" uses the conventions of factual journalism to hold its readers responsible for the facts of My Lai and to peel away further the persona of the relatively well-adjusted veteran that O'Brien had constructed for himself in his early nonfiction. *In the Lake of the Woods* forces its readers to negotiate a complicated interaction between invention and the factual record of the My Lai massacre.

O'Brien's narrator in *In the Lake of the Woods* continues to explore the possibility that O'Brien has more secrets in his Vietnam record than he has been willing to tell. In the same footnote that first reveals the identity of O'Brien's actual friend Chip Merricks and cites other key moments from O'Brien's war memories the narrator raises the possibility that we have not yet heard all he has done: "Behind us we left a wake of fire and smoke. We called in gunships and air strikes. We brutalized. We wasted. We pistol-whipped. We trashed wells. We kicked and punched. We burned all that would burn. Yes, and these too were atrocities—*the dirty secrets that live forever inside all of us*" (301n, emphasis added).

Although the narrator of *In the Lake of the Woods* surely is in part a fictional device, his confessions are mirrored in "The Vietnam in Me," which is presented as nonfiction in a newspaper anchored by a cadre of fact-checkers and libel attorneys. Here, during his return trip to Vietnam in 1994, while O'Brien listens to a survivor of the My Lai massacre recall her horror, he also amplifies his sense of personal responsibility in terms that directly echo the language from the *In the Lake of the Woods* footnote: "Wreckage was the rule. Brutality was S.O.P. Scalded children, pistol-whipped women, burning hootches, free-fire zones, body counts, indiscriminate bombing and harassment fire, villages in ash, M-60 machine guns hosing down dark green tree lines and any human life behind them. In a war without aim, you tend not to aim. You close your eyes, close your heart" (52–53).

Even as he confesses his involvement O'Brien uses "The Vietnam in Me" to fill in factual details raised earlier by his Vietnam narratives. In this text as well he discloses the name of his friend Chip Merricks and reveals other names of casualties in his unit that square with official Vietnam records. One of the most compelling passages sheds light on the death of Kiowa, which was dramatized (and undercut) in *The Things They Carried*'s "Speaking of Courage" and "Notes" chapters. O'Brien closes the *New York Times* narrative of his 1994 return to Vietnam by searching out the "shit field" where Kiowa died, "out along a narrow paddy dike, where suddenly the world shapes itself exactly as it was shaped a quarter-century ago" (56). Across the years O'Brien recalls "how Paige lost his lower leg, how we had to probe for McElhaney in the flooded paddy, how the gunfire went on and on" (56). The language closes the gap between Kiowa and McElhaney and points back toward a passage in *If I Die in a Combat Zone*. Official U.S. casualty records reveal that a Rodger Dennis McElhaney, an Army private first class from Jamestown, Pa., died on July 16, 1969. Thus, O'Brien reveals in the *New York Times* piece that, despite *If I Die in a Combat Zone*'s assurance that "names and physical characteristics of persons depicted in this book have been changed" (7), he had in fact used several real names in that book.

McElhaney's death was recounted in the "July" chapter of *If I Die in a Combat Zone*, in which an advance ordered by an incompetent Army captain had turned into panicked retreat across a flooded paddy after the unit took enemy fire. McElhaney apparently died when he was run over by a retreating U.S. tank ("track") and Paige lost his leg in the same way. The search for McElhaney's body was "horrible. No one really wanted to be the man to find Mac" (153). He was found under two feet of water. "Most of the blood was out of him," O'Brien recalls, adding with some irony, "He was little to begin with" (153).

Some of the links between *The Things They Carried* and "The Vietnam in Me" are even more complex, suggesting that O'Brien actually imagined key textual events in his "life" before he could live them. For example, O'Brien's return to the "shit field" in the February 1994 trip recorded in "The Vietnam in Me" mirrors a scene that the "O'Brien" narrator had constructed for himself four years earlier in the "Field Trip" chapter of *The Things They Carried*. There, "O'Brien" returns to Vietnam with his (fictional) daughter, finds the field, sits down at the spot where he believes Kiowa's rucksack was found, and mourns the fact that he cannot share this moment with Kiowa:

> The sun made me squint. Twenty years. A lot like yesterday, a lot like never. In a way, maybe, I'd gone under with Kiowa, and now *after two decades I'd finally worked my way out.* A hot afternoon, a bright August sun, and the war was over. For a few moments I could not bring myself to move. Like waking from a summer nap, feeling lazy and sluggish, the world collected itself around me. Fifty meters up the field one of the old farmers stood watching from along the dike. The man's face was dark and solemn. As we stared at each other, neither of us moving, I felt something go shut in my heart while something else swung open. (212, emphasis added)

At the time *The Things They Carried* was published in 1990, O'Brien had not returned to Vietnam. Indeed, an April 12, 1990, interview by Bruckner during O'Brien's postpublication book tour reveals that the author was only then planning his first trip back for "a conference of American and Vietnamese writers in Hanoi" (15). Whether O'Brien visited the Quang Ngai province later in 1990 is unclear, but it is certain that he did not return to the "shit field" near the hamlet of My Khe 3 until February 1994.

O'Brien writes of that return in "The Vietnam in Me" and records how he and his Vietnamese guides became lost looking for the "one piece of ground I wish to revisit above all others in the country" (56). O'Brien's guide, a Mr. Tan, seems anxious to confront O'Brien with the results of U.S. involvement in Vietnam, at one point on the journey taking him to meet a man whose legs had both been blown away. In language that echoes the silent look from the old Vietnamese farmer in *The Things They Carried* (which, of course, had only taken place in O'Brien's imagination), O'Brien records a silent communication with his guide Mr. Tan. "We try for smiles," he says. "Mr. Tan does not smile. He nods to himself—maybe to me. But I get the point anyway. Here is your paradise" (56). When at last they find the shit field, "we stand looking out on a wide and very lovely field of rice. The sunlight gives it some gold and some yellow. There is no wind at all. Before us is how peace would be described in a dictionary for the speechless. I don't cry. I don't know what to do. At one point I hear myself talking about what happened here so long ago, motioning out at the rice, describing chaos and horror beyond anything I would experience until a few months later" (56).

The later "chaos and horror" to which O'Brien refers is his subsequent break-up with Kate, the woman who had accompanied him on his return to Vietnam. He reveals in the *New York Times* article that he has become clinically depressed after the estrangement, even suicidal: the antitheses of the relatively well-adjusted veteran persona he had constructed for himself nonfictionally in *If I Die in a Combat Zone* and even fictionally in *The Things They Carried*. In essence O'Brien uses the public record of a relatively straightforward journalistic account to destabilize in his *nonfiction* the presence he had created for the first-person narrator "O'Brien" of his earlier texts.

No more do we hear of the "nice smooth glide—no flashbacks or midnight sweats" (179) that characterized the alter ego O'Brien had built for himself in *The Things They Carried*, the narrator who is sure that "by telling stories, you objectify your experience" (179). It turns out that O'Brien has been unable to work his way out of his implication in Vietnam as easily as he had believed during his imaginary return to the "Pinkville" district. Now, "on war time, the world is one long horror movie, image after image," O'Brien writes of his actual 1994 trip and its aftermath in the remarkably candid confessional published as "The Vietnam in Me," "and if it's anything like Vietnam, I'm in for a lifetime of wee-hour creeps. Meanwhile, I try to plug up the leaks and carry through on some personal resolutions. For too many years I've lived in paralysis—guilt, depression, terror, shame—and now it's either move or die" (56).

O'Brien, it seems, plans a similarly painful reckoning for his readers. His most recent novel, *In the Lake of the Woods,* was published shortly after his reunion visit to Vietnam's "Pinkville," and it seems designed to force its

American readers to come to terms with our own guilt for our involvement in Vietnam and, specifically, in the My Lai massacre. The novel weaves the tale of one John Wade, a My Lai veteran who has buried his past war crimes and has launched a successful political career in Minnesota. Wade's run for the United States Senate is derailed when a fellow My Lai veteran discloses Wade's culpability, particularly his killing of a fellow soldier who surprised Wade while he was hiding in a ditch. Returning with his wife, Kathy, to Minnesota's north country after the failed campaign, Wade increasingly is haunted by failure and guilt. One night Kathy Wade disappears, and John Wade becomes the subject of a criminal investigation. Typically complex, O'Brien's novel is at once a recounting of that investigation, an interweaving of several scenarios that might explain Kathy Wade's disappearance, and a reenactment of crucial scenes from the actual My Lai massacre and Wade's fictional past.

Although the novel's surface plot has been justly criticized for some clumsy characterizations (particularly its stereotyped rendering of the "party hack"), what interests me is how O'Brien constructs a narrative presence for himself that, as I have discussed earlier, dovetails in many respects with his actual history. For example, the narrator reveals that in researching the book, he returned to the My Lai area and found the ditch into which American G.I.s had herded scores of old men, women, and children during the slaughter. O'Brien's actual visit to that ditch makes up a compelling portion of "The Vietnam in Me," in which O'Brien feels "the guilt chills" (53) as he hears a Vietnamese survivor recall being buried alive under the bodies in the ditch. By most standards, he says, as *Times* photographer Edward Keating snaps pictures of the evidence, "this is not much of a ditch. A few feet deep. A few feet wide" (53).

Like a nonfiction novelist enfolded inside a fictional novel, the narrator of *In the Lake of the Woods* tells his readers that his project is to reconstruct the history of John Wade[6] as faithfully as possible. In so doing he interlaces the text with footnotes in the "evidence" chapters that document the sources of his knowledge and repeatedly bring into play his methodology as a reporter. There are "certain mysteries," he says: "that weave through life itself, human motive and human desire. Even much of what might appear to be fact in this narrative—action, word, thought—must ultimately be viewed as a diligent but still imaginative reconstruction of events. I have tried, of course, to be faithful to the evidence. Yet evidence is not truth. It is only evident" (30n). What infinitely complicates the book is that some of these footnotes certainly are invention—such as the sources for facts of the case of the fictional John Wade, who outside the text (it is relatively easy to prove) was never a candidate for United States senator. Others of O'Brien's footnotes, however, just as certainly are actual documentation.

With this strategy, O'Brien artfully snares the sort of reader who believes that outside facts can never be fixed and thus really don't matter either to fictional or nonfictional texts. For if the facts don't matter, and all is text, then O'Brien's careful documentation of how American soldiers murdered as many as 505 Vietnamese at My Lai assumes an identical "truth" status to his careful documentation of how the fictional John Wade may have (or may not have) murdered his fictional wife. We have already seen how all of O'Brien's writing about Vietnam seems designed to trap his readers in the guilt of involvement, even if specific facts remain slippery. *In the Lake of the Woods* continues that project, but seems to want to make the reader work even harder to uncover the evidence of what we actually did at My Lai.

O'Brien's developing strategy may have been a response, in part, to Michael Bilton and Kevin Sim's scrupulously researched *Four Hours in My Lai,* a 1992 text that the two British filmmakers expanded from their International Emmy and Golden Globe Award–winning documentary prepared for Yorkshire Television and for WGBH-Boston public broadcasting. Bilton and Sim tracked down many of the American G.I.s responsible for My Lai and documented how American policy in Vietnam helped to create the atrocities and how subsequent official policy has helped to discount them. In an advance review of the 1992 book printed on its dust jacket, O'Brien suggested the book should be "required reading" for every American voter, war recruit, politician, and general. "[T]his must be one of the most significant and compelling books in many, many years," he wrote. "I was stunned and horrified; I knew but I didn't know" (dust jacket, hardcover edition).

John Wade's flashbacks to My Lai events are documented by evidence from Bilton and Sim's book, as well as by evidence from the Department of the Army's Peers Commission report, Richard Hammer's *The Court-Martial of Lt. Calley,* explanations of post-traumatic stress syndrome and its effect on the partners of veterans, and the histories of other massacres from as long ago as the battles of Lexington or the Colorado militia massacre of a Cheyenne village in 1864. Each of the footnotes that discusses war histories checks out against actual texts; in all but one case O'Brien's narrator names actual names and depicts actual events drawn from eyewitness accounts of the My Lai massacre.

That one case presents one of the more intriguing mysteries of *In the Lake of the Woods* and shows how artfully O'Brien constructs the arc of documentation from the fictional (the "facts" of the John Wade murder investigation as invented from the police records and newspaper accounts of the Wade case) to the nonfictional (the facts drawn from the narratives of My Lai histories and investigations). At the apex of that arc is the testimony of one Richard Thinbill about the involvement of John Wade at My Lai, which O'Brien documents from the transcript of the Court-Martial of Lieutenant Calley, box 4, folder 8, pages 1734 and 1735 in the U.S. National Archives (*Lake of the Woods* 202, 263–64).[7] In several spiraling passages structurally characteristic of O'Brien's writing, the author imagines the facts of the shooting: how John "Sorcerer" Wade killed a man named Weatherby who peered into the ditch and started to smile, then made a funny jerking motion as Wade shot him (*Lake of the Woods* 64, 75, 112, 220). Wade at first blames Weatherby's death on the "fucking VC" but begins to giggle uncontrollably as his friend Thinbill tries to shake him out of his hysteria (220). O'Brien creates the following interplay between a government questioner and Thinbill at the Calley courtmartial:

Q: "This Sorcerer, you can't recall his name?"

A: "Not right at this exact moment."

Q: "And he giggled?"

A: "That was afterward. He was upset." (263–64)

Throughout the My Lai episodes, O'Brien ascribes atrocities to more than a dozen United States G.I.s whose names are found on official lists of soldiers present at My Lai. The exceptions are Richard Thinbill (the novel's witness against John Wade) and Pfc. Weatherby (the man Wade shot), who earlier had helped Calley slaughter Vietnamese civilians huddled in the ditch. At the novel's climax, fictional and nonfictional characters collide in the abject horror of the My Lai massacre:

Sorcerer watched a red tracer burn through a child's butt. He watched a woman's head open up. He watched a little boy climb out of the ditch and start to run, and he watched Calley grab the kid and give him a good talking to and then toss him back and draw down and shoot the kid dead. The bodies did twitching things. There were gases. There were splatterings and bits of bone. Overhead, the pastel sunlight pressed down bright and warm, hardly a cloud, and for a long time people died in piles and layers. Ammunition was a problem. Weatherby's weapon kept jamming. He flung the rifle away and borrowed someone else's and wiped the barrel and thumped in a fresh magazine and knelt down and shot necks and stomachs. (219)[8]

Ultimately Wade and Calley speak to each other across the generic boundaries of O'Brien's blurred text: "[Calley:] '. . . people blabbin' about a bunch of dead civilians. Personally, I don't understand it.' He smiled at Sorcerer. 'These folks here, they look like civilians?' [Wade:] 'No Sir.' [Calley:] 'Course not.' Calley crushed the flies in his fist, put his hand to his nose and sniffed it. 'Tear this place apart. See if we can find us some VC weapons.'" (216)[9]

Wrapped around this horrifying text is the story of how Wade possibly murdered his wife, Kathy, some twenty years later in the aftermath of political defeat. O'Brien presents the case in a series of hypothesis chapters, some of which imagine Kathy running away from her husband and disappearing in the lake country of northern Minnesota; others of which imagine her getting lost in the lake country and waiting to die; others of which imagine John and Kathy Wade running off together to forge new identities; and still others which imagine John murdering Kathy during a Vietnam-induced flashback during which he pours boiling water over her face then sinks her body two hundred yards out in the cold northern lake (274–78).

O'Brien's metafictional narrator muses over the evidence in footnotes written in his own voice, considering how "the human desire for certainty collides with our love of an enigma" (269n). In terms that recall the fictional Nicholas Branch's distress in the face of runaway intertextuality in DeLillo's *Libra,* the narrator considers "reams of data" that do not satisfy even his "primitive appetite for answers" (269n). Near the end of the book, when he has summoned all the "facts" of the Wade case, the narrator invites the reader to invent his own ending and concludes: "One way or another, it seems, we all perform vanishing tricks, effacing history, locking up our lives and slipping day by day into the graying shadows. Our whereabouts are uncertain. All secrets lead to the dark, and beyond the dark there is only maybe" (304n).

We have been this way before in the contemporary novel, a poststructural narrator exhausted by the effort to manage a text, ready to abandon the search to an equally lost reader. What makes O'Brien's text absolutely unique, however, is that he poses these standard metafictional dilemmas within the deeply implicating matrix of history and nonfiction. In fact he forces his conscientious readers toward the very sort of implicated reading for which I have been arguing in this book. If we are so ready to grant the Wade murder case investigator that exhausted indeterminacy, are we equally ready to efface the history of the My Lai massacre? There too, O'Brien suggests, are secrets that lead beyond the dark to only "maybe."

Of the novel's early reviewers, H. Bruce Franklin makes a compelling case that only one of the Kathy Wade disappearance scenarios (the one in which Wade pours scalding water over his wife's face and hides her body) is reinforced by chapter narratives that O'Brien does not specifically label as hypotheses in the text. Therefore, Franklin argues, O'Brien hides a "reality" within the fiction of the John Wade story that he forces his reader to uncover, much as realistic fiction has always had a "truth" standard that allowed readers to read the text with mimetic engagement *as if* it were true. The same sort of effort, O'Brien's complicated methodology suggests, will be required if we are to discover the nonfictional facts that matter within and behind the intertextual record of the massacre of My Lai and the larger tragedy of Vietnam. As Franklin notes: "Not everything, however, is fiction. There is another kind of reality—represented by My Lai in 1968 and O'Brien's own experience around My Lai the following year. And in this experience, as O'Brien tells us over and over again, he, like his fictive John Wade and like the American nation, committed acts so horrible that they continually evoke denial" (43).

Franklin's interpretation is consistent with the longest footnote in *In the Lake of the Woods:* the footnote that evokes the death of Chip Merricks and most clearly squares with what we know of the facts of O'Brien's own life. I will quote it at some length to recapture the full taste of its bitter lesson:

> All these years later, like John Wade, I cannot remember much, I cannot feel much. Maybe erasure is necessary. Maybe the human spirit defends itself as the body does, attacking infection, enveloping and destroying those malignancies that would otherwise consume us. Still, it's odd. On occasions, especially when I'm alone, I find myself wonder-

ing if these old tattered memories weren't lifted from
someone else's life or from a piece of fiction I once read or
heard about. My own war does not belong to me. In a peculiar way, even at this very instant, the ordeal of John
Wade—the long decades of silence and lies and secrecy—
all this has a vivid, living clarity that seems far more authentic than my own faraway experience. Maybe that's
what this book is for. To remind me. To give me back my
vanished life. (301n)

The silence, the lies, and the secrecy are what O'Brien seems driven to force
himself, his readers, and his nation to face.

Read in tandem with the more scrupulously "public" self that
O'Brien constructs in the *New York Times* piece published the same year,
the narratives drive toward a similar point. O'Brien understands "the wick-
edness that soaks into your blood" and the "boil that precedes butchery"
(53). Yet not all stories of Vietnam are the same, and not all actions have the
same result; there are facts outside the texts that will force their readers to
acknowledge that facts *matter,* even if they are difficult to discover. In "The
Vietnam in Me" O'Brien contemplates a now ordinary-looking ditch near the
My Lai villages, the same ditch in which Lieutenant Calley once confronted
a two-year-old child who—separated from its mother—had managed to
crawl toward the lip of the ditch away from the bodies. Eyewitnesses recall
that Calley "picked the child up, shoved it back down the slope and shot it"
(Bilton and Sim 122).

Now, at least as recently as 1992, Calley runs his parents-in-law's
jewelry store in the Cross Plaza Shopping Mall in Columbus, Georgia (Bilton
and Sims 2), his legal appeals successful and his few months under house
arrest long ago served. Meanwhile, the child he shot is dead in history *and*
in text in a way that surpasses the fictional deaths depicted in a thousand war
novels. He is like Ralph Rugoff staring at a corpse on a slab, unprepared for
the experience after watching a thousand fictional deaths. O'Brien is still
trying to make sense of the history of that ditch in My Lai, trying to sort out
the facts that separated his own Alpha Company's actions from those of
Calley's Charlie Company. At last he concludes with evident irony: "I know
what occurred here, yes, but I also feel betrayed by a nation that so widely
shrugs off barbarity, by a military judicial system that treats murderers and
common soldiers as one and the same. Apparently we're all innocent—those

who exercise moral restraint and those who do not, officers who control their troops and officers who do not. In a way, America has declared *itself* innocent" (53).[10]

In text after text across the decades since his service in Vietnam, O'Brien has never declared that innocence for himself; each text has begun with a confession of his personal culpability and cowardice for fighting a war he knows he should not have fought. He asks only the same responsibility of his readers. The Vietnam texts, despite (and because of) their challenge to generic certainty, build a body of deeply implicated writing for their author, a body of writing whose sum is far greater and more unsettling than its parts. Each text that the author and reader together create burrows toward the same lesson: there is a body buried "in the blending twilight of in between" (*Lake of the Woods* 291). And if you ask if the story is true, and if the answer matters, you've got your answer.

Notes

1. Later in her book, Frus provisionally adopts a use of the word *text* that is much closer to my own, at least in her first usage of the term in the following statement (though not her second): "[T]he text as read is constantly being produced by the interaction between reader and text, and by the resistance of each" (229). But two sentences later, she reiterates her belief that checking the narrative against outside facts is "hopeless" (229).

2. Nabokov himself, of course, complicates the text by composing a forward "written" by the didactic John J. Ray, Ph.D., which argues for the book's instructional value (7). Nabokov then undercuts Ray's pronouncements both by the novel's dazzling lyricism and by his own afterword to the Putnam edition, wherein he argues that "despite John Ray's assertion, *Lolita* has no moral in tow. For me a work of fiction exists only insofar as it affords me what I shall bluntly call aesthetic bliss" (286). Although a full reading lies outside the scope of this study, my sense is that Nabokov creates a delightfully articulate scoundrel in Humbert but ultimately subverts Humbert's inventiveness in the second half of the book as he forces Humbert (and the reader) to come to terms with Humbert's guilt. The ultimate effect, I would argue, is neither the self-assured didacticism of John J. Ray nor the self-ironic aesthetic formalism of Nabokov's afterword.

3. The computer-enhanced mock-up of the death photos had inserted a black band over the "Nicole Brown Simpson throat wound" even though the actress playing the part had no such wound. The *Globe,* which published the actual death scene photos, retained the black box and made it larger because the severity of the actual wound was much greater than the earlier computer-enhanced mock-up had anticipated. Why did not the *Globe* simply publish the photos unedited, since they had decided already to defy a court order? "If you

could see what was underneath that box, you would understand," *Globe* vice-president Terry Raskyn told *Editor and Publisher* reporter Dorothy Giobbe. My argument is that although the black boxes introduced staged narrative elements to both photographs, which rendered neither photograph "true" in one sense, the photographs were not identically "untrue." Even though each woman's throat is obscured by a black band in the photographic narratives, the uncut throat of the model playing the victim has a much different material presence than the deep slash that caused the death of the actual Nicole Brown Simpson. The recognition of those sorts of differences within varying narratives is central to the sorts of arguments this book will be making.

4. My sense of genre, of course, is simply one of many. I am not arguing for its universality, although I believe it will be of particular value for those interested in the referential nature of nonfictional narrative and in the power struggle between its construction of outside experience and the operation of outside experience on the narrative itself. More specifically, the "interpretive strategies" and "political edge" I bring as a student of literature to this task are those I learned as a journalist: (1) that one cannot assume the thoughts of another living human being without accounting for how those thoughts are gained; (2) that access to scenes is always complicated because even when access is gained, the very presence of the observer can alter that scene dramatically (documentary journalism's version of the Heisenberg Uncertainty Principle); and (3) that decisions to grant voice to characters through direct quotes never can be innocent because they raise questions of transcription as well as decisions on whom to quote and how often. My argument is that considerations such as these are rarely faced as directly in fictional depictions, even those of high realism.

5. In a footnote to his *Modern Fiction Studies* essay, Heyne seems to make some room for this sort of blurring narrative, though he won't agree that it is pervasive or even common. "There are certain instances," he says, "in which the factual status of a text is problematic" because the author's intent is not clear or because she deliberately blurs the fact/fiction boundary. "But even such experimentation is defined by a norm from which to deviate" (484n).

6. Tim O'Brien's Vietnam narratives—which I shall examine in detail in chapter 5—offer as close to a refutation of Foley's gestalt theory as any I could cite. O'Brien also offers insurmountable challenges, in my judgment, to those critics who depend primarily on authorial intent for definitions of fact and fiction.

7. Indeed, it has become a sort of ritual in nonfiction theory to dismiss Zavarzadeh's "zero degree claim" (see Weber's *The Art of Fact*, Hellmann's *Fables of Fact*, Heyne's "Toward a Theory of Literary Nonfiction," and Frus's *The Politics and Poetics of Journalistic Narrative*), but beyond that relatively easy

dismissal, no engaged reading of Zavarzadeh's most perceptive ideas has been produced to date.

NOTES TO CHAPTER 2

1. In distinguishing my approach from Booth's, I want to be clear that whatever I know about the way narrative works began with him. Booth's *The Rhetoric of Fiction* showed me as a college student that it was impossible to divorce the artistry of a text from the message it was communicating. Booth's careful attention to the differing presences of author, narrator, and reader informs every approach I have taken since that time. But he has not yet devoted his considerable talents to a specific reading of nonfictional narrative, and I believe his treatment of nonfictional texts is flattened by what I identified in the previous chapter as a common critical "embarrassment" with the actual work of nonfictional documentation and access.

2. Wolfe habitually uses ellipses and/or emphases; unless otherwise noted all such devices in Wolfe quotes in this chapter are his.

3. I am indebted to the analyses of recent feminist critics—particularly many published in the collection *In Dora's Case: Freud, Hysteria, Feminism,* edited by Charles Bernheimer and Claire Kahane, who unmask the power agenda inherent in Freud's treatment of Dora. Maria Ramos's discussion of Freud's dominance of Dora during the analysis is insightful. Kahane concentrates on how Freud's voice as narrator organizes dialogue and events to his advantage; Suzanne Gearhart, Jacqueline Rose, and Jane Gallop write suggestive analyses of the transference and countertransference in the case. Toril Moi in particular demonstrates persuasively how Freud's compulsion to fill the gaps of Dora's history ultimately reveals that the analyst "clings to his dream of complete elucidation" (187) of the Dora case.

4. Postmodern novelists regularly play with this division: John Fowles in *The French Lieutenant's Woman* wonders if his hero is real and if an author can control a character's life; Italo Calvino creates his reader as a character in *If on a winter's night a traveler;* Joan Didion and Paul Auster present, even "discover," themselves as characters in *Democracy* and *City of Glass,* and so on. As I have said before, I am not arguing a strict genre approach in this study, but I shall address specifically the differences among these sorts of characterized authors in my extended discussion of the work of Tim O'Brien.

5. I am strongly indebted to Marcus's argument, particularly his recognition of "Freud's own unsettled and ambiguous role in the case" (67) and his

argument that "in the cause of psychoanalytic treatment, nothing less than 'reality' itself is made, constructed or reconstructed" (71). Where I break with Marcus is in his insistence that the case study is a "story or a fiction" because it has been rendered in language (71). Certainly it is a story, but my approach means to explore the special consequences of regarding it as a narrative that Freud meant to be read, however much it resembles a modern novella, specifically as nonfiction.

6. Many readings, of course, including the present study and many of those published in the Bernheimer and Kahane collection, rebel against direct authorial control and attempt to approach Dora outside the spell of Freud's intent. But the development and practice of reader-reception theory does not alter the author's *intent* that I am outlining in this chapter. Freud's case-study methodology does circumscribe some of the evidence that we can bring to those readings, most particularly in his denial of a voice and historical identity to the subject of his case study.

7. As the chapter turns toward a close reading of Freud's style, I shall refer, on most occasions, both to Freud's original German text as well as to the standard translation by James Strachey, which Freud, by 1923, had personally corrected and which he termed the work of "my excellent English translators" (*Dora* 28n). Throughout this section, quote citations in English are from the Collier edition and those in German are from "Bruchstuck einer Hysterie-Analyse" in volume 5 of the *Gasammelte Werke* (Collected Works), published by Imago.

8. Rosette C. Lamont has shown that Hélène Cixous's play, *Portrait of Dora,* fashions a response to Freud's text by placing the character of Dora on center stage and relegating Freud to the margins. The stage representation constructs a "present-tense" body for Dora that allows her to escape Freud's narrative sublimation. "Dora occupies center stage," Lamont writes, "while Freud is off to the side, superseded by events he is unable to control. Sitting with his back to the audience, he recounts what we are about to witness. The plot, however, will not be structured by the account" (88).

NOTES TO CHAPTER 3

1. The task of assessing Wolfe's many public statements over the years has been made immensely more easy by the 1990 publication of *Conversations with Tom Wolfe,* a collection of his interviews over twenty-four years, edited by Dorothy M. Scura.

2. Weber's collection of contemporary articles from New Journalism's

leading practitioners provides a valuable look at the theories and practices of New Journalism and, as such, is the only book length work specifically about New Journalism published during the 1960s or 1970s that really helps the current scholar explore the form's social and political controversies.

3. Paul Perry's *On the Bus* account, published in 1990 with copious photographs of the original Pranksters taken during the 1960s by Ron "Hassler" Bivert, quotes from many of Kesey's contemporaries and associates as well as presenting narrative "flashbacks" by former Prankster Ken Babbs. The book both readjusts and in some respects enhances the Prankster record and in that way reveals the manner by which nonfiction affects its subjects. The strong subtext of the book, though never overtly stated, is that the lives of each of these people have been construed not only by their experience with Kesey but also by their experience of being named characters in a book that by 1990 had gone through thirty-one printings.

4. Although the fiction/nonfiction status of some of Reed's tales is murky, Floyd Dell, Reed's fellow editor at *The Masses* and the editor most likely to have supervised the publication of Reed's dispatches from Mexico, classified the narrative among Reed's "stories" rather than among his "journalistic accounts" in *Daughters of the Revolution and Other Stories,* Dell's 1927 collection of Reed's narratives (viii).

5. Vitali Tselischev was a visiting lecturer in philosophy at Ashland University during the 1993 spring semester. During a June 6, 1993, interview in Ashland, Ohio, Tselischev, who teaches at Novosibirsk State University in Russia and has translated the writings of philosopher Richard Rorty into Russian, translated key words for me and also recalled that when he was a youngster of sixteen in 1958 the long ban on *Ten Days* was lifted in the Soviet Union. He recalls reading the narrative with relish as a lad, particularly its depiction of the taking of the Russian Winter Palace. "He was there," Tselischev said of Reed. "He was an important witness. We have never been permitted to read him before."

NOTES TO CHAPTER 4

1. Fred Fedler's Harcourt Brace Jovanovich text, *Reporting for the Print Media,* calls the standards timeliness, importance, prominence, proximity, and oddities (116–17). The four University of Missouri School of Journalism professors (Brian S. Brooks et al.) who write St. Martin's *News Reporting and Writing* call them impact, proximity, timeliness, prominence, novelty, and conflict (6–14). Melvin Mencher's text for William C. Brown identifies news values as impact, timeliness, prominence, proximity, conflict, the bizarre, and currency

(58–60). As an example of the latter, he says that "although starvation is common in several countries in the Third World" it lacked currency until a television crew brought images back to the United States. "For a while a massive outpouring of aid went to the country. Then the interest slackened" (60).

2. Dickens imagines his reader walking idly along the street just outside Newgate, separated by only a wall from the squalor and death inside. As such, Dickens's effort to draw that reader from the "sidewalk" safety into an experience from which he will be released functions somewhat like a sidewalk newspaper vending machine that "summons" the reader from routine travel into the world of media representation where exotic "news values" are consumed.

3. Former *Los Angeles Times* and *Wall Street Journal* reporter A. Kent MacDonald, a socialist, has written of a reporter's ability to get controversial topics into mainstream newspapers so long as the reporter remembers the standards of news value and delivers fresh, readable, ostensibly objective stories. Even though they are committed to capitalism, MacDonald says, few editors are conscious ideologues. "Most just want to print good stories and get the paper out on time. In their mind, a good story is one that is read and commented on, whatever its message" (13). Yet reporters seldom are able to propose thoroughgoing economic solutions to the problems that their reporting uncovers, MacDonald says. He recalls his long series on economic inequality for the *Times:* "understandably, there was no concluding piece on remedies. . . . [R]edistribution of wealth was more than the wealthy *Los Angeles Times* was prepared to contemplate" (17).

4. Republican strategists tried to add an actual dimension to the fictional death in *Philadelphia* during the 1994 race for the U.S. Senate in Ohio by pointing out the similarities between the Tom Hanks character and an HIV-positive lawyer who was dismissed by the national law firm owned by Democratic candidate Joel Hyatt. Tracking polls showed that the charges had a temporary impact, but voters appeared to have forgotten about the issue by the November election. G.O.P. candidate Mike DeWine did handily defeat Hyatt for U.S. Senate; DeWine swept into office in the midst of a nationwide Republican landslide.

NOTES TO CHAPTER 5

1. Historiographers who insist that the past can only be constructed through narrative traditionally have faced these questions, as have literary theorists, like Phyllis Frus, who argue that fictional and nonfictional texts essentially have the same textual status. For her part, Frus seems to abandon her insistence

elsewhere that "arguing over which parts a writer 'got right' in terms of accuracy is a hopeless exercise because we have no primary or original text to compare later versions to" (229) and grants a special—though still textual—factual authority to the Holocaust. "The fact that historians can say irrefutably that millions of Jews were killed in gas chambers in Germany in a few short years is the result of having established those historical facts by amassing documents, survivors' accounts, stories, and witnessing of all kinds," Frus says. "Because it is historically verifiable, this sequence of events to which we give the interpretive and symbolic name 'the Holocaust' is meaningful" (176). My contention, of course, is that it is no more "hopeless" to reach outside a nonfiction text like O'Brien's *If I Die in a Combat Zone* or "The Vietnam in Me" to argue their truth against texts like the official Vietnam casualty list, Seymour Hersh's *My Lai: A Report on the Massacre and Its Aftermath*, Richard Hammer's *The Court-Martial of Lt. Calley*, Michael Bilton and Kevin Sim's *Four Hours in My Lai*, or even the *Report of the Department of the Army on My Lai* (The Peers Commission).

2. O'Brien's other three novels are *Going after Cacciato, Northern Lights*, and *The Nuclear Age*. Each of the three would offer insights to O'Brien's Vietnam experience, but none of them blurs the status of fiction and nonfiction in a way that would make them as relevant to my study. One good reading of *Going after Cacciato* in light of O'Brien's nonfiction is provided by Maria S. Bonn in her "Can Stories Save Us? Tim O'Brien and the Efficacy of the Text." Bonn considers the character of Paul Berlin as a storyteller in *Going after Cacciato* and traces the commonality of his project with that of O'Brien. She concludes that both believe "stories can save us," but only by preserving our experience, not by offering any ultimate salvation (14).

3. All names, ranks, addresses, and dates of death for United States military personnel killed in Vietnam are taken from the official listing at the Vietnam War Memorial in Washington, D.C.

4. The list of U.S. servicemen killed in Vietnam has no Curt or Curtis Lemon. Although there was an Army Pfc. Richard Keith Lemmon, who was killed on April 12, 1969, during the period O'Brien served in Vietnam, there appears to be no historical link between that soldier and the name O'Brien chose for his story.

5. Lorrie N. Smith presents an intriguing reading of the "gendered subtext" of both this story and of *The Things They Carried* as a whole. She finds it significant that the narrator calls his misguided listener a "dumb cooze" and says that, in general, O'Brien presents war as "an inevitable, natural phenomenon deeply meaningful to the male psyche and hostile to femininity" (38). Smith's reading demonstrates the way in which O'Brien's strategy causes readers to collapse the distinction between the author and the "O'Brien" narrator of the

book. Whatever O'Brien's personal politics, the narrator is partly a victim of a war machine whose overwhelming sexism O'Brien has critiqued with bitter irony in his discussion of boot camp mentality in *If I Die in a Combat Zone:* "There is no thing named love in the world. Women are dinks. Women are villains. They are creatures akin to Communists and yellow-skinned people and hippies. We march off to learn about hand-to-hand combat" (52).

6. Although O'Brien seems clearly to align himself most closely with the unnamed narrator of the novel, he also seems to identify his own dilemma as a Vietnam veteran in key scenes constructed for his fictional John Wade. Wade, like O'Brien, is recycled to the back lines at the end of a long tour near My Lai; like O'Brien, Wade discovers some refuge in a fishing village near the South China Sea. And O'Brien recreates for Wade a key scene that O'Brien himself had lived: changing his Army clothes to civilian ones in the rear lavatory of the last air flight home from Vietnam.

O'Brien wrote in *If I Die in a Combat Zone* of his own last flight into Minneapolis: "When the no-smoking lights come on, you go into the back of the plane. You take off your uniform. You roll it into a ball and stuff it into your suitcase and put on a sweater and blue jeans. You smile at yourself in the mirror. You grin, beginning to know you're happy" (205). In *In the Lake of the Woods* John Wade's flight home to Minneapolis was "lost time. Jet lag, maybe, but something else too. He felt dangerous. In the skies over North Dakota he went back into the lavatory, where he took off his uniform and put on a sweater and slacks, quietly appraising himself in the mirror. After a moment he winked. 'Hey, Sorcerer,' he said. 'How's tricks?'" (273). Given that John Wade's carefully constructed public image as a well-adjusted war veteran and politician is even more convincing in the novel than O'Brien's real life persona, the doubling effect between author and character here assumes chilling implications for O'Brien's own identity.

7. The records of the Calley court-martial are stored at the National Archives in record group 153, a collection that runs to some thirty boxes and consumes some twelve linear feet of documents (Bilton and Sim 388). Bilton and Sim examined the documents as well as reviewing a collection of sixty-four sound tapes encompassing Calley's trial. No witness named Richard Thinbill is mentioned in their book.

8. Ample documentation exists for the facts of the slaughter at the ditch. In preparing his account O'Brien most certainly relied on the straightforwardly written evidence presented by the Peers Commission ("At approximately, 0900–0915 hours, Vietnamese personnel who had been herded into the ditch were shot down by members of the 1st Platoon" [Goldstein 136]) and on Bilton and Sim's narrative, which was taken directly from the testimony supplied to the

Peers Commission and to the Army Criminal Investigation Division by Dennis Conti, an American G.I. who witnessed the killing (393n). Bilton and Sim's version of the same scene at the ditch:

> Conti stood behind them as Calley and [Lt. Paul] Meadlo, standing side by side, blazed away. They stood only ten feet from their hapless victims, changing magazines from time to time. The Vietnamese screamed, yelled, and tried to get up. It was pure carnage as heads were shot off along with limbs; the fleshier body parts were ripped to shreds. Meadlo had taken twenty-three fully loaded magazines for his M-16 in his pack when they left [the landing zone]. He fired in a spraying motion. He noticed one man dressed in red fall dead as he fired the rifle on automatic until the magazine was exhausted. Then he reloaded. He then switched to semiautomatic fire and loaded the third magazine. After a minute or so Meadlo couldn't continue. Tears flooded down his cheeks. He turned, stuck his rifle in Conti's hand, and said: "You shoot them."

Additional evidence of the massacre at the ditch was provided by photographs taken by Army photographer Ronald Heaberle, published in the *Cleveland Plain Dealer,* and aired on CBS News in November 1969 (Bilton and Sim 260).

    9. O'Brien's depiction of Calley is one of the most unusual moves in recent American fiction in that Calley is still alive (and thus able to initiate a defamation claim against O'Brien) and in that O'Brien not only uses Calley's real name but constructs his character quite closely to what we know of the actual Calley. Naomi Jacobs's careful study of historical figures in contemporary fiction traces the ramifications of this combination. "According to the law, no one has an exclusive right to a name; it is the name in conjunction with a recognizable portrayal of a person's individual characteristics that allows us to say that a collection of words 'refers to' an individual; the name is the least important constituent in that reference" (186). To prove a libel claim Calley would have to establish that the text was false, that it referred to him, and that it imputed a crime or shameful behavior that would bring him into shame and ridicule or harm his ability to earn a living. O'Brien's depiction of Calley is drawn quite closely from protected testimony at his court-martial and from the government investigation of My Lai. But when Calley addresses the fictional character of Wade and tells him to "Tear this place apart" (216), O'Brien has caused Calley to take an action that he could not have taken in life. "Oddly enough, then, a writer who attempts to 'Tell the truth, but tell it slant,' in a disguised version of real-life experience,"

concludes Jacobs after her extensive study of case law, "may be more liable to prosecution than a writer who tells open, outrageous lies about a real person— so long as they are clearly lies" (159). Such considerations reveal the way that O'Brien's fictional text is strikingly different from many deeply implicating fictional depictions of war that do not engage actual living antagonists.

10. Franklin links the American impulse of forgetfulness that O'Brien identifies to the inaugural address of President George Bush: "The final lesson of Vietnam is that no great nation can long afford to be sundered by a memory" (44).

WORKS CITED

Agee, James. *Let Us Now Praise Famous Men*. Boston: Houghton Mifflin, 1939.

Anderson, Chris. *Style as Argument: Contemporary American Nonfiction*. Carbondale: Southern Illinois P, 1987.

Aristotle. *Poetics. The Critical Tradition*. Ed. David H. Richter. New York: St. Martin's, 1989. 21–29.

Auerbach, Erich. *Mimesis: The Representation of Reality in Western Literature*. Garden City: Doubleday Anchor, 1957.

Auster, Paul. *The Art of Hunger*. New York: Penguin, 1992.

Bakhtin, M. M. *The Dialogic Imagination*. Austin: U of Texas P, 1981.

Banaszynski, Jacqui. "AIDS in the Heartland." Friedlander and Lee 259–70.

Barsam, Richard M. *Non-Fiction Film*. Bloomington: Indiana UP, 1992.

Barthes, Roland. *Camera Lucida*. New York: Noonday, 1981.

———. "Historical Discourse." *Introduction to Structuralism*. Ed. Michael Lane. New York: Basic Books, 1970.

———. *The Pleasure of the Text*. New York: Hill and Wang, 1975.

Baskin, Alex. *John Reed: The Early Years in Greenwich Village*. New York: Archives of Social History, 1990.

Bellamy, Joe David. "Sitting Up with Tom Wolfe." Scura 56–72.

———. "Tom Wolfe." Scura 36–72.

Bernheimer, Charles, and Claire Kahane, eds. *In Dora's Case: Freud, Hysteria, Feminism*. New York: Columbia UP, 1985.

Bilton, Michael, and Kevin Sim. *Four Hours in My Lai*. New York: Viking, 1992.

Bonn, Maria S. "Can Stories Save Us? Tim O'Brien and the Efficacy of the Text." *Critique* 36.1 (1994): 2–15.

Booth, Wayne C. *The Company We Keep: An Ethics of Fiction*. Berkeley: U of California P, 1988.

———. *The Rhetoric of Fiction*. 2nd ed. Chicago: U of Chicago P, 1983.

———. *A Rhetoric of Irony*. Chicago: U of Chicago P, 1983.

Brooks, Brian S., et al. *News Reporting and Writing.* 3rd ed. New York: St. Martin's, 1988.

Bruckner, D.J.R. "A Storyteller for the War That Won't End." *New York Times* 3 Apr. 1990, natl. ed.: C15.

Carey, James. "Mass Communication and Cultural Studies." *Communication as Culture: Essays on Media and Society.* Boston: Unwin Hyman, 1988. 37–68.

Case, Tony. "Staged Journalism." *Editor and Publisher* 25 Mar. 1995: 11–12.

Connery, Thomas B., ed. *A Sourcebook of American Literary Journalism.* New York: Greenwood, 1992.

Davis, Walter A. *Inwardness and Existence.* Madison: U of Wisconsin P, 1989.

Dean, Michael. "Pop Writer of the Period—Tom Wolfe Talks to Michael Dean." Scura 24–29.

DeLillo, Don. *Libra.* New York: Penguin, 1989.

De Quincey, Thomas. *Confessions of an English Opium Eater.* New York: Appleton, 1917.

Deutsch, Felix. "A Footnote to Freud's 'Fragment of an Analysis of a Case of Hysteria.'" Bernheimer and Kahane 35–55.

Dickens, Charles. "A Visit to Newgate Prison." In *Sketches by Boz.* New York: Harper, 1954.

Didion, Joan. *After Henry.* New York: Vintage, 1993.

———. *Democracy.* New York: Simon and Schuster, 1984.

———. *Miami.* New York: Pocket Books, 1987.

———. "On Morality." *Slouching Towards Bethlehem.* 157–63

———. *Salvador.* New York: Simon and Schuster, 1983.

———. *Slouching Towards Bethlehem.* New York: Farrar, Straus and Giroux, 1968.

———. *White Album.* New York: Simon and Schuster, 1979.

———. "Why I Write." *Joan Didion: Essays and Conversations.* Ed. Ellen G. Friedman. Princeton: Ontario Review P, 1984. 5–10.

Dietz, Lawrence. "Tom Wolfe on the Search for the Real Me." Scura 18–23.

Dillard, Annie. "To Fashion a Text." Zinsser 39–59.

Duke, David C. *John Reed.* Boston: G. K. Hall, 1987.

Dundy, Elaine. "Tom Wolfe . . . But Exactly, Yes!" Scura 6–17.

Dutka, Elaine. "Hollywood Jumps at Cooke's Life Story." *Cleveland Plain Dealer* 4 June 1996, final ed.: 12E. Rpt. from *Los Angeles Times.*

Dyer, Katie. "What Critical Reading Might Be, or Feeling *The Malady of Death.*" Unpublished essay, 1992.

Eco, Umberto. *Travels in Hyperreality.* New York: Harcourt, Brace, Jovanovich, 1986.

Elbow, Peter. "Desperation Writing." *The Bedford Reader.* Ed. X. J. Kennedy and Dorothy M. Kennedy. 3rd ed. New York: St. Martin's, 1988. 263–68.

Fedler, Fred. *Reporting for the Print Media.* 5th ed. New York: Harcourt, Brace, Jovanovich, 1993.

Fishkin, Shelley Fisher. *From Fact to Fiction: Journalism and Imaginative Writing in America.* Baltimore: Johns Hopkins UP, 1985.

Fiske, John. *Introduction to Communications Studies.* 2nd ed. London: Routledge, 1990.

Flippo, Chet. *Everybody Was Kung-Fu Dancing.* New York: St. Martin's, 1991.

Foley, Barbara. *Telling the Truth: The Theory and Practice of Documentary Fiction.* Baltimore: Johns Hopkins UP, 1985.

Foucault, Michel. *Discipline and Punish.* New York: Vintage, 1977.

———. *The History of Sexuality: An Introduction.* New York: Vintage, 1978.

Frankfort, Ellen. *Life at the Village Voice.* New York: William Morrow, 1976.

Franklin, H. Bruce. "Plausibility of Denial." *Progressive* 58.12 (1994): 40–44.

Frazier, Ian. "Looking for My Family." Zinsser 121–39.

Freud, Sigmund. "Bruchstuck einer Hysterie-Analyse." *Gesammelte Werke.* Vol 5. London: Imago, 1942. 161–286.

———. *Dora: An Analysis of a Case of Hysteria.* New York: Collier, 1963.

Friedlander, Edward J., and John Lee. *Feature Writing for Newspapers and Magazines.* New York: HarperCollins, 1993.

Frus, Phyllis. *The Politics and Poetics of Journalistic Narrative.* Cambridge: Cambridge UP, 1994.

Furst, Lillian R. *All Is True: The Claims and Strategies of Realist Fiction.* Durham: Duke UP, 1995.

Gagnier, Regenia. *Subjectivities.* New York: Oxford UP, 1991.

Gallop, Jane. "Keys to Dora." Bernheimer and Kahane 19–33.

Gates, Henry Louis Jr., ed. *"Race," Writing, and Difference.* Chicago: U of Chicago P, 1985.

Gebauer, Gunter, and Christoph Wulf. *Mimesis: Culture, Art, Society.* Berkeley: U of California P, 1995.

Giobbe, Dorothy. "Covering Executions." *Editor and Publisher* 24 Feb. 1996: 8–9.

———. "Supermarket Tab Runs Gory Murder Scene Photos." *Editor and Publisher* 7 Oct. 1995: 10, 33.

Goldstein, Joseph, Burke Marshall, and Jack Schwartz. *The My Lai Massacre and Its Coverup: Beyond the Reach of the Law? The Peers Commission Report.* London: Free Press, 1976.

Hannaham, James. "The Elements of Kyle: The Timely Death of an Online Hero." *Village Voice* 8 Oct. 1995: 46.

Hazlitt, William. "The Fight." *The Norton Anthology of English Literature*. Rev. ed. New York: W. W. Norton, 1968. 637–44.

Hellmann, John. *Fables of Fact*. Urbana: U of Illinois P, 1981.

Hemingway, Ernest. *A Farewell to Arms*. New York: Scribner's, 1929.

Hentoff, Nat. "Behold the New Journalism—It's Coming after You." Weber, *Reporter* 49–53.

Herr, Michael. *Dispatches*. New York: Knopf, 1977.

Heyne, Eric. "Toward a Theory of Literary Nonfiction." *Modern Fiction Studies* 33.3 (1987): 479–90.

Hicks, Granville. *John Reed: The Making of a Revolutionary*. New York: Macmillan, 1936.

Homberger, Eric. *John Reed*. Manchester: Manchester UP, 1990.

Homberger, Eric, and John Biggart, ed. *John Reed and the Russian Revolution: Uncollected Articles, Letters, and Speeches on Russia*. New York: St. Martin's, 1992.

Humphrey, Robert E. "John Reed." Connery 151–60.

Jacobs, Naomi. *The Character of Truth: Historical Figures in Contemporary Fiction*. Carbondale: Southern Illinois UP, 1990.

Jameson, Fredric. *The Political Unconscious*. Ithaca: Cornell UP, 1981.

Kaplan, Steven. "The Undying Uncertainty of the Narrator in Tim O'Brien's *The Things They Carried*." *Critique* 35.1 (1993): 43–51.

Kendrick, Thomas R. "Introduction." *Writing in Style*. Ed. Laura Langley Babb. Washington: Washington Post Writer's Group, 1975. i–xi.

Kramer, Jane. "Cowboy." *The Literary Journalists*. Sims 127–44.

———. *The Last Cowboy*. New York: Harper and Row, 1977.

Lamont, Rosette C. "The Reverse Side of a Portrait: The Dora of Freud and Cixous." *Feminine Focus: The New Women Playwrights*. Ed. Enoch Brater. New York: Oxford UP, 1989. 79–93.

Lehman, Daniel W. "Missing: After a Year, Mother Hopes." *Charlottesville Daily Progress* 13 Apr. 1986: A1, A12.

Lesser, Wendy. *Pictures at an Execution: An Inquiry into the Subject of Murder*. Cambridge: Harvard UP, 1993.

Lippmann, Walter. "Legendary John Reed." *New Republic* Dec. 1914: 15–16.

Lounsberry, Barbara. *The Art of Fact: Contemporary Artists of Nonfiction*. New York: Greenwood, 1990.

MacDonald, A. Kent. "Boring from within the Bourgeois Press: Part One." *Monthly Review* Nov. 1988: 13–24.

Mailer, Norman. *Executioner's Song*. Boston: Little, Brown, 1979.

Malcolm, Janet. *The Journalist and the Murderer*. New York: Vintage, 1990.

Marcus, Steven. "Freud and Dora: Story, History, Case History." Bernheimer and Kahane 56–91.

Mayhew, Henry. *London Labor and the London Poor.* 4 vols. London: Augustus M. Kelley, 1895.

McAuliffe, Ken. *The Great American Newspaper.* New York: Scribner's, 1978.

McGinniss, Joe. *Fatal Vision.* New York: Putnam, 1983.

McLeod, Mary. "*CA* Interview." Scura 178–85.

Mencher, Melvin. *News Reporting and Writing.* 5th ed. New York: William C. Brown, 1991.

Mewborn, Brant. "Tom Wolfe." *Rolling Stone* 5 Nov.–10 Dec. 1987: 214–20. Rpt. in Scura 230–40.

Miller, J. Hillis. "Narrative and History." *ELH* 41 (1974): 455–73.

Moi, Toril. "Representation of Patriarchy: Sexuality and Epistemology in Freud's *Dora.*" Bernheimer and Kahane 181–99.

Morrison, Toni. "The Site of Memory." Zinsser 83–102.

Muggli, Mark Z. "Joan Didion and the Problem of Journalistic Travel Writing." *Temperamental Journeys: Essays on the Modern Literature of Travel.* Ed. Michael Kowalewski. Athens: U of Georgia P, 1992. 176–94.

———. "The Poetics of Joan Didion's Journalism." *American Literature* 59 (Oct. 1987): 402–21

Nabokov, Vladimir. *Lolita.* New York: Berkley, 1966.

Newfield, Jack. "Journalism: Old, New and Corporate." Weber, *Reporter* 54–65.

Nichols, Bill. *Representing Reality.* Bloomington: Indiana UP, 1991.

O'Brien, Tim. *Going after Cacciato.* New York: Dell, 1978.

———. *If I Die in a Combat Zone.* New York: Dell, 1973.

———. *In the Lake of the Woods.* Boston: Houghton Mifflin, 1994.

———. *The Things They Carried.* New York: Penguin, 1990.

———. "The Vietnam in Me." *New York Times Magazine* 2 October, 1994: 48–57.

Overbeck, Wayne. *Major Principles of Media Law.* Fort Worth: Harcourt, Brace, Jovanovich, 1992.

Pauly, John J. "The Politics of New Journalism." Sims, *Literary Journalism* 110–29.

Perry, Paul. *On The Bus.* New York: Thunder's Mouth, 1990.

Phelan, James. *Narrative as Rhetoric: Technique, Audiences, Ethics, Ideology.* Columbus: Ohio State UP, 1996.

———. "Present Tense Narration, Mimesis, the Narrative Norm, and the Positioning of the Reader in *Waiting for the Barbarians.*" *Understanding Narrative.* Ed. James Phelan and Peter Rabinowitz. Columbus: Ohio State UP, 1994. 222–45.

———. *Reading People. Reading Plots.* Chicago: U of Chicago P, 1989.

Pratt, Mary Louise. *Imperial Eyes: Travel Writing and Transculturation.* London: Routledge, 1992.

———. "Scratches on the Face of the Country; or, What Mr. Barrow Saw in the Land of the Bushmen." *"Race," Writing and Difference.* Ed. Henry Louis Gates Jr. Chicago: U of Chicago P, 1985. 138–62.

Rabinowitz, Peter. "Reader Response, Reader Responsibility: *Heart of Darkness* and the Politics of Displacement." *Case Studies in Contemporary Criticism.* Ed. Ross C Murfin. 2nd ed. Boston: Bedford-St. Martin's, 1996. 131–47.

Ramos, Maria. "Freud's Dora, Dora's Hysteria." Bernheimer and Kahane 149–80.

Reagan, Ron. "*GEO* Conversation: Tom Wolfe." Scura 186–98.

Reed, John. "Almost Thirty." *Adventures of a Young Man: Short Stories from Life.* Berlin: Seven Seas, 1963; San Francisco: City Lights, 1975. 125–44.

———. *Daughter of the Revolution and Other Stories.* Ed. Floyd Dell. Freeport: Books for Libraries P, 1927.

———. *The Education of John Reed.* Ed. John Stuart. New York: International Publishers, 1955.

———. "Foreign Affairs." Homberger and Biggart 147–51.

———. *Insurgent Mexico.* New York: International, 1969.

———. "Mac-American." *Daughter of the Revolution and Other Stories.* 43–49.

———. "Seeing Is Believing." *Daughter of the Revolution and Other Stories.* 133–37.

———. "A Taste of Justice." *Daughter of the Revolution and Other Stories.* 125–30.

———. *Ten Days That Shook the World.* New York: Vintage, 1960.

———. "This Unpopular War." *The Education of John Reed.* 166–75.

———. "A Visit to the Russian Army" Homberger and Biggart 28–56.

———. *The War in Eastern Europe.* New York: Charles Scribner's Sons, 1916.

———. "With the Allies." *The Education of John Reed.* 77–88.

Richter, David. *The Critical Tradition.* New York: St. Martin's, 1989.

Rieff, Philip. "Introduction." *Dora: An Analysis of a Case of Hysteria.* New York: Collier, 1963. 7–20.

Rose, Jacqueline. "*Dora:* Fragment of an Analysis." Bernheimer and Kahane 128–47.

Rosenbaum, Ron. *Travels with Dr. Death.* New York: Penguin, 1991.

Rosenstone, Robert A. *Romantic Revolutionary: A Biography of John Reed.* New York: Vintage, 1975.

Rosmarin, Adena. *The Power of Genre.* Minneapolis: U of Minnesota P, 1985.

Rugoff, Ralph. *Circus Americanus.* London: Verso, 1995.

Sager, Michael. "Janet's World." *GQ* June 1996: 200–211.

Schmaltz, Jeffrey. "Chronicler of Gay Life in Own Battle with AIDS." *Cleveland Plain Dealer.* 9 May 1993, early ed: G6.

Scura, Dorothy M., ed. *Conversations with Tom Wolfe.* Jackson: UP of Mississippi, 1990.

Searle, John. "The Logical Status of Factual Discourse." *New Literary History* 6 (1975): 319–32.

Shilts, Randy. "Talking AIDS to Death." *The Best American Essays 1990.* Ed. Justin Kaplan and Robert Atwan. New York: Ticknor and Fields, 1990. 231–46.

Sims, Norman., ed. *Literary Journalism in the Twentieth Century.* Oxford: Oxford UP, 1990.

———. *The Literary Journalists.* New York: Ballantine, 1984.

Smith, Lorrie N. "'The Things Men Do': The Gendered Subtext in Tim O'Brien's *Esquire* Stories." *Critique* 36.1 (1994): 16–40.

Sprengnether, Madelon. "Enforcing Oedipus: Freud and Dora." Bernheimer and Kahane 254–75.

Stallybrass, Peter, and Allon White. *The Politics and Poetics of Transgression.* Ithaca: Cornell UP, 1986.

Stamberg, Susan. "Cautionary Tales." *Joan Didion: Essays and Conversations.* Ed. Ellen G. Friedman. Princeton: Ontario Review P, 1984. 22–28.

Stone, Gerald. *Newswriting.* New York: HarperCollins, 1992.

Taylor, A. J. P. "Introduction." *Ten Days That Shook the World.* Middlesex: Penguin, 1966. vii–xix.

Thompson, Toby. "The Evolution of Dandy Tom." Scura 199–220.

Tompkins, Jane. "'Indians': Textuality, Morality, and the Problem of History." Gates, *"Race," Writing and Difference,* 59–77.

Towers, Robert. "Libra." *New York Review of Books* 18 Aug. 1988: 13.

Tselischev, Vitali. Personal interview. 6 June 1993.

Turkle, Sherry. "Ghosts in the Machine." *The Sciences* Nov./Dec. 1995: 36–39.

Vincent, Richard C. "CNN: Elites Talking to Elites." *Triumph of the Image.* Ed. Jamid Mowlana, George Gerbner, and Herbert I. Schiller. Boulder: Westview, 1992.

Virilio, Paul. *The Vision Machine.* Bloomington: Indiana UP, 1994.

Weber, Ronald. *The Literature of Fact.* Athens: Ohio UP, 1980.

———. *The Reporter as Artist: A Look at the New Journalism Controversy.* New York: Hastings House, 1974.

White, Hayden. *The Content of the Form.* Baltimore: Johns Hopkins UP, 1987.

Wilson, James C. ed. *John Reed for the Masses.* Jefferson, NC: McFarland, 1987.

Wolfe, Tom. *The Electric Kool-Aid Acid Test.* New York: Farrar, Straus and Giroux, 1970.

———. *The Kandy-Kolored Tangerine-Flake Streamline Baby.* New York: Farrar, Straus and Giroux, 1965.

————. "The New Journalism." *The New Journalism.* Ed. E. W. Johnson and Tom Wolfe. New York: Harper and Row, 1973. 3–52.

Zavarzadeh, Mas'ud. *The Mythopoeic Reality.* Urbana: U of Illinois P, 1976.

Zelenko, Lori Simmons. "What Are the Social Pressures Affecting the Art World Today?" Scura 172–77.

Zinsser, William. *Inventing the Truth.* Rev. ed. Boston: Houghton Mifflin, 1995.

Index

THE THEORY AND INTERPRETATION OF NARRATIVE SERIES

James Phelan and Peter J. Rabinowitz, Editors

Because the series editors believe that the most significant work in narrative studies today contributes both to our knowledge of specific narratives and to our understanding of narrative in general, studies in the series typically offer interpretations of individual narratives and address significant theoretical issues underlying those interpretations. The series does not privilege any one critical perspective but is open to work from any strong theoretical position.